n8n Agents in Action

Building and Automating Smart Workflows for Developers

Written By

Henry Finley

Copyright

Title: *n8n Agents in Action: Building and Automating Smart Workflows for Developers*

Author: Henry Finley

Copyright © 2025 by Henry Finley. All rights reserved.

Disclaimer

Trademark Notice

Table of Contents

Chapter 1: Introduction

1.1. What is n8n?

n8n is an **open-source automation platform** that allows users to automate workflows, integrate apps, and handle data processing tasks without needing extensive programming knowledge. With its **visual interface**, users can build and automate workflows by connecting different services and applications together.

Key Features of n8n:

- **No-Code and Low-Code**: While n8n is designed to be accessible for users without coding experience, it also offers the flexibility of writing custom scripts for more advanced tasks.
- **Extensive Integrations**: n8n supports a wide variety of third-party applications and APIs, including popular services like Google Sheets, Slack, and Salesforce, and even custom HTTP API integrations.
- **Self-Hosting and Cloud Options**: You can choose to self-host n8n or use it via cloud providers, ensuring flexibility in how you run your automation workflows.
- **Custom Nodes**: Users can extend n8n's functionality by building custom nodes for unique integrations, giving complete control over automation.
- **Open-Source**: Being open-source means that n8n is free to use and constantly evolving, with contributions from a growing community of developers.

How Does n8n Work?

n8n functions through workflows, which are created using nodes. A **node** is a single task or action (e.g., sending an email, writing data to a database, or triggering an HTTP request). **Workflows** consist of one or more nodes connected in sequence to perform a series of tasks automatically.

A workflow can be triggered in various ways:

- **Manual triggers**: e.g., clicking a button or using a web interface.

- **Scheduled triggers**: e.g., running a workflow every hour or every day.
- **Event-based triggers**: e.g., when a new record is created in a database or when an email is received.

By dragging and connecting nodes on the platform's user-friendly interface, users can design a flow that handles complex tasks like data processing, notifications, and API calls, all without writing significant amounts of code.

1.2. The Role of Agents in Automation

Agents in the context of n8n are specialized automation processes that handle repetitive tasks, decision-making, and complex workflows on behalf of the user. They can be thought of as the **"workers"** within n8n that execute tasks autonomously, based on pre-set triggers and rules.

The Role of Agents:

- **Autonomy**: Agents can operate independently, carrying out tasks based on the workflow you've set up. They ensure that tasks happen automatically, without requiring human intervention.
- **Process Automation**: In automation systems, agents streamline workflows by taking over manual tasks, reducing the chances of errors, and improving the efficiency of repetitive processes.
- **Data Handling and Processing**: Agents in n8n can collect, process, and send data to various systems, making data workflows seamless. They enable real-time data integration between different applications, such as syncing customer data across platforms or automating data reporting.
- **Decision Making**: Agents can be programmed to make decisions based on **conditionals**, data changes, or events. This feature makes them valuable for handling dynamic tasks, such as changing workflows depending on certain conditions (e.g., if a specific value exceeds a threshold, send an alert).
- **Multi-Agent Workflows**: Complex tasks often require collaboration between multiple agents. In n8n, you can design workflows that involve **multiple agents** working together, each handling a specific part of a process. For example, one agent might extract data from a CRM, while another processes that data and a third sends notifications based on certain triggers.

Examples of Agent Roles in n8n:

- **Notification Agent**: This agent could send an email or SMS notification whenever a task is completed or a new event occurs.
- **Data Sync Agent**: This agent could be responsible for syncing data between two platforms, ensuring they are always up-to-date.
- **Decision Agent**: This agent could monitor conditions (like checking if a sales goal has been met) and make decisions accordingly (e.g., triggering a specific action if the goal is met).

In the next chapters, we'll explore how to set up n8n agents, use them to build automation workflows, and integrate them with external systems.

1.3. Why Automate with n8n?

Automation is a powerful tool for improving efficiency, accuracy, and productivity in business processes. With **n8n**, automation becomes accessible and highly customizable, offering users the ability to design and manage workflows without extensive coding knowledge. Below are key reasons why automating with n8n can be a game-changer for individuals and organizations:

1.3.1. Eliminate Repetitive Tasks

Manual, repetitive tasks are often time-consuming and prone to errors. **n8n automation** helps eliminate the need for manual intervention in tasks such as:

- Data entry
- Report generation
- Sending routine emails or notifications
- Social media updates
- Syncing data across systems

By automating these tasks, n8n frees up time for more strategic and valuable work, allowing employees to focus on higher-level goals.

1.3.2. Improve Efficiency and Speed

n8n allows businesses to automate workflows that would normally require several steps and human intervention. This leads to:

- **Faster decision-making**: Automated processes trigger actions in real-time, leading to quicker responses.
- **Continuous operation**: Automations can run 24/7 without breaks, ensuring that processes are handled consistently, regardless of time zones.

With n8n, workflows run at the speed of automation, which significantly accelerates business operations.

1.3.3. Reduce Human Error

Humans can make mistakes due to fatigue, distraction, or miscommunication. With **n8n workflows**, the risk of error is drastically reduced:

- **Consistent results**: Once set up, n8n workflows execute tasks in a repeatable, error-free manner.
- **Accurate data processing**: Automation ensures that data is processed and transferred without discrepancies.

By removing manual data handling, n8n ensures a higher degree of accuracy and consistency across all operations.

1.3.4. Increase Flexibility and Customization

Unlike traditional off-the-shelf automation tools, **n8n is highly flexible** and allows you to:

- **Integrate a wide variety of services**: From cloud platforms like Google Sheets to communication tools like Slack, n8n connects to over 200 different applications.
- **Build custom solutions**: Whether you need a specific workflow or need to create custom integrations, n8n provides the flexibility to design automation that fits your unique needs.

This flexibility makes n8n an ideal solution for businesses of all sizes and industries.

1.3.5. Cost-Effective

n8n is **open-source**, which means there are no licensing fees for the platform itself. This makes it an affordable alternative to many proprietary automation tools, which often come with steep subscription costs.

1.3.6. Improve Collaboration

With n8n, teams can collaborate more efficiently by automating cross-department workflows. For example:

- **Sales and marketing**: Automatically sync leads from marketing campaigns to your CRM system.
- **Customer support**: Automatically create support tickets based on customer inquiries.
- **Product teams**: Automatically update product databases when changes occur.

By automating these workflows, departments can operate more smoothly and with better communication.

1.3.7. Seamless Integration

n8n connects with numerous third-party applications, enabling seamless data flow between different systems. Whether it's pulling data from an API or sending notifications through Slack, n8n ensures that all your tools and services work together in harmony.

1.4. Benefits of n8n Agents in Workflow Automation

n8n agents are the cornerstone of **automation workflows**, allowing businesses and developers to automate a wide range of tasks. Agents serve as the **"workers"** that handle tasks autonomously, according to the predefined logic and triggers set by users. Here are the key benefits of using n8n agents in automation:

1.4.1. Increased Automation Efficiency

By utilizing agents in n8n, businesses can automate entire workflows from start to finish. Instead of relying on manual triggers and intervention, agents handle the full task:

- **Autonomous Task Execution**: Once configured, agents can perform tasks like sending emails, processing data, or triggering APIs on their own.
- **Continuous Operation**: Agents can run continuously in the background, ensuring that tasks are completed on time, without the need for human oversight.

1.4.2. Flexibility and Customization

n8n agents can be customized to handle specific tasks based on your needs. Whether it's automating a simple workflow or creating a complex, multi-agent process, n8n agents are highly adaptable.

- **Conditional Logic**: Agents can be programmed to make decisions based on incoming data or triggers. For example, an agent can decide whether to send an email based on the value of a data field or time of day.
- **Custom Workflows**: n8n allows you to create highly tailored workflows where agents can collaborate or handle individual tasks in different systems (e.g., one agent might process payment data while another sends confirmation emails).

1.4.3. Collaboration Between Multiple Agents

n8n allows for **multi-agent workflows**, where different agents work together in a coordinated manner. This is ideal for complex workflows that require multiple steps and processes.

- **Distributed Task Management**: Complex workflows can be broken down into smaller, manageable tasks handled by different agents. This enables better organization and ensures each agent is working on a specific part of the process.
- **Parallel Execution**: Agents can run in parallel, improving the speed of workflows and reducing bottlenecks.

1.4.4. Streamlined Decision-Making

Agents in n8n can handle **conditional logic** and **decision-making**, allowing workflows to adapt dynamically based on the conditions of incoming data.

- **Example**: An agent could be programmed to process customer orders based on inventory levels. If an item is out of stock, the agent could trigger a notification to the sales team, update the customer, and initiate a backorder process.

1.4.5. Error Handling and Recovery

n8n agents are equipped with built-in mechanisms for **error handling and retries**, ensuring that workflows are not interrupted by minor failures.

- **Retry Logic**: If an agent encounters an error (e.g., an API request fails), it can be set to retry the task automatically, preventing workflow disruptions.
- **Fallback Actions**: You can define alternative actions if an agent encounters issues, such as sending an alert or logging the error for review.

1.4.6. Improved Scalability

Using agents enables businesses to scale automation as they grow. Since agents handle tasks independently and autonomously, the system can handle an increased workload without additional manual intervention.

- **Multiple Agents for Larger Workflows**: As workflows grow more complex, multiple agents can collaborate seamlessly to perform an increasing number of tasks, ensuring that automation scales with your business needs.

1.4.7. Cost-Effectiveness

n8n agents reduce the need for manual labor, leading to substantial cost savings. By automating routine processes and data management, businesses can reduce operational costs while increasing output.

1.4.8. Ease of Maintenance and Monitoring

n8n provides a centralized platform to monitor the performance of agents and workflows. You can track agent activity, view logs, and quickly identify and resolve issues, all through n8n's user-friendly interface.

- **Real-Time Monitoring**: With n8n's monitoring tools, you can keep an eye on agent performance and ensure they are running efficiently.
- **Centralized Error Reporting**: All issues are logged in one place, making it easier to resolve problems quickly.

With these benefits, **n8n agents** are not just a tool for automating tasks but an essential component in building sophisticated and efficient **automated workflows**. They help organizations streamline processes, reduce human error, and free up valuable time for more strategic work.

1.5. Target Audience and Use Cases

1.5.1. Target Audience

This book is designed for professionals, developers, and organizations looking to leverage **automation** to streamline workflows, integrate disparate systems, and improve operational efficiency. Specifically, the target audience includes:

- **Developers and Engineers**: Those who are comfortable with or looking to integrate automation into their development processes. They will appreciate the **hands-on tutorials**, **real-world examples**, and **technical depth** that this book offers.
- **Automation Engineers**: Professionals who focus on automating workflows, handling data processing tasks, and integrating multiple tools and systems. They'll find value in learning how to automate sophisticated workflows using **n8n agents** and enhance their automation strategies.
- **Data Scientists and Analysts**: Individuals working with data who need to automate tasks like data fetching, processing, and reporting. n8n's integration with databases, APIs, and external services will be of particular interest.

- **Product Managers**: Those managing systems or teams where automation can lead to greater productivity, efficiency, and collaboration. They can use n8n agents to reduce manual operations, improve decision-making, and speed up process execution.
- **Small and Medium Enterprises (SMEs)**: Organizations looking for cost-effective automation solutions. n8n's **open-source nature** makes it an attractive tool for businesses that want to integrate and automate tasks without significant licensing or development costs.
- **Tech Enthusiasts and AI Enthusiasts**: People passionate about automation and AI who want to understand how to build and deploy **intelligent workflows** using tools like **n8n agents**.

This book will provide the knowledge and skills needed to **design, implement, and scale automation workflows** using **n8n agents**, regardless of technical skill level.

1.5.2. Key Use Cases for n8n Agents

n8n agents can be utilized in a wide variety of real-world scenarios to automate repetitive tasks, integrate data, and enhance workflows. Below are a few key **use cases** for n8n agents:

- **Automated Data Processing and Integration**: Agents can pull data from multiple sources (APIs, databases, web scraping) and process it for downstream tasks such as reporting, analytics, or storage in different systems.
  - **Example**: Automating the import of sales data from an e-commerce platform (e.g., Shopify), cleaning and transforming it, and then pushing it to a data warehouse for analysis.
- **CRM Automation**: n8n agents can automate customer relationship management (CRM) tasks such as lead scoring, customer notifications, and status updates across multiple systems.
  - **Example**: Automatically updating customer information in a CRM tool like Salesforce when a user fills out a contact form on a website.
- **Marketing Automation**: Automating tasks such as email marketing campaigns, customer segmentation, and social media management. Agents can trigger personalized email sequences, automate posting on social media, or send notifications based on user behavior.
  - **Example**: Creating a workflow that sends welcome emails to new subscribers or automating social media content posting based on blog content.

- **DevOps Automation**: n8n agents can manage tasks like continuous integration/continuous deployment (CI/CD), error tracking, cloud resource provisioning, or deployment pipelines.
  - **Example**: Automatically deploying updates to a web application whenever changes are pushed to a GitHub repository, or provisioning cloud instances based on predefined criteria.
- **Customer Support Automation**: Automating ticket creation, notification sending, and status updates in customer support systems. Agents can also fetch data from customer queries and trigger relevant actions in the support workflows.
  - **Example**: Automatically opening support tickets when customers email a certain address or creating notifications when a certain ticket status is reached.
- **Monitoring and Alerts**: n8n agents can monitor different systems, services, or data streams and trigger notifications when thresholds are met or when certain conditions are met.
  - **Example**: Setting up an agent to send alerts when a website goes down, or when there's a significant spike in server usage.

By using **n8n agents**, these use cases become streamlined, reducing the need for manual tasks and ensuring that systems and workflows run smoothly in the background.

1.6. Overview of the Book Structure

This book is structured to provide a **progressive learning experience**, guiding you from the basics of **n8n agents** to building advanced workflows that automate tasks, integrate multiple services, and scale operations. Each chapter builds on the previous one, starting with fundamental concepts and moving towards more complex workflows and deployment strategies.

Chapter 1: Introduction

- **Overview** of **n8n** and the **role of agents** in automation. We will introduce the platform, explain its key features, and provide examples of how **n8n agents** fit into real-world automation workflows.

- **Target audience** and **use cases** are discussed to ensure readers understand how they can apply what they learn in their professional context.

Chapter 2: Getting Started with n8n

- **Installation and setup** instructions for n8n and the initial configuration.
- **Introduction to the n8n interface**, including how to create your first workflow using the platform's drag-and-drop functionality.

Chapter 3: n8n Agents: The Core Concept

- A deep dive into **n8n agents**, what they are, and how they work within the broader automation framework of n8n.
- **Basic agent setup**, how to create, configure, and deploy agents in your workflows.

Chapter 4: Building Your First n8n Agent Workflow

- A **step-by-step tutorial** on creating your first agent workflow, with examples of basic tasks like sending notifications and connecting different nodes.

Chapter 5: Advanced Agent Features

- Explore advanced topics such as **looping**, **conditional logic**, and **error handling**.
- Techniques to scale up your workflows and build **more complex automations**.

Chapter 6: Integrating External Systems with n8n Agents

- Learn how to connect n8n to external APIs, databases, and services using agents to extend workflow capabilities.
- **Practical examples** of integrating third-party tools such as **Google Sheets**, **Salesforce**, and **Slack**.

Chapter 7: Managing Complex Workflows with Multiple Agents

- Building workflows that involve **multiple agents**, **dependencies**, and **inter-agent communication** for more complex automation scenarios.

Chapter 8: Deploying and Scaling n8n Agents in Production

- Guide on **deploying** and **scaling n8n agents** in real-world environments, including cloud deployment, performance optimization, and handling large-scale workflows.

Chapter 9: Real-World Use Cases of n8n Agents

- Detailed examples of how n8n agents are used across different industries for **marketing**, **customer support**, **data processing**, and **DevOps automation**.
- **Case studies** showcasing successful agent-driven workflows in real-world applications.

Chapter 10: Troubleshooting and Optimization

- Learn how to troubleshoot **common errors**, optimize workflow performance, and ensure that your agents run smoothly without disruptions.

Chapter 11: Extending n8n Agents

- How to extend n8n's capabilities by **writing custom nodes**, building **advanced integrations**, and **adding new functionality** to your automation workflows.

Chapter 12: Advanced Topics in Automation with n8n Agents

- Explore cutting-edge automation topics like **AI-powered workflows**, **IoT integrations**, and the future of **multi-agent systems**.

Chapter 13: Future of n8n and Automation with Agents

- A look at the **evolving landscape** of automation technologies and how **n8n agents** fit into the future of intelligent workflows.

Chapter 14: Conclusion

- **Recap of the journey** from beginner to advanced automation with n8n agents.
- Next steps and how to continue building and refining your **automated workflows**.

This structure ensures that readers will **gradually build their skills** and **expand their knowledge**, with each chapter offering valuable takeaways that can be applied immediately to their own automation projects.

Chapter 2: Getting Started with n8n

2.1. Installing n8n

Before you can start automating workflows with **n8n agents**, the first step is to install and set up **n8n**. In this section, we'll walk you through the installation process, so you can get **n8n** up and running on your local machine or server.

System Requirements

n8n supports several installation methods depending on the environment you want to work in (local machine, cloud, or Docker). Here are the **minimum system requirements** for running n8n:

- **Operating System**: Linux, macOS, Windows (via WSL for Windows)
- **Node.js**: Version 16 or later (as n8n is built on Node.js)
- **Database**: SQLite (default) or PostgreSQL/MySQL for larger or production environments
- **Memory**: At least **2GB RAM** for smooth operation

Installation Methods

There are several ways to install **n8n**. You can choose the one that suits your needs best.

Method 1: Install with npm (Node.js Package Manager)

1. **Prerequisites:**
   - Ensure **Node.js** and **npm** are installed on your system. You can download and install Node.js from Node.js website.
   - Verify installation:

     ```bash

     node -v
     npm -v
     ```

2. **Install n8n using npm**:

- o Open your terminal or command prompt.
- o Run the following command to install **n8n** globally:

```bash
npm install -g n8n
```

3. **Start n8n**:
   - o Once installed, you can start **n8n** by running the following command:

```bash
n8n
```

   - o By default, **n8n** will be available at `http://localhost:5678`. Open your browser and go to this URL to access the n8n interface.

Method 2: Install via Docker

If you prefer to use **Docker** for containerization, you can run n8n without worrying about dependencies and environment issues.

1. **Prerequisites:**
   - o Install **Docker** from Docker website.
2. **Pull the n8n Docker image**:
   - o Open your terminal and run the following command to pull the official **n8n Docker image**:

```bash
docker pull n8nio/n8n
```

3. **Run n8n in Docker**:
   - o Run the following command to start the **n8n** container:

```bash
docker run -d --name n8n -p 5678:5678 -v
~/.n8n:/root/.n8n n8nio/n8n
```

4. **Access n8n**:
   - o As with the npm installation, open your browser and navigate to `http://localhost:5678`.

Method 3: Install on Cloud (n8n Cloud)

1. You can also use **n8n Cloud**, a hosted version of **n8n** that offers pre-configured environments with no installation required. Simply sign up on the n8n Cloud platform and start automating directly in the cloud.

Post-Installation Check

Once you've installed **n8n**, you can verify the installation by opening a web browser and navigating to `http://localhost:5678`. If everything is set up correctly, you should see the n8n web interface.

2.2. Initial Setup and Configuration

Now that **n8n** is installed, the next step is to configure it. This will include setting up the basic preferences for your environment, as well as configuring any integrations you'll use in your workflows.

2.2.1. First-Time Launch

When you first run **n8n**, the web interface will guide you through a **one-time setup** process. This will include:

- **Creating an Admin User**: During the initial setup, you'll be prompted to create an admin user with a username and password to access the n8n dashboard. This is important for securing your environment.
- **Choosing Database**: By default, n8n uses **SQLite** for local development. However, for production environments, you may want to configure **PostgreSQL** or **MySQL** for better performance and scalability.

2.2.2. Setting Up Environment Variables

To customize your n8n setup (e.g., change default ports, database configuration, security settings), you can use **environment variables**.

- **Set Up .env File**:
  - o Create a `.env` file in the root directory of your **n8n installation**.
  - o Common variables you may want to configure:
    - ▪ **Database Settings**:

      bash

      ```
      DB_TYPE=postgresdb
      DB_POSTGRESDB_HOST=your_host
      DB_POSTGRESDB_PORT=5432
      DB_POSTGRESDB_USER=your_user
      DB_POSTGRESDB_PASSWORD=your_password
      DB_POSTGRESDB_DATABASE=your_database
      ```

    - ▪ **Server Configuration** (Change port or host):

      bash

      ```
      N8N_PORT=5678
      N8N_HOST=localhost
      ```

    - ▪ **Security Settings** (optional but recommended for production):

      bash

      ```
      N8N_BASIC_AUTH_ACTIVE=true
      N8N_BASIC_AUTH_USER=your_username
      N8N_BASIC_AUTH_PASSWORD=your_passwor
      d
      ```

2.2.3. Configuring Authentication and Access Control

If you plan to use **n8n** in a team environment or want to restrict access to your workflows, you should set up **authentication** and **access control**.

- **Basic Authentication**: You can set up basic authentication (username/password) by configuring the environment variable **N8N_BASIC_AUTH_ACTIVE**.
- **OAuth2 Authentication**: For integrations with third-party services (such as Google, Slack, or GitHub), you'll need to configure OAuth2 credentials within n8n. This can be done directly in the n8n interface.

2.2.4. Setting Up External Integrations

To start building workflows, you'll need to integrate **external services** (APIs, databases, etc.):

1. Go to the **Credentials** section in the n8n interface.
2. Choose the service (e.g., **Google Sheets**, **Slack**, **Twitter**).
3. **Authenticate and configure the API keys** as required for the service.

For example, if you're connecting to **Google Sheets**, you will need to set up **OAuth2 credentials** by linking your Google account and authorizing n8n to access your Sheets.

2.2.5. Running Workflows

Once n8n is configured, you can start creating and running workflows. A workflow is a sequence of tasks that n8n will automate, such as pulling data from an API, processing that data, and then sending a report to your team via email.

- To create a workflow, simply click the **"New Workflow"** button on the dashboard.
- Add nodes (e.g., **HTTP Request**, **Google Sheets**, **Slack**) and connect them logically based on your automation needs.
- Once a workflow is created, you can test it by clicking **Execute Workflow**.

2.2.6. Monitoring and Debugging Workflows

Once your workflows are running, **n8n** provides tools to monitor their execution:

- The **Workflow Execution Log** shows real-time updates on tasks, any errors, and the outcome of each step in the workflow.

- Use the **Error Node** to handle failures and troubleshoot any issues.

This section ensures that readers understand how to install, configure, and begin using **n8n** effectively. From setting up a development environment to integrating external systems, this chapter provides all the foundational knowledge needed to start automating tasks with n8n.

2.3. n8n Interface Overview

The **n8n interface** is designed to be intuitive and user-friendly, enabling users to create and manage **automated workflows** without requiring extensive technical knowledge. This section will walk you through the various components of the n8n interface, explaining their functions and how to use them effectively.

2.3.1. The Main Navigation Menu

At the top of the n8n interface, you'll find the **Main Navigation Menu**, which includes the following key sections:

- **Workflows**: The primary area where you create and manage workflows.
  - **Create New Workflow**: Click this button to start building a new workflow from scratch.
  - **My Workflows**: Here, you can view, edit, and manage all the workflows you've created.
- **Credentials**: The section where you store credentials for various third-party services and APIs.
  - **Create New Credential**: This allows you to add authentication details for external services like Google Sheets, Slack, or any custom API.
- **Executions**: Shows a log of all executed workflows, with their results, timestamps, and any error details.
  - You can **filter** and **search** past executions to monitor your workflows' success or failure.
- **Settings**: Provides access to global settings such as authentication, environment variables, and other administrative configurations.

2.3.2. The Workflow Editor

The **Workflow Editor** is the core area where you'll spend most of your time. It's a visual environment that allows you to drag and drop **nodes** (individual tasks or actions) to build workflows. Key elements of the Workflow Editor include:

- **Canvas Area**: This is the large space where you design your workflows. You'll drag nodes into this space and connect them in sequence to define your workflow's logic.
- **Nodes Panel**: Located on the left side, this panel contains all available nodes. You can search for specific nodes or browse through categories like **HTTP Request**, **Database**, and **Cloud Services**. Nodes represent individual tasks such as sending an email, making an API call, or processing data.
    - **Node Types**: You can create nodes for a wide variety of services, like Google Sheets, Slack, APIs, and databases, or even custom-built nodes.
- **Node Properties Panel**: Once you drag a node to the canvas, you'll see its configuration options in the **Node Properties Panel** on the right. Here, you'll define the settings for that node, such as the API endpoint, authentication credentials, or input parameters.
    - **Inputs and Outputs**: The properties panel also lets you set up **inputs** (what data the node receives) and **outputs** (what data the node passes to the next step in the workflow).

2.3.3. Workflow Controls

Once you have designed your workflow, you can control its execution using the following buttons located in the top-right corner:

- **Execute Workflow**: This button runs the workflow and shows real-time progress in the **Execution Log**. It's useful for testing your workflow.
- **Save Workflow**: Once you're happy with your workflow, click this button to save it for future use.
- **Activate Workflow**: Activating the workflow means it will begin running automatically according to the triggers you've set (e.g., an API request, a time schedule, or an event).
- **Stop Workflow**: If you need to halt a running workflow, click this button to stop its execution.

- **Undo/Redo**: If you make a mistake while editing the workflow, use the undo and redo buttons to revert changes.

2.3.4. Workflow Execution Log

The **Execution Log** displays detailed information about the current workflow run, showing each step's input and output, along with any **errors** or **successes**. If an error occurs during the workflow execution, you can view the error message here and debug the workflow.

2.3.5. Node Connections

In the Workflow Editor, you will connect nodes to define the sequence of actions. Each node has **input** and **output** ports:

- **Output Ports**: Send data from one node to another.
- **Input Ports**: Receive data from previous nodes.

When you create a connection between nodes, you're essentially defining the flow of data from one task to another. This is the core of how workflows are automated in n8n.

2.3.6. Search and Filter

The interface includes search functionality for quick access to workflows, nodes, credentials, and execution logs. You can filter through workflows, node types, or past executions based on different criteria, helping you stay organized.

2.4. Understanding the n8n Dashboard

The **n8n Dashboard** provides an overview of your entire automation environment, offering easy access to the most important aspects of your workflows, credentials, and execution logs. Here's a breakdown of the **main components** of the n8n dashboard:

2.4.1. Dashboard Overview

When you first log in to **n8n**, you are greeted with the dashboard. The dashboard provides a high-level overview of your workflows and system status.

Key Dashboard Features:

- **Workflows Overview**: The central area of the dashboard displays all your saved workflows in a grid view. Here, you can see:
  - **Active/Inactive Status**: Whether a workflow is currently active (running automatically) or inactive.
  - **Last Execution**: The time when the workflow was last triggered or executed.
  - **Execution Status**: Whether the last execution was successful or had errors.
- **Create New Workflow Button**: At the top-right corner, there's a button that allows you to create a new workflow quickly.
- **Workflow Management**: You can **edit**, **delete**, or **duplicate** existing workflows directly from the dashboard. To manage workflows in detail, you can click on each workflow to open the **Workflow Editor**.

2.4.2. Active Workflows Section

This section shows all workflows that are actively running or waiting to be triggered. You can view the following:

- **Status**: Whether each workflow is active, paused, or failed.
- **Execution History**: A quick overview of the most recent executions, including success/failure notifications.

2.4.3. Credentials Management

On the **Credentials tab**, you can manage the **authentication details** required to interact with third-party services (e.g., Google Sheets, Slack, etc.).

- **View Credentials**: The credentials list shows the credentials you've set up, including their type (API key, OAuth, etc.) and their status.
- **Create/Manage Credentials**: You can add new credentials or edit/delete existing ones from this section.

2.4.4. Execution Logs

This section allows you to monitor **workflow executions**. It shows the logs for each workflow run, including:

- **Execution Status**: Whether the workflow executed successfully or encountered errors.
- **Execution Details**: Logs of each step in the workflow, including any errors or issues that occurred.

You can filter executions by date, success/failure status, or workflow name.

2.4.5. Settings Access

On the dashboard, you can access the **Settings** section to configure global settings for your n8n instance:

- **User Settings**: Update user details, passwords, and access roles.
- **System Settings**: Configure general system settings such as SMTP configuration for emails, environment variables, and security settings.
- **Integrations**: Set up external services and manage connections to databases, cloud storage, and APIs.

2.4.6. Notifications and Alerts

n8n provides real-time **notifications** on the dashboard for:

- **Errors**: Alerts you if a workflow fails.
- **Successful Executions**: Confirmation when workflows run as expected.
- **Scheduled Jobs**: Notifications for workflows that are scheduled to run at specific times.

These notifications help you stay informed about the state of your workflows, ensuring you're aware of any potential issues as they arise.

With these sections in mind, the **n8n interface** becomes a powerful tool for designing, managing, and automating workflows. Understanding the various components of the interface and how to navigate the dashboard is critical to using **n8n** effectively.

2.5. First Workflow Creation: Your First Steps with n8n

Now that you understand the n8n dashboard, it's time to create your very first workflow! This section will guide you through the basic steps of **creating and running a simple workflow** in n8n, from scratch.

2.5.1. Overview of a Workflow

A workflow in **n8n** is a series of **nodes** connected together to automate a task or a process. Each node represents an individual action (e.g., sending an email, making an API request, processing data). Workflows are event-driven and can be triggered by actions like:

- **Manual triggers** (button clicks, API calls).
- **Scheduled triggers** (e.g., run daily, weekly).
- **Event-based triggers** (e.g., new data in a database).

2.5.2. Starting a New Workflow

1. **Create a New Workflow**: From the n8n dashboard, click the **"Create New Workflow"** button.
   - This will open the **Workflow Editor**, where you'll be able to design and build your workflow visually.
2. **Name Your Workflow**: Give your workflow a **descriptive name** that reflects the task it automates. This will help you organize and easily identify it later.

2.5.3. Adding Your First Node

1. **Select a Node**: In the **Nodes Panel** on the left side of the editor, you will see a list of available node types. Start with a simple node such as **HTTP Request** or **Set** (used to define data).
   - Click and drag the node onto the **Canvas Area** to add it to the workflow.
2. **Configure the Node**: After adding the node to the canvas, the **Node Properties Panel** on the right will open, allowing you to configure its settings.

o   For example, for the **HTTP Request** node, you would specify the **URL**, **HTTP method** (GET, POST), and any necessary **parameters** or **headers**.

2.5.4. Connecting Nodes

To create a sequence of tasks, you need to **connect nodes**:

1. Click on the **output port** of one node and drag the line to the **input port** of the next node.
2. Each node's output will be passed as input to the next node, enabling data flow between steps in the workflow.

2.5.5. Adding a Trigger

Next, we need to add a **trigger** to start the workflow. You can choose from several types of triggers:

- **Manual Trigger**: A simple button you can click to manually run the workflow.
- **Cron Trigger**: If you want the workflow to run on a schedule (e.g., every day at midnight).
- **Webhook Trigger**: If you want the workflow to run when it receives an HTTP request.

For your first workflow, let's use a **manual trigger** for simplicity:

1. Search for **"Start"** in the Nodes Panel.
2. Drag the **Start Node** onto the canvas. This will serve as your **workflow trigger**.

2.5.6. Running Your Workflow

Once your workflow is set up, you can **test it**:

1. Click on the **"Execute Workflow"** button in the top-right corner of the screen.
2. If everything is set up correctly, you should see your nodes execute sequentially.
3. The results of each node will be displayed in the **Execution Log**, showing whether it was successful or if any errors occurred.

2.5.7. Saving and Activating Your Workflow

Once you've created and tested your workflow:

- **Save Your Workflow**: Click the **Save Workflow** button to preserve your work.
- **Activate Your Workflow**: To have the workflow run automatically based on its triggers, click **Activate**. Now, your workflow is ready to run as per its trigger conditions.

2.5.8. Example: A Simple Email Notification Workflow

To tie everything together, here's an example of a basic workflow:

1. **Start Node**: Trigger the workflow manually.
2. **Send Email Node**: Use the **Send Email** node to send an email to a recipient. Configure the **SMTP** settings (such as **host**, **port**, **username**, and **password**) under the **Node Properties Panel**.
3. **Test**: When you run the workflow, it will send an email notification to the configured recipient.

This section ensures that readers can easily get started with **n8n** and **create their first automated workflow**. By walking through the process step by step, beginners will feel comfortable designing and testing simple workflows.

2.6. Introduction to Nodes, Triggers, and Actions

In **n8n**, **nodes**, **triggers**, and **actions** are the foundational building blocks used to create and manage workflows. Understanding how these components work together is essential for building efficient and effective automation solutions. Let's break them down:

2.6.1. Nodes in n8n

A **node** represents a single task or operation within a workflow. Each node can perform one or more actions like sending an email, making an API request, or processing data.

Types of Nodes:

- **Service Nodes**: These nodes represent **third-party services** or applications, such as Google Sheets, Slack, or Trello. They allow n8n to interact with external systems.
  - **Example**: A **Google Sheets** node can add a new row of data to a sheet or read values from a specified range.
- **Utility Nodes**: These are nodes that provide utility functions, such as manipulating text, formatting dates, or splitting and combining data.
  - **Example**: A **Set** node can be used to assign or modify values that will be used in other nodes.
- **Trigger Nodes**: These nodes are responsible for starting workflows. They "listen" for certain events and initiate the workflow when those events occur (e.g., a webhook request, a scheduled time, or an incoming message).
- **Action Nodes**: These are nodes that perform a specific action after receiving data from the workflow, such as sending data to another service, making an API call, or processing information.
  - **Example**: An **HTTP Request** node can make a GET or POST request to an API endpoint.

Node Configuration:

Each node comes with a **properties panel** on the right, where you can configure settings such as:

- Input data (parameters for the action)
- Authentication details (e.g., API keys)
- Output data (what happens after the node runs)

Nodes are **connected** to each other, creating a **data flow** through the workflow. You can configure each node to process and pass data to the next node in sequence.

2.6.2. Triggers in n8n

A **trigger node** is a special type of node used to start a workflow. It listens for specific events and activates the workflow when those events occur. Triggers are essential for creating workflows that run automatically without manual intervention.

Types of Triggers:

- **Manual Trigger**: This type of trigger is activated manually by clicking a button. It's ideal for testing or for workflows that need to be run on-demand.
  - ○ **Example**: Clicking a button to start a workflow that processes data or sends notifications.
- **Scheduled Trigger**: A scheduled trigger runs a workflow at specific times or intervals (e.g., every hour, every day at midnight).
  - ○ **Example**: A workflow that checks the weather every morning at 8 AM and sends a daily weather report.
- **Webhook Trigger**: This trigger listens for an incoming HTTP request (e.g., a webhook from a third-party service or application). It's commonly used in workflows that interact with external APIs or services.
  - ○ **Example**: A trigger that listens for a webhook from a payment service when a user makes a purchase.
- **Event-based Trigger**: Event-based triggers are activated when a specific event happens, like new data being added to a database or a file being uploaded to cloud storage.
  - ○ **Example**: A trigger that activates when a new file is uploaded to a Google Drive folder.

Trigger Configuration:

Each trigger has settings for defining how and when it will activate the workflow:

- **Frequency** (for scheduled triggers)
- **Webhooks** (for receiving data from external systems)
- **Conditions** (for event-based triggers)

2.6.3. Actions in n8n

An **action** is the operation performed by a node once it is triggered. Once a trigger starts a workflow, the action nodes execute specific tasks like sending an email, interacting with a database, or calling an external API.

Types of Actions:

- **Data Actions**: These nodes manipulate or process the data. For example, you can use a **Set** node to define variables or a **Function** node to run JavaScript code.
- **Service Actions**: Nodes that interact with external services. These nodes could send data to a third-party service (like an **HTTP Request** node), update a Google Sheet, or send a Slack message.

Example Action Workflow:

1. **Trigger**: A scheduled trigger runs every day at 9 AM.
2. **Action**: The workflow sends an **HTTP Request** to fetch data from an external API.
3. **Action**: The fetched data is processed, and a **Slack message** is sent to a team channel with the updated information.

Each action is a step in the **data flow**, and it's important to configure these nodes correctly to ensure the workflow runs smoothly.

2.7. Key Terminologies in n8n (Workflows, Variables, Connections)

Understanding the core **terminologies** used in **n8n** is crucial for navigating the platform and building successful workflows. Here's a breakdown of some key terms:

2.7.1. Workflows

A **workflow** is a sequence of nodes connected together to automate a specific task or process. Workflows can contain a combination of **trigger nodes**, **action nodes**, and **service nodes**, which work in tandem to carry out the desired automation.

- **Workflow Example**: A workflow could be triggered by a new email, which triggers an HTTP request to fetch data, processes the data, and finally sends a notification to a Slack channel.

Workflows can also be set to run automatically based on triggers (e.g., scheduled, event-based) or manually by the user.

2.7.2. Variables

In n8n, a **variable** refers to a piece of data that is passed between nodes throughout the workflow. Variables store dynamic data (such as input from an API call, user inputs, or processed results) that can be used in subsequent steps.

- **Types of Variables**:
  - **Static Variables**: Fixed values like a text string or number (e.g., "Hello World").
  - **Dynamic Variables**: Values that change based on workflow execution, such as data fetched from an API or user input.

Variables are particularly useful in workflows where one node's output needs to be passed to another node for processing.

- **Example**: A variable containing a user's email address fetched from a database could be passed to a **Send Email** node to notify the user.

2.7.3. Connections

Connections define the flow of data between nodes. When you connect one node to another, you're essentially passing the output data of one node to the input of the next node.

- **Node Connections**: In the **Workflow Editor**, you visually connect nodes by clicking the **output port** of one node and dragging it to the **input port** of the next node.
  - This **connection** indicates the order in which tasks are executed.
- **Data Flow**: The data that is passed between connected nodes is referred to as the **data flow**. Each node in the workflow can either process, modify, or pass along this data.

Connections ensure that data flows correctly through the entire workflow, from trigger to action, and that each node gets the data it needs to perform its task.

2.7.4. Execution Context

Every time a workflow runs, n8n processes the **execution context** which refers to the current state of the workflow, including the input data, variables, and configuration. Understanding this context is essential for troubleshooting and ensuring that workflows run as expected.

- **Example**: If a workflow runs on a schedule, n8n will pass the current date and time as part of the execution context to nodes that require it.

Understanding **nodes**, **triggers**, **actions**, and **key terminologies** is crucial for successfully using **n8n** to automate tasks. By mastering these core concepts, you'll be able to design efficient, robust workflows that integrate seamlessly with various services and APIs.

3.3. How Agents Enhance Workflow Automation

n8n agents are integral to enhancing the power of workflow automation. By automating tasks and handling processes independently, they offer numerous advantages in terms of scalability, flexibility, and efficiency. In this section, we will explore how **agents** amplify the effectiveness of **workflow automation** in n8n.

3.3.1. Reducing Manual Intervention

One of the key benefits of **n8n agents** is their ability to **automate repetitive tasks** that would otherwise require human intervention. For example, without agents, you would need to manually check data sources, send emails, or make API requests. By using agents, these tasks become fully automated.

- **Example**: An agent that checks a database every hour for new customer orders and automatically sends confirmation emails. Once set up, it operates autonomously, eliminating the need for manual checks or emails.

3.3.2. Enhanced Efficiency and Speed

With **n8n agents**, tasks that previously required human attention can now be completed **instantly** and **reliably**. This leads to improved **efficiency**, as agents can handle large volumes of repetitive work without tiring or needing breaks.

- **Example**: An agent that processes form submissions, validates data, stores it in a database, and sends notifications—all automatically. This speeds up processes that would normally take hours if done manually.

3.3.3. Handling Complex Workflows

While n8n's basic workflow design allows for easy task automation, agents make it possible to manage **complex workflows** that require multiple steps, decision-making, and interactions with external systems. Agents can handle multiple branches, conditions, and actions in parallel, ensuring that workflows are more **dynamic**.

- **Example**: In a customer support workflow, one agent might receive and categorize customer queries, another might send automatic responses, while a third escalates issues to a support team based on the severity of the problem.

3.3.4. Scaling and Flexibility

As workflows grow in complexity or volume, **n8n agents** can be scaled to meet increasing demands. Multiple agents can work together, each performing a specific task. This flexibility ensures that automation is not constrained by the limitations of manual processes.

- **Example**: An e-commerce site uses multiple agents: one agent monitors stock levels, another checks customer payment statuses, and a third one processes orders. As traffic increases, agents can be scaled horizontally to handle more operations in parallel.

3.3.5. Integration and Cross-System Automation

n8n agents excel in integrating multiple systems and tools. By using agents, you can ensure seamless data exchange between different applications and services. Agents manage the complexity of data extraction, transformation, and communication between systems, making it easier to automate cross-platform workflows.

- **Example**: An agent can fetch customer data from an e-commerce platform (like Shopify), process it, and update the CRM system (like Salesforce) automatically. Similarly, data can be sent to a marketing platform (like Mailchimp) to trigger personalized email campaigns.

3.3.6. Decision-Making Capabilities

Agents enhance workflows by incorporating decision-making logic. Using conditionals, agents can evaluate data and choose the appropriate path or action based on the results. This allows workflows to be **adaptive** and handle changing conditions automatically.

- **Example**: A lead scoring agent checks if a new lead meets specific criteria (e.g., budget, interest level). If the lead qualifies, the agent triggers a sales follow-up email. Otherwise, the agent may send an informational email or store the lead for future consideration.

3.3.7. Error Handling and Recovery

Another critical advantage of agents is their ability to handle **errors** and **failures** gracefully. When an agent encounters an error, it can retry actions, alert administrators, or switch to fallback operations. This ensures smooth operation and prevents workflows from getting disrupted.

- **Example**: If an agent fails to send an email due to a server issue, it can automatically retry the action after a set interval. If the issue persists, the agent can send an alert or log the error for investigation.

3.4. n8n Agent Lifecycle: Setup, Execution, and Termination

Understanding the lifecycle of an **n8n agent** is critical to managing and optimizing workflows. From **setup** to **execution** and eventual **termination**, the agent lifecycle provides insights into how agents function and how you can control them within your workflows.

3.4.1. Agent Setup

The lifecycle of an **n8n agent** begins with **setup**. This is the stage where you define the configuration, parameters, and connections that the agent will use to perform its tasks.

Steps in Agent Setup:

1. **Trigger Definition**: The first step in the agent setup is defining the **trigger**. This could be a time-based schedule (e.g., every hour), an

event-based trigger (e.g., when a webhook is received), or a manual trigger (e.g., button click).

2. **Node Configuration**: Once the agent is triggered, you configure the **nodes** it will use. This might include setting up API endpoints, data sources, credentials, and actions the agent will perform (e.g., sending an email, making a database query).

3. **Authentication and Credentials**: During setup, the agent will often need **authentication credentials** to interact with external systems (e.g., API keys, OAuth tokens, or database connection details). These credentials are stored securely in n8n's **credentials manager**.

4. **Variables and Data Flow**: Set up any **variables** that the agent will need to process, such as user data, timestamps, or external API responses. These variables are crucial for defining how the agent processes incoming data and interacts with other nodes.

5. **Conditional Logic**: If the agent requires decision-making, configure any **conditionals** or logic to guide the agent's behavior based on data inputs (e.g., use an if-else node to decide the course of action based on a variable).

3.4.2. Agent Execution

After setup, the agent is ready to execute its task. Execution refers to the phase where the agent actively performs the tasks it's been assigned based on the defined workflow.

Steps in Agent Execution:

1. **Trigger Activation**: When the specified **trigger** occurs (e.g., time, event, or manual), the agent starts executing its workflow. This could involve fetching data, making API calls, or processing inputs.

2. **Node Execution**: The agent performs the actions associated with the **nodes** in its workflow. For example, it may fetch data from a database, process the data, and then send the result to a different service.

3. **Data Passing**: Data flows from one node to another, with each node using the data passed from the previous step to perform its task. This process can continue through multiple nodes in the workflow until the agent completes its assigned task.

4. **Error Handling**: If any step encounters an issue (e.g., failed API request or data validation error), the agent will follow predefined error-handling rules, such as retrying the action or logging the error for review.

5. **Logging**: Throughout the execution, **logs** are generated to track the agent's progress, actions performed, and any errors encountered. This helps with debugging and performance monitoring.

3.4.3. Agent Termination

Once the agent has completed its task, it goes through the **termination** phase. This is where the agent ends its execution, and the workflow either stops or continues to the next set of actions.

Steps in Agent Termination:

1. **Completion of Task**: After the agent performs all its actions (e.g., sending an email, saving data), the workflow may either be completed or proceed to additional steps based on the workflow design.
2. **Final Status**: The agent will update its status, marking it as **completed**, **failed**, or **pending**, depending on the results of the workflow execution.
3. **Release Resources**: Any resources (e.g., database connections, memory) that were used during the agent's execution are **released** or cleaned up. This ensures that the system remains efficient and ready for the next execution.
4. **Notify or Alert**: If configured, the agent can **notify users** of completion, such as sending a success message, alerting for errors, or triggering follow-up actions.
5. **Reactivation**: If the agent is set to run periodically (via a scheduled trigger), it will **reactivate** after a specified time and repeat the setup-execution-termination cycle.

By understanding the lifecycle of **n8n agents**, you can more effectively **design, execute, and manage workflows**. Each stage—**setup, execution, and termination**—ensures that agents perform their tasks autonomously and efficiently, enabling you to automate even the most complex processes.

3.5. Key Components of an n8n Agent

An **n8n agent** is a modular unit of automation designed to perform tasks autonomously within a workflow. The agent's core components work together to define its behavior, interact with other nodes, and automate processes. In this section, we will break down the key components that make up an **n8n agent**.

3.5.1. Trigger

The **trigger** is the first component of the agent and is responsible for starting the workflow. Without a trigger, an agent would not know when to begin its task. There are various types of triggers, and they can be selected based on the specific needs of the workflow.

Types of Triggers:

- **Manual Trigger**: Activated by the user, usually through a button press or manual interaction in the n8n interface.
- **Scheduled Trigger**: Runs the agent at predefined intervals (e.g., every day at a specific time).
- **Webhook Trigger**: Activated when a specific HTTP request is received. This is ideal for integrating external services into the workflow.
- **Event-Based Trigger**: Triggers when an event happens, such as a new entry in a database or when a file is uploaded to cloud storage.

The trigger defines when and how the agent will start performing its task, and it ensures the automation is initiated at the right moment.

3.5.2. Nodes

Nodes are the individual tasks or actions that the agent will perform once triggered. They can interact with a variety of systems and services, process data, and execute logic.

Types of Nodes in an Agent:

- **Action Nodes**: These nodes perform specific tasks like sending data to another system (e.g., sending an email, making an API request, or adding a row to a spreadsheet).
- **Utility Nodes**: These nodes help manipulate or modify data, such as formatting text, splitting data into different variables, or performing calculations.

- **Service Nodes**: These nodes are pre-configured to interact with popular services, such as Google Sheets, Salesforce, or Slack, allowing agents to automate tasks across platforms.

Each node is connected in sequence to form a workflow that defines the agent's behavior. The data flows from one node to another, where each node processes and passes data to the next.

3.5.3. Variables

Variables are essential for passing dynamic data between nodes and across different parts of the agent's workflow. They store information that can be used to modify the agent's behavior or decision-making logic.

Types of Variables in n8n:

- **Input Variables**: Data that is received by the agent when it is triggered, such as form submissions, API responses, or external event data.
- **Output Variables**: Data that is generated by the agent after completing an action, such as the result of a calculation or the response from an external API.
- **Temporary Variables**: Used to store data for use within the workflow, such as intermediate processing results.

Variables are passed between nodes as part of the **data flow** within the workflow, ensuring that each node has the necessary data to perform its task.

3.5.4. Conditional Logic

Conditional logic allows an agent to make decisions based on the data it receives. With the help of if-else conditions, switches, and loops, agents can follow different paths based on specific conditions or data values.

Types of Conditional Logic:

- **If-Else Conditions**: Allows the agent to make decisions based on data. For example, "If the order amount is greater than $100, send a discount email."
- **Switch Nodes**: A more flexible decision structure that lets the agent choose from multiple paths depending on the data it encounters.

- **Loops**: Used to repeat actions for multiple items (e.g., processing a list of customers or performing the same task for each file in a directory).

Conditional logic makes n8n agents **dynamic**, enabling them to adapt to changing data or workflows and automate complex processes.

3.5.5. Error Handling

Error handling is a critical part of any agent. It ensures that the agent can respond to issues in the workflow, such as failed API requests, missing data, or unexpected conditions.

Key Components of Error Handling:

- **Error Nodes**: These nodes capture errors that occur during the execution of a workflow and allow you to define actions to handle them (e.g., retrying the action, sending an alert, or logging the issue).
- **Retry Logic**: Some agents may be set to **automatically retry** failed actions a predefined number of times, especially for temporary issues like network failures.
- **Fallback Actions**: If an error cannot be resolved, the agent can be configured to take a **fallback action**, such as notifying the user, logging the error, or performing an alternative task.

Error handling ensures that your workflows are resilient and can continue running even when unexpected issues arise.

3.6. Configuring an n8n Agent

Now that we've explored the key components of an **n8n agent**, it's time to dive into how to **configure** these agents in n8n. This section will guide you through the process of setting up an agent, configuring its nodes, and managing its settings to ensure it runs as intended.

3.6.1. Setting Up the Agent Trigger

The first step in configuring an **n8n agent** is defining the **trigger**. The trigger tells the agent when to start performing its task. Here's how you can configure it:

1. **Choose a Trigger Type**: From the **Nodes Panel**, drag a **Trigger node** (e.g., **Webhook, Cron, Manual Trigger**) onto the canvas.
2. **Configure Trigger Settings**: Each trigger node will have its own set of configuration options. For instance:
   - For a **Webhook Trigger**, you'll need to define the **HTTP method** (GET/POST) and the **URL path** for the webhook endpoint.
   - For a **Cron Trigger**, you can specify the **frequency** (e.g., every hour, daily at midnight).

Once the trigger is configured, the agent will begin its workflow when the specified conditions are met (e.g., a webhook is received or a scheduled time arrives).

3.6.2. Configuring Nodes

After setting up the trigger, you need to configure the **action nodes** that will perform the actual tasks. Here's how you can configure the nodes:

1. **Select a Node**: From the **Nodes Panel**, drag a node (e.g., **HTTP Request, Send Email, Set**) onto the canvas.
2. **Configure the Node Properties**:
   - **Input**: Define the **data** that the node needs to execute. For example, in an **HTTP Request** node, specify the API endpoint, request method, and parameters.
   - **Output**: Define what data should be returned after the node completes its task, such as the response from an API or a success message.

Each node in the workflow can use data from previous nodes, passed via **variables**, to perform its task.

3.6.3. Adding Conditional Logic

To create dynamic agents that can respond to different data inputs, you need to configure **conditional logic** in your workflow:

1. **Add If-Else or Switch Nodes**: Use these nodes to define conditions based on variables or input data.
2. **Configure Condition Logic**: For example, an **If-Else** node might check if a value is greater than a threshold and take different actions depending on the result.

3. **Link Conditional Nodes**: Connect the **conditional nodes** to other nodes that will execute based on the condition's outcome.

3.6.4. Configuring Variables and Data Flow

Define any variables that your agent will use to store data across nodes:

1. **Create Variables**: Use the **Set node** to define static or dynamic variables (e.g., email addresses, API keys, calculation results).
2. **Pass Data Between Nodes**: Configure nodes to use data stored in these variables. For example, you can pass a dynamically generated email address from one node to a **Send Email** node.

3.6.5. Error Handling and Retry Logic

Configure the **error handling** for your agent to ensure it can recover from failures:

1. **Error Nodes**: Attach an **Error node** to handle potential failures. You can configure it to **log errors**, **retry**, or **send alerts** when something goes wrong.
2. **Retry Logic**: In the **Node Properties Panel**, configure the **retry behavior** for nodes that may encounter intermittent failures, such as network issues.

3.6.6. Testing and Activating the Agent

Once your agent is configured, you need to test it to ensure it behaves as expected:

1. **Execute Workflow**: Use the **Execute Workflow** button to run your workflow manually and see the results in real-time.
2. **Debugging**: Check the **Execution Log** for any errors or issues during testing.
3. **Activate Workflow**: After testing, click the **Activate** button to enable your agent to run automatically based on its trigger conditions.

Configuring an **n8n agent** involves setting up triggers, nodes, variables, and conditional logic to create powerful workflows that run autonomously. Once configured, agents can handle complex automation tasks, making them invaluable tools for improving efficiency, accuracy, and scalability in your workflows.

3.7. Creating an Agent with the n8n UI

Creating an agent in **n8n** is a simple process that leverages the platform's intuitive, **drag-and-drop interface**. In this section, we will guide you step-by-step on how to **create and configure an agent** using the **n8n UI**. By the end of this section, you'll be able to create agents that perform automated tasks seamlessly.

3.7.1. Getting Started with the n8n UI

Before you start creating an agent, ensure you are logged into the **n8n** dashboard and are familiar with the **Workflow Editor**. The **n8n UI** is where you'll design workflows and configure agents.

Here's a quick recap of the **n8n UI** components that will be involved in creating an agent:

- **Nodes Panel**: Contains all available nodes you can use in your workflow.
- **Canvas Area**: The workspace where you drag and drop nodes to create workflows.
- **Node Properties Panel**: Allows you to configure the properties of each node (e.g., API endpoints, credentials, and input/output settings).
- **Execution Log**: Shows real-time updates of each node's progress when the workflow is running.

3.7.2. Step-by-Step Guide to Creating an n8n Agent

To create an **n8n agent**, follow these steps:

Step 1: Create a New Workflow

1. On the **n8n dashboard**, click the **"Create New Workflow"** button.
   - o This will open the **Workflow Editor** where you can design and configure your workflow.

Step 2: Choose a Trigger for Your Agent

1. **Add a Trigger Node**: Triggers tell your agent when to start executing. In the **Nodes Panel** on the left, search for a trigger type (e.g., **Cron, Webhook, Manual Trigger**).
    - **Example**: For a simple agent that runs daily, select the **Cron** trigger.
2. **Configure the Trigger**: Once you drag the trigger node to the **Canvas Area**, the **Node Properties Panel** on the right will display the settings for that node.
    - For a **Cron trigger**, you will specify the schedule (e.g., every day at 9 AM).

Step 3: Add Action Nodes

Now that your agent has a trigger, it's time to define the actions the agent will perform.

1. **Choose Action Nodes**: In the **Nodes Panel**, search for an **action node** that the agent should perform. For example:
    - **Send Email**: If your agent is supposed to send an email.
    - **HTTP Request**: If your agent needs to make an API call.
    - **Set**: If you want the agent to set a variable or manipulate data.
2. **Add Action Node to Canvas**: Drag the action node onto the canvas. Each node can have one or more actions that it performs, and you can link them to other nodes in sequence.
3. **Configure the Action**: Click on the node you just added to the **Canvas Area**, and in the **Node Properties Panel**, configure the settings.
    - For example, if you're sending an email, input the **SMTP server settings** (host, port, username, password) and the **recipient's email address**.
    - If it's an **HTTP Request** node, enter the **URL, HTTP method** (GET, POST), and any **parameters** or **headers** the request requires.

Step 4: Configure Variables (if needed)

If your agent requires dynamic data or **variables**, you will configure them during this step.

1. **Add a Set Node**: Use the **Set** node to define and assign values to variables. These can be simple values (e.g., a string or number) or data retrieved from other nodes (e.g., from an API call).
2. **Pass Variables Between Nodes**: Once variables are set, you can use them in subsequent nodes. For example, you could use a variable containing the **recipient's email** in the **Send Email** node.

Step 5: Adding Conditional Logic

To make your agent more **dynamic**, add **if-else** or **switch nodes** to create decision-making logic based on the data processed by the agent.

1. **Add an If Node**: The **If** node allows you to branch the workflow based on specific conditions.
   - For example, if the agent fetches data from an API, you could use the **If** node to check if the data meets certain criteria (e.g., "If status = 'success', send an email").
2. **Configure the Logic**: In the **Node Properties Panel**, define the condition (e.g., check if a variable equals a certain value).

Step 6: Connect the Nodes

Once all your nodes are in place, **connect them** in sequence to define the workflow:

1. Click on the **output port** (small circle) of one node and drag the line to the **input port** of the next node.
2. The connections determine the order in which the tasks will be executed. For example:
   - The **Cron trigger** node will be connected to the **HTTP Request** node.
   - The **HTTP Request** node can then be connected to a **Set** node, which will modify the data.

Step 7: Configure Error Handling (Optional)

You can add error handling to ensure the agent handles failures gracefully:

1. Add an **Error Node** if you want to catch and handle any failures (e.g., a failed API request or a missing parameter).
2. You can configure the **Error Node** to either retry the task or log the error for future review.

Step 8: Test Your Agent

After configuring your agent, it's essential to test it to ensure it behaves as expected:

1. Click the **"Execute Workflow"** button at the top-right of the screen.
   o This will run the workflow in test mode and allow you to monitor the agent's actions in real-time.
2. Check the **Execution Log** to see the agent's progress and verify if any errors occurred.
3. If everything works correctly, the agent will perform its task (e.g., send an email, make an API request).

Step 9: Save and Activate the Agent

Once the agent has been tested and is working as expected:

1. **Save the Workflow**: Click the **Save Workflow** button to preserve your configuration.
2. **Activate the Workflow**: If the agent is ready to run automatically, click **Activate**. This ensures that the workflow will run according to the trigger (e.g., on a schedule, upon receiving a webhook, etc.).

Example: Creating a Simple Notification Agent

Here's an example of a **simple notification agent** using n8n:

1. **Trigger**: Use the **Cron Trigger** node to schedule the agent to run at 9 AM every day.
2. **Action**: Use the **Send Email** node to send an email notification to a specified address.
3. **Variable**: Define the email body using the **Set** node, incorporating dynamic data (e.g., today's date).
4. **Conditional Logic**: Optionally, add a **Switch Node** to send different emails based on certain conditions (e.g., send a summary email on weekdays and a full report on weekends).
5. **Test and Activate**: After testing, save and activate the agent to ensure it runs at the scheduled time.

Creating an **n8n agent** using the **n8n UI** involves defining a trigger, adding nodes for the actions the agent will perform, connecting those nodes, and ensuring proper error handling and conditional logic. Once set up, you can test the agent and activate it to run automatically.

This flexible and intuitive approach allows you to build complex workflows with minimal effort. As you become more familiar with the platform, you can expand on these basic agents to create sophisticated, intelligent workflows that automate tasks across multiple systems.

Chapter 4: Building Your First n8n Agent Workflow

4.1. Setting up a Simple Agent

Creating a simple agent workflow in **n8n** is an excellent way to understand how automation works. In this section, we'll walk you through setting up a basic agent that performs a simple task—like sending a notification or fetching data from an API.

Step 1: Start a New Workflow

1. From the **n8n Dashboard**, click the **"Create New Workflow"** button. This will open the **Workflow Editor**.
2. You'll see an empty canvas area where you can start building your agent.

Step 2: Choose the Trigger for the Agent

The first component of any agent is the **trigger**, which defines when the agent will start its task. For this example, we'll use a **manual trigger**, which allows us to run the workflow manually from the **n8n UI**.

1. In the **Nodes Panel**, search for the **Start** node (this is the manual trigger).
2. Drag the **Start** node onto the canvas.

Now, we have a **trigger** to initiate the workflow. You can use a **Cron** or **Webhook** trigger in future examples for more advanced agents.

Step 3: Add the Action Node

Now that we have a trigger, the next step is to define the action the agent will perform. For this example, let's create an agent that sends an email notification.

1. In the **Nodes Panel**, search for the **Send Email** node (this will be our action).

2. Drag the **Send Email** node onto the canvas, and connect it to the **Start** node by clicking the **output port** of the **Start** node and connecting it to the **input port** of the **Send Email** node.

Step 4: Configure the Action Node

Click on the **Send Email** node to configure it:

1. **SMTP Settings**: You need to configure the SMTP settings for sending the email. In the **Node Properties Panel**, enter the following:
   - **SMTP Server**: The SMTP server address (e.g., `smtp.gmail.com` for Gmail).
   - **Port**: The SMTP port (e.g., 587 for Gmail).
   - **User**: Your email address or the SMTP user.
   - **Password**: The password or an app-specific password (if using Gmail or another provider with 2FA).
2. **Email Details**: In the same panel, configure the following email details:
   - **From**: The email address from which the email will be sent.
   - **To**: The recipient's email address.
   - **Subject**: The subject of the email.
   - **Text**: The content of the email (e.g., "Hello, this is a notification from your n8n agent!").

Step 5: Test the Agent

1. Click on the **Execute Workflow** button in the top-right corner to test the agent. The workflow will execute, and you should receive an email notification.
2. If you don't receive the email, check the **Execution Log** to see if there were any issues with the configuration or credentials.

Step 6: Save the Workflow

Once everything is working correctly, click **Save** to store the workflow.

4.2. Connecting Triggers and Actions

Now that you've set up a basic agent, let's explore how to connect multiple **triggers** and **actions** in a more complex workflow. The flow of data and tasks between triggers and actions is what makes **n8n** so powerful.

Step 1: Adding a Trigger

Let's add a more complex trigger. For this example, we'll use the **Cron Trigger** to schedule the agent to run at a specific time.

1. In the **Nodes Panel**, search for **Cron** and drag it onto the canvas.
2. **Connect the Cron Trigger to the Start Node**:
   - The **Cron** node will now trigger the workflow based on the scheduled time. You can configure it to run every day at a specific time (e.g., 9 AM).
3. **Configure the Cron Node**:
   - In the **Node Properties Panel**, set the **Cron Expression** for the desired schedule. For example:
     - **Every day at 9 AM**: Use the cron expression 0 9 * * * (This means "run at 9 AM every day").
   - Once configured, the **Cron Trigger** will automatically start the workflow every day at 9 AM.

Step 2: Adding Multiple Action Nodes

In this section, let's add **two action nodes** that the agent will execute sequentially. We will use the **HTTP Request** node to pull data from an API and the **Send Email** node to send a notification with the data.

1. **Add the HTTP Request Node**:
   - Drag the **HTTP Request** node onto the canvas.
   - Connect the **Cron Trigger** to the **HTTP Request** node.
   - In the **Node Properties Panel**, configure the HTTP request by entering the **API URL**, **HTTP Method** (GET, POST), and any parameters you need to pass in the request.
   - **Example**: You can make an API request to a weather service (like OpenWeather) to get the current temperature:
     - **URL**: https://api.openweathermap.org/data/

```
2.5/weather?q=London&appid=YOUR_API_
KEY
```
- **Method**: GET
2. **Add the Send Email Node**:
    o Drag the **Send Email** node onto the canvas.
    o Connect the **HTTP Request** node to the **Send Email** node.
    o In the **Node Properties Panel**, configure the email settings to send the result of the API request as the content of the email.
    o **Example**: The email body can include the temperature data retrieved from the **HTTP Request** node.

Step 3: Data Passing Between Nodes

Once you've connected the nodes, n8n will pass data from one node to another:

1. The **Cron Trigger** starts the workflow at the specified time.
2. The **HTTP Request** node fetches data from the API (e.g., weather information).
3. The **Send Email** node sends an email, using the data retrieved from the HTTP request (e.g., including the current temperature in the email body).

Step 4: Testing the Full Workflow

1. Click **Execute Workflow** to test the entire process. The workflow will execute in sequence, starting with the **Cron Trigger** at the scheduled time.
2. After the workflow runs, check the **Execution Log** to ensure that data is passed correctly between the nodes and that the email was sent successfully.

Step 5: Save and Activate the Workflow

Once the workflow is working as expected:

1. Click **Save** to store the workflow.
2. Click **Activate** to have the workflow run automatically based on the **Cron Trigger** schedule.

In this chapter, we covered how to set up a **simple agent** using a **manual trigger** and **send email** action, as well as how to **connect multiple triggers and actions** to create more complex workflows. By connecting **triggers** (like **Cron**) with **action nodes** (such as **HTTP requests** and **email notifications**), you can create a wide variety of automated processes to streamline your tasks and operations.

4.3. Working with Data Flows in Agent Workflows

In **n8n**, **data flow** is the process by which information moves from one node to another in a workflow. Understanding how to handle and pass data between nodes is essential for building efficient and functional agent workflows. In this section, we will explore how to manage **data flows**, including how to **set**, **pass**, and **use** data in different nodes of the workflow.

4.3.1. What is Data Flow in n8n?

Data flow refers to the way information is passed from one node to another in the workflow. Each node in **n8n** can send **data outputs** that serve as **inputs** for subsequent nodes. This dynamic data exchange enables **agents** to perform complex tasks based on real-time information, making workflows adaptable and efficient.

Key Components of Data Flow:

- **Input Data**: Data that comes into the workflow, typically from an external source or a trigger.
- **Output Data**: Data generated or processed by a node, passed to the next node for further processing.
- **Variables**: Data that is **stored** temporarily during workflow execution and used by other nodes. Variables can hold values such as strings, numbers, or complex JSON objects.

4.3.2. Setting Data for Nodes

In **n8n**, you can define and set data at various stages of the workflow. You can either input data manually or allow the workflow to generate dynamic data as it executes.

- **Using the Set Node**: The **Set node** is useful for defining and passing static or dynamic values.
  - o **Static Data**: You can hard-code values such as specific email addresses, dates, or API keys that will be used in subsequent nodes.
  - o **Dynamic Data**: You can use data from previous nodes (e.g., an API response or user input) and set it as a variable to be used in later nodes.

Example: You might want to set a variable with a **user's name** that is then passed to an **email** node to send a personalized message. In the **Set node**, you can set the variable as:

```json
json

{
   "user_name": "John Doe"
}
```

4.3.3. Passing Data Between Nodes

Data is passed automatically from one node to another in n8n based on the connections you make between the nodes. Each node's **output** becomes the **input** for the next node in the workflow.

- **Connecting Nodes**: You connect nodes by dragging a line from the **output port** of one node to the **input port** of another. This defines the path data will take through the workflow.

Example: In a basic workflow, data retrieved by an **HTTP Request** node (e.g., customer order details) will be passed to the next node, such as a **Send Email** node. The order details will be used as part of the email content, which the agent sends automatically.

- **Using Expressions**: Data passed between nodes can be accessed through **expressions** (dynamic data paths). For instance, if an API returns a JSON response containing a `name` field, you can reference that data in another node as `{{$json["name"]}}`.

Example: If you retrieved customer data from an API, you could send a personalized email by referencing the customer's name:

```json
{
  "to": "{{$json["email"]}}",
  "subject": "Your Order Confirmation",
  "body": "Hello {{$json["name"]}}, your order has
been processed."
}
```

4.3.4. Manipulating Data in Nodes

You can manipulate data at each stage of the workflow to fit the needs of subsequent nodes. Some common ways to manipulate data include:

- **Text Transformation**: Use the **Set node** or **Function node** to manipulate strings, such as converting text to uppercase, trimming spaces, or joining strings.
- **Data Filtering**: The **IF node** lets you filter data based on conditions. For example, you could check if an order total is above a certain threshold and trigger different actions accordingly.
- **Formatting Data**: The **Set node** and **Function node** can also format data, like changing the date format or converting values from one type to another.

Example: You could use a **Set node** to format the retrieved date into a readable string:

```json
{
  "formatted_date": "{{ $json['date'] | date('YYYY-
MM-DD') }}"
}
```

4.4. Basic Error Handling in n8n Agents

Error handling is essential for ensuring that **n8n workflows** run smoothly and can recover from issues that may arise during execution. **n8n agents** are capable of **gracefully handling errors** by implementing mechanisms for retries, notifications, and fallbacks.

4.4.1. Why is Error Handling Important?

In any automation system, things can go wrong—whether it's a failed API request, an invalid user input, or a network issue. **Error handling** ensures that the workflow doesn't crash or stop unexpectedly, and it provides mechanisms to recover from failures.

Without proper error handling, your agent may halt execution, leaving tasks incomplete or failing to notify users when something goes wrong.

4.4.2. Configuring Error Handling in n8n

n8n provides several tools and nodes for handling errors during workflow execution:

Step 1: Error Trigger Nodes

1. **Error Trigger**: You can create an **Error Trigger** node that is activated when an error occurs in the workflow. This node can notify the relevant parties or take alternative actions (e.g., retrying the failed action, logging the issue).
    - o **Example**: You could configure the error trigger to send a message via Slack or email whenever an error occurs in the workflow.

Step 2: Retry Logic

1. **Retrying Failed Actions**: For certain actions (like HTTP requests or database operations), you can configure **retry logic** to automatically retry a failed action a number of times before reporting the error.
    - o **Example**: If an HTTP request fails due to network issues, n8n can automatically retry the request up to three times before logging an error.
2. **Configure Retry Delay**: You can set a delay between retries, allowing the system time to recover from temporary issues before attempting the task again.

Step 3: Using the Error Workflow Node

1. **Error Node**: Use the **Error Workflow node** to handle errors at a higher level. This node allows you to define custom behavior in case of failure. It can be connected to any step in the workflow to catch errors or failures.
   - You can configure this node to send a **failure report** or initiate an **alternate workflow** to handle the error.

Step 4: Notifications on Failure

1. **Notifying on Failure**: When an error occurs, you can configure n8n to send notifications to relevant stakeholders. Common notification methods include:
   - **Slack messages** to a specific channel
   - **Emails** to notify administrators or users
   - **Webhook calls** to trigger external error management systems
2. You can use the **Set node** or **Function node** to format the error message before sending it out, ensuring that it provides useful information for debugging.

Step 5: Fallback Logic

1. **Fallback Actions**: If a node encounters a failure and retrying the task doesn't resolve the issue, you can define fallback actions. This might include notifying an administrator, redirecting the workflow to a different path, or simply logging the error for future review.

Example: If an API request fails, you could have the workflow fallback to an alternative node that sends a **default response** or logs the error in a database for further inspection.

4.4.3. Best Practices for Error Handling in n8n

- **Always Use Error Nodes**: Whenever possible, use error nodes to catch any issues and gracefully handle failures.
- **Retry Logic for Critical Actions**: For operations that are essential to the workflow (e.g., API calls, database updates), enable retry logic with appropriate delays.

- **Notify Relevant Stakeholders**: Set up notifications to alert the right people when errors occur, so they can take timely action.
- **Document Errors**: Make sure that errors are logged and stored for future analysis. This can be helpful for troubleshooting and improving workflows.

In this chapter, we've explored how to **manage data flows** in n8n agent workflows, including how to pass and manipulate data between nodes. Additionally, we've covered the importance of **error handling** and how to set up retry logic, fallback actions, and notifications to ensure your workflows remain reliable and resilient to failures.

With this foundation, you can now build more robust and dynamic **n8n agent workflows** that can handle real-world conditions and errors while automating complex tasks seamlessly.

4.5. A Hands-on Example: Automating a Basic Task

In this section, we will walk through a **hands-on example** of automating a basic task using **n8n**. This will help solidify your understanding of how to set up workflows, connect nodes, and pass data between them.

Let's create a simple agent that automates the task of **sending a welcome email** whenever a new customer registers on a website. The agent will perform the following tasks:

1. Receive a new user registration through a **Webhook** trigger.
2. Retrieve user details such as name and email.
3. Send a welcome email to the user.

Step 1: Create a New Workflow

1. From the **n8n Dashboard**, click the **"Create New Workflow"** button to open the **Workflow Editor**.
2. This opens a new, blank canvas where we can start adding nodes to build our workflow.

Step 2: Add a Webhook Trigger

The **Webhook** trigger will allow the workflow to listen for incoming HTTP requests, which is how we simulate receiving a new user registration.

1. In the **Nodes Panel**, search for **Webhook** and drag it onto the canvas.
2. Click on the **Webhook node** to configure it.
   - **HTTP Method**: Select **POST** (this is the method the new user registration will use to send data to the webhook).
   - **Path**: Set the webhook path, such as `/new-user`.
   - This path will be the endpoint URL that other systems can send data to, such as a form submission or API request from your website.

Step 3: Add a Set Node to Capture User Data

Next, we need to capture the data coming from the webhook, which will contain user details like name and email. We'll use the **Set node** to define and manipulate the data.

1. In the **Nodes Panel**, search for **Set** and drag it onto the canvas.
2. Connect the **Webhook node** to the **Set node**.
3. Click on the **Set node** and configure it:
   - Add two fields:
     - **Name**: `user_name` (set the value to `{{$json["name"]}}`, assuming the webhook contains a `name` field).
     - **Email**: `user_email` (set the value to `{{$json["email"]}}`, assuming the webhook contains an `email` field).

   This ensures that we store the **user's name** and **email** in variables for use in the next steps.

Step 4: Add an Email Node to Send the Welcome Message

Now, let's set up the agent to send a welcome email to the user.

1. In the **Nodes Panel**, search for **Send Email** and drag it onto the canvas.
2. Connect the **Set node** to the **Send Email node**.

3. Click on the **Send Email node** and configure it:
   o **SMTP Configuration**: Enter the **SMTP server details** for the email service (e.g., Gmail, Outlook, or your own SMTP server).
   o **To**: Use the `user_email` variable (`{{$node["Set"].json["user_email"]}}`).
   o **Subject**: "Welcome to Our Service, {{$node["Set"].json["user_name"]}}!"
   o **Text**: "Hello {{$node["Set"].json["user_name"]}}, welcome to our service! We're excited to have you onboard."

By using the variables `user_name` and `user_email` in the email body and recipient fields, we personalize the email with the new user's information.

Step 5: Save and Test the Workflow

1. Click **Save** to store your workflow.
2. Click **Execute Workflow** to test the workflow manually. You can test it by simulating a **Webhook request** using a tool like **Postman** or **cURL**.
   o Send a POST request to `http://localhost:5678/webhook/new-user` with a JSON body like this:

   ```json
   json

   {
      "name": "John Doe",
      "email": "johndoe@example.com"
   }
   ```

3. Check the **Execution Log** to verify that the data was passed correctly between the nodes, and the **welcome email** was sent successfully.

Step 6: Activate the Workflow

Once everything is working:

1. Click **Activate** to allow the workflow to run automatically whenever the **Webhook** trigger is invoked (for example, whenever a new user registers on your website).

4.6. Testing and Debugging Your First Agent Workflow

Once you have created your first **n8n agent workflow**, it's important to test and debug it to ensure that it works as expected. **n8n** provides powerful tools for testing workflows, tracking execution logs, and troubleshooting errors.

4.6.1. Testing the Workflow

Before you deploy the agent to production, you need to thoroughly **test** it to ensure that it performs as expected.

Manual Testing

1. **Execute Workflow**: Click the **Execute Workflow** button at the top-right corner to run the workflow manually.
2. **Trigger the Workflow**: If you're using a **Webhook trigger**, you can simulate a trigger (like the new user registration example) using tools like **Postman** or **cURL**. You can send a test HTTP request to the **Webhook URL** with test data.
   - Example with **Postman**:
     - Method: POST
     - URL:
       `http://localhost:5678/webhook/new-user`
     - Body:

       ```json

       {
          "name": "Jane Doe",
          "email": "janedoe@example.com"
       }
       ```

Check the Execution Log

Once the workflow executes, you'll see a real-time log of each node's progress:

1. **Execution Log**: The log shows each step of the workflow and highlights any **errors** or **issues** encountered.

2. **Data Passing**: The log also provides a detailed view of the **data** passed between nodes. You can check whether the **user's name** and **email** were correctly retrieved and passed to the email node.

4.6.2. Debugging Workflow Errors

If something goes wrong during execution (e.g., the email is not sent, or the Webhook doesn't trigger), you can use **n8n's debugging tools** to troubleshoot the issue.

Using Execution Log for Debugging

1. In the **Execution Log**, you will see whether each node executed successfully. If there's an error, n8n will display the error message in the log.
2. **Common Issues to Look for**:
    o **Missing Credentials**: If an action like sending an email fails, make sure your SMTP settings are correctly configured.
    o **Invalid Data**: If the data passed between nodes is incorrect or missing, double-check the node configurations, especially if you are using dynamic variables or expressions.

Node-Level Debugging

1. **Debugging Node Outputs**: Each node displays its input and output data in the **Node Properties Panel**. If an error occurs, check the data that was passed into the node to ensure that all required fields are present and correctly formatted.
2. **Error Handling**: If a node fails, **error nodes** or **retry logic** can help you handle the failure. You can also use **conditional nodes** (like **If** or **Switch**) to catch specific errors and redirect the workflow to an alternative path.

Testing with Different Inputs

For more comprehensive testing, try sending **different data inputs** to simulate real-world conditions:

*   Test edge cases (e.g., empty fields, incorrect email formats).
*   Test how the workflow behaves under different conditions (e.g., when no data is received or when the API request fails).

In this chapter, we've walked through the process of creating a **basic agent workflow** to automate a simple task (sending a welcome email). We also covered the process of **testing** and **debugging** workflows to ensure they run smoothly.

n8n provides a robust platform for building workflows, and with the tools available for testing and debugging, you can ensure that your automation works reliably. The next steps will focus on handling more complex workflows, adding advanced features, and optimizing workflows for performance and scalability.

4.7. Best Practices for Workflow Design

Designing efficient, maintainable, and scalable workflows is crucial for ensuring that **n8n** automation runs smoothly. Adhering to best practices not only improves workflow performance but also makes it easier to debug, expand, and collaborate on workflows. In this section, we will explore the best practices for designing workflows in **n8n** to maximize effectiveness and minimize issues.

4.7.1. Plan Your Workflow Before Implementation

Before diving into the workflow editor, it's essential to **plan your workflow** thoroughly. A clear understanding of the task you're automating helps you define each step accurately.

Best Practices:

- **Map the Workflow**: Sketch out a diagram or outline of the workflow before starting. This can be as simple as a flowchart showing the steps, triggers, actions, and expected outcomes.
  - **Example**: For an email notification system, plan how data flows from the trigger (e.g., webhook or schedule) through the various actions (e.g., data fetching, conditional logic, email sending).

- **Identify Data Sources**: Understand where your data is coming from and how it will be processed. Know whether the data is static, dynamic, or coming from external APIs.
- **Define Expected Outputs**: Think through the final result that you want the workflow to produce. This will guide your node selections and conditions.

4.7.2. Keep Workflows Simple and Modular

While it's tempting to create large workflows with many nodes, it's important to **keep workflows modular and simple**. A simpler workflow is easier to manage, debug, and scale.

Best Practices:

- **Break Down Complex Workflows**: Instead of building one massive workflow, break it into smaller, modular workflows. Each workflow can handle a specific task (e.g., one for sending an email, another for database queries).
  - **Example**: A large workflow that processes customer data can be broken into smaller workflows, such as one for gathering data, one for transforming the data, and one for sending notifications.
- **Reuse Workflows and Sub-Workflows**: Create reusable workflows or **sub-workflows** for tasks that appear in multiple workflows. For example, you might have a standard **error handling workflow** that can be reused across different workflows.
- **Use Sub-Workflows for Long or Repetitive Tasks**: For complex tasks, consider using the **Execute Workflow node**, which allows you to trigger another workflow. This keeps your main workflow clean and ensures modularity.

4.7.3. Minimize Data Duplication

Duplicating data unnecessarily can lead to performance degradation and errors. Ensure data flows efficiently through the workflow, and avoid redundancy.

Best Practices:

- **Avoid Storing Data Repeatedly**: If the same data is needed across multiple nodes, pass it from one node to another instead of duplicating it in multiple places.
  - ○ **Example**: Use variables to store data that needs to be accessed across multiple nodes rather than setting the same data multiple times.
- **Optimize Data Handling**: If your workflow involves fetching large datasets, make sure you're processing only the necessary information to avoid performance bottlenecks.

4.7.4. Use Conditional Logic Wisely

Conditional logic (e.g., **If-Else**, **Switch** nodes) is a powerful tool for making workflows dynamic. However, overusing complex conditionals can make workflows harder to follow and debug.

Best Practices:

- **Keep Conditions Simple**: Use conditionals to check for basic conditions like data presence or simple comparisons. Avoid overly complex logic in a single node.
- **Use Default Paths**: Whenever possible, include **default actions** for unexpected conditions to ensure that the workflow doesn't break.
  - ○ **Example**: If a particular condition isn't met, use a fallback action that logs the issue or sends an alert instead of causing the entire workflow to fail.
- **Avoid Deep Nesting of Conditions**: While n8n allows multiple levels of conditions, try to keep the logic **flat** and easy to follow. Deeply nested conditionals can be hard to maintain and debug.

4.7.5. Ensure Error Handling is in Place

Error handling is crucial for building reliable workflows. Without proper error handling, an unexpected failure could stop the entire workflow or lead to undetected issues.

Best Practices:

- **Use the Error Workflow Node**: Always include an **Error Node** or define **fallback actions** for scenarios where things might go wrong. This ensures the workflow is resilient and can recover from failures.
- **Log Errors for Later Review**: Ensure that errors are logged for future analysis. You can use the **Set node** or **Function node** to log detailed error messages to a database or external system.
- **Set Retry Logic**: For tasks that are prone to temporary failures (e.g., network requests), enable **retry logic** to automatically attempt the task again.
- **Fail Gracefully**: If an error is unavoidable, the workflow should **fail gracefully**. This means notifying relevant parties and providing clear information on what went wrong.

4.7.6. Test Early and Often

Testing is a critical part of workflow design. As you build, you should frequently test the workflow to ensure that each step is functioning as expected.

Best Practices:

- **Test Individual Nodes**: Test each node separately to make sure it's performing its task as expected. This is especially important for API calls, integrations, and complex logic nodes.
- **Use the Execution Log**: The **Execution Log** provides real-time feedback about each node's execution. If an error occurs, it will be logged, which helps in quickly diagnosing issues.
- **Run Small Tests**: Before deploying an entire workflow, run smaller tests with sample data to make sure everything works end-to-end. Start with basic workflows and expand as you gain confidence.
- **Use the Test Feature in n8n**: The **"Execute Workflow"** button lets you test workflows manually. For workflows triggered by webhooks or events, simulate those triggers using tools like **Postman** or **curl**.

4.7.7. Use Naming Conventions and Comments

Organizing your workflow with **clear naming conventions** and **comments** makes it easier to understand and maintain. This is particularly important when sharing workflows with teammates or revisiting them after some time.

Best Practices:

- **Name Nodes Clearly**: Use descriptive names for your nodes that explain what each part of the workflow does. For example, use names like "Fetch User Data," "Send Confirmation Email," or "Process Payment."
- **Comment Nodes**: Use comments to explain complex logic or parts of the workflow that may need clarification. Comments are a great way to document your workflows for future reference.
- **Organize Workflow Layout**: Keep your workflow layout **clean and organized**. Align nodes logically to make the workflow easy to follow. Use the **Zoom** feature to zoom out for better visual organization.

4.7.8. Optimize for Performance

As workflows grow in complexity, performance can become an issue. Optimizing workflows can help ensure they run smoothly, even with large amounts of data.

Best Practices:

- **Minimize Redundant Operations**: Avoid repetitive tasks that don't add value, like repeatedly querying the same data or sending duplicate notifications.
- **Limit External API Calls**: API calls can slow down workflows if they're too frequent or unnecessary. Ensure that API requests are necessary and that data is cached or reused where appropriate.
- **Batch Data**: If processing large datasets, consider using **batch processing** to break the data into smaller, more manageable chunks. This helps prevent timeouts and improves performance.
- **Use Caching for Data**: Cache frequently used data whenever possible to avoid repeated requests for the same data.

By following these **best practices** for workflow design, you'll be able to build **efficient, scalable**, and **maintainable workflows** in **n8n**. The combination of planning, simplicity, modularity, error handling, and testing will help you create workflows that are not only reliable but also adaptable to evolving requirements.

Chapter 5: Advanced Agent Features

5.1. Implementing Loops and Branching Logic in n8n Agents

In **n8n**, you can create **advanced workflows** by using **loops** and **branching logic**. These features enable you to handle repetitive tasks and complex decision-making processes, making your agents more dynamic and adaptive. In this section, we'll explore how to implement **loops** and **branching logic** within **n8n agents**.

5.1.1. What Are Loops in n8n?

A **loop** allows you to repeat a set of actions multiple times within a workflow. This is useful for tasks that involve processing multiple items, such as iterating over a list of customer records or processing files in a directory.

Types of Loops:

- **Loop Through Data (Iterate)**: This loop type allows you to iterate over a collection of data (e.g., an array or list) and execute the same task for each item in the list.
- **Set a Fixed Number of Iterations**: You can loop a specific number of times, which is helpful for scenarios where the number of iterations is predetermined.

5.1.2. Implementing a Simple Loop with n8n

Here's how to implement a basic loop in n8n:

1. **Create a Set Node** to define the data you want to iterate over (e.g., an array of customer records).
   - Example:

```json
{
  "customers": [
    {"name": "John Doe", "email":
"john@example.com"},
```

```
    {"name": "Jane Smith", "email":
"jane@example.com"},
    {"name": "Robert Brown", "email":
"robert@example.com"}
  ]
}
```

2. **Add the "Loop" Node**: Drag the **Loop node** (called **"SplitInBatches"** in n8n) onto the canvas.
   o Connect the **Set node** to the **SplitInBatches node**.
   o Configure the **SplitInBatches** node to loop over the customer data array.
3. **Configure the Loop**:
   o Set the **Batch Size** to 1, meaning the loop will process one customer at a time.
   o Each iteration will pass one customer to the next node in the workflow.
4. **Add Action Nodes**: After the **SplitInBatches node**, add an action node (e.g., **Send Email**) to send an email to each customer in the list.
   o Use the variables set in the loop, such as `{{$json["name"]}}` and `{{$json["email"]}}`, to customize the email for each customer.
5. **Test the Loop**: Run the workflow and verify that each customer receives their own email.

5.1.3. Use Cases for Loops

- **Email Campaigns**: Sending personalized emails to a list of customers.
- **Data Processing**: Iterating through a list of data entries, such as invoices or orders, and performing the same operation on each one.
- **Batch Updates**: Updating records in a database in small batches to avoid timeouts or performance issues.

5.1.4. What is Branching Logic in n8n?

Branching logic allows you to create **conditional workflows** where the flow of the workflow diverges based on certain criteria. This enables dynamic decision-making, allowing agents to respond to different data or conditions.

Types of Branching Logic:

- **If-Else Conditions**: Simple decision-making based on a condition. If the condition is true, one set of actions occurs; if false, another set of actions takes place.
- **Switch Node**: A more advanced branching mechanism where you can check multiple conditions and route the workflow based on the outcome.
- **Multiple Branches**: You can create multiple branches within a workflow, where different paths are taken based on data or logic.

5.1.5. Implementing Branching Logic with n8n

Here's how to implement a basic **if-else** branching logic in n8n:

1. **Add an If Node**: In the **Nodes Panel**, search for and drag the **If** node onto the canvas.
2. **Connect the Previous Node**: Connect the node that outputs data (e.g., an **HTTP Request** node) to the **If** node.
3. **Configure the Condition**: Set a condition that the workflow will check. For example:
   - **Condition**: Check if a field `{{$json["status"]}}` equals `"active"`.
   - This means the workflow will follow different paths depending on whether the status is `"active"` or not.
4. **Add Action Nodes for Both Conditions**: You can add different actions for the **True** and **False** conditions. For example:
   - **True**: Send a confirmation email if the status is active.
   - **False**: Trigger an alert or log the issue if the status is inactive.
5. **Test the Workflow**: When the workflow runs, it will process the condition and take the appropriate action based on the data provided.

5.1.6. Use Cases for Branching Logic

- **Dynamic Email Responses**: Send different emails based on user actions or preferences (e.g., send a confirmation email if an order is placed, or send a discount email if the user has abandoned their cart).
- **Order Processing**: Different actions for processing orders based on the order status (e.g., if the order is paid, proceed to shipment; if not, send a reminder).

5.2. Working with Conditionals and Filters

Conditionals and filters allow you to control the flow of data and actions in **n8n workflows**. By applying filters and conditions, you can ensure that only specific data triggers actions or decisions.

5.2.1. What are Conditionals in n8n?

Conditionals are used to evaluate data and determine the flow of the workflow. With conditionals, you can perform checks like:

- Is a value equal to something?
- Is a value greater than or less than a certain number?
- Is a field not empty?

Types of Conditional Nodes:

- **If Node**: Evaluates a single condition and branches the workflow based on true or false.
- **Switch Node**: A more advanced version of the **If Node**, which allows for multiple branches based on different values or conditions.

5.2.2. Using the If Node for Conditional Logic

The **If node** allows you to set up simple conditions to control the flow of the workflow.

1. **Configure the If Node**:
   - Add an **If Node** and connect it to the node that outputs the data you want to evaluate.
   - In the **Node Properties Panel**, set the **Condition Type**. You can check conditions like:
     - **Value equals**: For example, `{{$json["status"]}}` equals `"paid"`.
     - **Value greater than**: For example, checking if an amount is greater than a certain threshold.
2. **Define Actions for Both Conditions**: You can add different actions for when the condition is **true** and **false**. For example:
   - **True**: Proceed with order fulfillment.
   - **False**: Send an email to the customer requesting payment.

5.2.3. Using the Switch Node for Multiple Conditions

The **Switch node** allows you to evaluate multiple conditions at once. This is useful when you want to create different paths for different data values.

1. **Add the Switch Node**: Search for and drag the **Switch node** onto the canvas.
2. **Configure Multiple Conditions**: In the **Node Properties Panel**, you can set multiple conditions, such as:
   - **Case 1**: If `{{$json["status"]}}` equals `"pending"`, perform Action 1.
   - **Case 2**: If `{{$json["status"]}}` equals `"completed"`, perform Action 2.
3. **Add Actions for Each Condition**: Connect actions to each condition branch. This allows you to handle multiple scenarios in one workflow.

5.2.4. Using Filters to Limit Data

In n8n, you can use filters to limit the data passed between nodes or restrict actions to only occur when certain criteria are met. Filters are particularly useful in data processing workflows.

- **Example of a Filter**:
  - You can use the **IF node** to check whether a field is empty or matches a specific pattern. For example, only continue with the workflow if a field contains a value greater than zero.

5.2.5. Combining Conditions and Filters

In more complex workflows, you can **combine conditionals and filters** to ensure the right actions are taken based on precise conditions. For example:

- **If the status is "active"** and the **order total is greater than $100**, then proceed to send an email.
- If either condition fails, the workflow could log an error or send a different email.

In this chapter, we've explored how to implement **loops, branching logic**, and **conditionals** in **n8n agents** to build more **dynamic, adaptive workflows**. With loops, your agents can iterate over data, and with branching logic, they can make decisions based on the data they encounter. Conditionals and filters allow for precise control over which actions are executed in the workflow.

These advanced features allow you to create intelligent workflows that can respond to different conditions and data, enabling powerful automation capabilities.

5.3. Creating Custom Actions for Agents

One of the most powerful features of **n8n** is its ability to create **custom actions** for your agents. Custom actions give you the flexibility to extend the platform's capabilities beyond built-in integrations and tailor your workflows to specific use cases.

In this section, we will walk through how to create **custom actions** for **n8n agents** and integrate them into your workflows. These custom actions can be written using **JavaScript** in **n8n's Function nodes** and can interact with external systems, process data, or perform any custom task you need.

5.3.1. What are Custom Actions?

Custom actions in **n8n** allow you to:

- **Run custom scripts**: You can write **JavaScript code** to define how data is processed or transformed in a workflow.
- **Extend functionality**: If **n8n** doesn't have a built-in integration for a specific service or action, you can create your own by using custom code in nodes.
- **Interact with external APIs**: Use JavaScript to make requests to APIs, process the responses, and send data to other services.

5.3.2. Creating a Custom Action Using the Function Node

The **Function node** in **n8n** allows you to write custom JavaScript code to define the logic of your actions. Here's how to create a basic custom action using the **Function node**:

1. **Add the Function Node**:
   o In the **Nodes Panel**, search for **Function** and drag it onto the canvas.
   o Connect the previous node (e.g., **Webhook Trigger** or **HTTP Request** node) to the **Function node**.
2. **Configure the Function Node**:
   o Click on the **Function node** to open the **Node Properties Panel**.
   o In the **JavaScript Code** section, you can write your custom code. This can involve manipulating data, calling APIs, or performing calculations.

Example of a simple custom action to process incoming data:

```javascript
// Custom Action: Process Incoming Data
const input = $json["input_data"];  //
Retrieve input data
const output = input.toUpperCase(); // Process
data (example: convert to uppercase)

return [{ json: { output_data: output } }];
```

   o In this example, we are transforming the input data into uppercase and passing it as output.
3. **Pass Data Between Nodes**:
   o The **Function node** can pass processed data to the next node in the workflow. The data returned from the **Function node** will be available to the next node via the {{$json}} object.
4. **Test the Custom Action**:
   o Click on **Execute Workflow** to test your custom action. Check the **Execution Log** to see if the custom action processed the data as expected.

5.3.3. Use Cases for Custom Actions

- **Custom Data Processing**: You may need to process incoming data before sending it to another service. For example, you could clean up user input data (removing unnecessary spaces or correcting formatting).

- **External API Calls**: If you need to interact with a service that's not directly supported by **n8n** (for instance, an internal API), you can make an API request using custom JavaScript in the **Function node**.
- **Advanced Logic**: Use **custom actions** to implement advanced business logic, such as performing calculations, validating data, or creating custom decision trees.

5.3.4. Using Custom Actions for Complex Automation

You can combine custom actions with other **n8n nodes** to build more complex workflows. For instance, a **Webhook Trigger** node can trigger a custom action to fetch data from an external service, which is then passed to other nodes for further processing (e.g., sending emails, storing data in databases).

5.4. Using Webhooks and APIs with Agents

Webhooks and **APIs** are integral components of **n8n agents**, allowing them to integrate with external systems and trigger workflows based on events or external data. Webhooks enable **n8n agents** to listen for incoming HTTP requests, while APIs allow agents to interact with other services and send or receive data.

In this section, we will explore how to use **webhooks** and **APIs** with **n8n agents** to create dynamic, event-driven workflows.

5.4.1. What is a Webhook?

A **webhook** is an HTTP endpoint that allows your **n8n agent** to **receive data** from external systems or services. When a specific event occurs in an external system (e.g., a new order is placed, or a customer submits a form), that system sends an HTTP request to the webhook URL, triggering the workflow in **n8n**.

How Webhooks Work in n8n:

1. **Webhooks Listen for Events**: A **Webhook Trigger** node listens for incoming HTTP requests from external systems. This node contains a URL that external systems can use to send data to **n8n**.

2. **Triggering Workflows**: When the webhook receives a request, it activates the workflow. The data sent by the external system is then processed through the workflow nodes.
3. **Flexible Payloads**: Webhooks can send data in various formats, such as **JSON, XML,** or **form data**. The data is passed to subsequent nodes for further processing, such as filtering, transforming, or sending notifications.

5.4.2. Setting Up a Webhook Trigger in n8n

1. **Create a Webhook Trigger**:
   - Drag the **Webhook** node onto the canvas from the **Nodes Panel**.
   - The **Webhook node** will generate a unique URL that you can use to receive data from external systems.
2. **Configure the Webhook**:
   - **HTTP Method**: Set the **HTTP method** (typically **POST** for webhooks).
   - **Webhook Path**: Set a custom path (e.g., `/new-order`). This URL will be used by the external system to send data to **n8n**.

   Example Webhook URL:
   `http://localhost:5678/webhook/new-order`

3. **Test the Webhook**:
   - Use a tool like **Postman** or **cURL** to send a test POST request to the webhook URL. The request should contain sample data, such as:

   ```json
   {
     "order_id": "12345",
     "customer_name": "John Doe",
     "total_amount": 100
   }
   ```

   - After sending the request, check the **Execution Log** to see if the data was received and processed by the workflow.
4. **Processing the Data**:

o The data sent by the webhook will be available in subsequent nodes using expressions like `{{$json["order_id"]}}` or `{{$json["customer_name"]}}`.

5.4.3. Working with External APIs

In addition to receiving data via webhooks, **n8n agents** can also interact with external APIs by making **HTTP requests**. This allows your workflows to retrieve or send data to other systems, such as third-party services, databases, or cloud platforms.

Using the HTTP Request Node

1. **Add an HTTP Request Node**: In the **Nodes Panel**, search for **HTTP Request** and drag it onto the canvas.
2. **Configure the API Request**:
   o **URL**: Set the API URL (e.g., `https://api.example.com/data`).
   o **HTTP Method**: Choose the appropriate HTTP method (GET, POST, PUT, DELETE).
   o **Headers**: Set any required headers, such as **Authorization** tokens or **Content-Type**.
   o **Body**: If needed, provide the data to be sent in the request body (for POST requests).

   Example of API request configuration:

   o **Method**: POST
   o **URL**: `https://api.example.com/send-email`
   o **Headers**: `{ "Authorization": "Bearer YOUR_API_KEY" }`
   o **Body**: `{ "email": "johndoe@example.com", "subject": "Welcome!", "message": "Thanks for signing up!" }`
3. **Test the API Request**:
   o Click **Execute Workflow** to test the API request. The **HTTP Request** node will make the call to the external API and return the response, which can be processed in subsequent nodes.

5.4.4. Use Cases for Webhooks and APIs

- **Webhook Triggers**: Automatically start workflows when events occur in external systems, such as new form submissions, orders, or data changes.
- **API Integration**: Send data to or retrieve data from external services like payment gateways, CRMs, or marketing platforms. For example, after receiving a new order via webhook, an agent can call a payment processing API to charge the customer's credit card.

Webhooks and APIs are powerful tools that enable **n8n agents** to interact with external systems and trigger workflows based on real-time data. By using **webhooks**, you can listen for events from third-party systems, while **HTTP requests** allow you to interact with APIs to send or retrieve data.

In this chapter, we've learned how to set up webhooks and API interactions within **n8n agents** to create highly dynamic and responsive workflows. These integrations open up a wide range of automation possibilities, allowing you to connect various services and perform actions based on external triggers and data.

5.5. Handling External Data with n8n Agents

In **n8n**, handling external data is a core capability that allows agents to interact with various services, APIs, databases, and other external sources. Properly managing this external data is essential for creating effective workflows that process, transform, and use the data in meaningful ways. In this section, we'll explore how to handle external data within **n8n agents**, focusing on data retrieval, processing, and passing data between nodes.

5.5.1. Retrieving External Data

n8n agents are highly capable of interacting with external data sources, such as third-party APIs, databases, or cloud services. The **HTTP Request node** is typically used to make API calls, while **database nodes** can retrieve data directly from SQL or NoSQL databases.

Using the HTTP Request Node:

To fetch external data from an API:

1. **Add the HTTP Request Node**: In the **Nodes Panel**, search for **HTTP Request** and drag it onto the canvas.
2. **Configure the API Request**:
   o Set the **URL** of the API endpoint.
   o Choose the appropriate **HTTP method** (GET, POST, etc.).
   o Set any **headers** required by the API, such as **Authorization** or **Content-Type**.
   o Define the **parameters** in the request body if needed (for POST requests).

Example of retrieving weather data from a weather API (like OpenWeather):

json

```
{
  "URL":
"https://api.openweathermap.org/data/2.5/weather?q=
London&appid=YOUR_API_KEY",
  "Method": "GET",
  "Headers": {"Content-Type": "application/json"}
}
```

3. **Test the Request**: After setting the parameters, click **Execute Workflow** to run the request and see the data returned by the API.

Working with External Databases:

For workflows that interact with **external databases** (e.g., MySQL, PostgreSQL, MongoDB), n8n provides specific nodes to fetch data.

1. **Add Database Node**: Search for a **database node** (e.g., **MySQL, PostgreSQL**), and drag it to the canvas.
2. **Configure the Database Connection**: Enter the database connection details (host, username, password, database name).
3. **Run Queries**: Use SQL queries (or query builder tools in n8n) to retrieve data from the database.

Example for querying a PostgreSQL database:

```sql
sql

SELECT * FROM customers WHERE status = 'active';
```

Once configured, data from the database will be available as JSON objects that can be used in subsequent nodes.

5.5.2. Processing External Data

After retrieving data from external sources, you may need to process it before passing it to other nodes. Common processing tasks include filtering, transforming, and formatting the data to fit the needs of the workflow.

Transforming Data with the Set Node:

The **Set node** allows you to define and manipulate variables, transforming external data into a desired format or extracting specific fields.

1. **Add a Set Node**: Drag the **Set node** onto the canvas and connect it to the node that retrieves the external data (e.g., **HTTP Request node**).
2. **Define Variables**: In the **Node Properties Panel**, define the variables that will hold the transformed data.
   - You can **rename fields, format dates**, or **combine values** to create new variables.

Example: Extracting and renaming fields from the weather API response:

```json
json

{
  "city": "{{$json['name']}}",
  "temperature": "{{$json['main']['temp']}}",
  "humidity": "{{$json['main']['humidity']}}"
}
```

This extracts the **city name, temperature**, and **humidity** from the API response and assigns them to new variables.

Manipulating Data with the Function Node:

If you need to perform more complex operations on the data (e.g., calculations, conditionals, or loops), you can use the **Function node**. This node allows you to write **JavaScript code** to manipulate data.

1. **Add the Function Node**: Drag the **Function node** onto the canvas and connect it to the node that outputs external data.
2. **Write JavaScript Code**: In the **Node Properties Panel**, write custom JavaScript code to process the data.

Example: Converting temperature from Kelvin to Celsius:

```javascript
const temperatureKelvin = $json["temperature"];
const temperatureCelsius = temperatureKelvin -
273.15;
return [{ json: { temperature_celsius:
temperatureCelsius } }];
```

5.5.3. Passing Data Between Nodes

Once external data is processed, it can be passed between nodes as variables, making it available for other actions in the workflow.

1. **Data Flow**: After transforming or manipulating data, the results can be passed to the next node using expressions like `{{$json["temperature_celsius"]}}` or `{{$node["Set"].json["humidity"]}}`.
2. **Actions Based on External Data**: You can now use the processed data in subsequent nodes, such as sending a personalized **email**, posting to **Slack**, or storing it in a **database**.

Example: Using the temperature value in an email body:

```json
{
  "to": "{{$json["email"]}}",
  "subject": "Weather Update",
```

```
"body": "Hello, the current temperature in your
city is {{$json["temperature_celsius"]}}°C."
}
```

5.6. Building Complex Agent Workflows with Multiple Paths

Building complex agent workflows often involves dealing with multiple decision points and branching logic. n8n provides powerful features like **conditional logic, loops,** and **parallel execution** to help you manage these complexities.

In this section, we will explore how to create workflows with **multiple paths, conditional branches,** and **parallel executions** to handle sophisticated automation tasks.

5.6.1. Using Conditional Logic to Branch Workflows

Conditional logic allows workflows to take different paths depending on data or input conditions. This is useful for scenarios where different actions need to be taken based on the data processed by the agent.

Step 1: Add an If Node

The **If node** lets you define conditions and route the workflow based on whether the condition evaluates to true or false.

1. **Configure the If Node**:
   o In the **Node Properties Panel**, set the **condition** you want to check. For example, check if the **order amount** is greater than $100:

   ```json
   json

   "order_amount": {{$json["order_amount"]}} >
   100
   ```

2. **Branch the Workflow**:
   o After adding the **If node**, connect two different paths: one for when the condition is **true** and another for when it is **false**.
   o For example:
     ▪ **True**: Proceed with processing the payment.

- **False**: Send a notification that the order is too small.

Step 2: Handling Multiple Conditions with the Switch Node

The **Switch node** allows for more complex branching logic with multiple conditions. You can define several possible outcomes based on the value of a field.

1. **Add a Switch Node**:
   - In the **Node Properties Panel**, configure multiple conditions (e.g., check the **order status** and take different actions based on whether it's "pending", "shipped", or "completed").
2. **Branch the Workflow Based on Conditions**:
   - Each condition in the **Switch node** represents a different path in the workflow. This allows you to handle multiple scenarios within a single workflow.

5.6.2. Using Loops for Repetitive Tasks

Loops in **n8n** allow you to repeat actions for each item in a list or collection. This is particularly useful when you need to process a set of data or perform a task multiple times.

Step 1: Use the SplitInBatches Node

The **SplitInBatches node** is commonly used to split a large dataset into smaller chunks, allowing you to process them one at a time.

1. **Configure the SplitInBatches Node**:
   - Connect it to a **Set node** or **HTTP Request node** that outputs an array of data (e.g., a list of customer records).
   - Configure the **Batch Size** to define how many items will be processed per iteration.
2. **Process Data in Batches**:
   - After splitting the data into batches, you can use a **loop** (e.g., using the **Function node**) to process each item in the batch, such as sending an email for each customer.

Step 2: Use a Loop with the Function Node

In some cases, you may want to implement custom loops in the **Function node** using JavaScript. For example:

```javascript
const customers = $json["customers"]; // Array of
customers
let emails = [];

for (let i = 0; i < customers.length; i++) {
  const customer = customers[i];
  emails.push({ email: customer.email });
}

return emails;
```

This loop iterates over the customers' list and processes each one.

5.6.3. Running Multiple Tasks in Parallel

Parallel execution is useful when you want to run multiple tasks simultaneously to improve workflow efficiency. **n8n** allows you to execute independent tasks in parallel without waiting for one task to finish before starting the next.

Step 1: Use the Execute Workflow Node

1. The **Execute Workflow node** allows you to trigger other workflows in parallel.
2. By configuring multiple **Execute Workflow nodes**, you can run different tasks at the same time, improving performance and scalability.

Step 2: Configure Parallel Execution

1. Set up multiple nodes (e.g., one for making an API request and another for processing data) and connect them in parallel by using **Execute Workflow nodes**.

In this chapter, we covered how to build **complex agent workflows** by using **multiple paths, loops,** and **parallel execution**. These advanced features allow you to create intelligent and adaptable workflows capable of handling a wide range of tasks and decision-making processes.

By implementing **conditional logic** and **loops**, you can create workflows that process data dynamically based on specific conditions. Additionally, **parallel execution** ensures that tasks run efficiently, even for complex workflows with multiple steps.

5.7. Advanced Error Handling and Retries

In any complex automation system, errors are inevitable. How you handle those errors can make a significant difference in the reliability and efficiency of your workflows. **n8n** provides several tools and strategies for managing errors and automatically retrying tasks when failures occur. In this section, we'll dive into **advanced error handling** and **retry mechanisms** to ensure that your **n8n agents** can handle unexpected failures gracefully.

5.7.1. What is Advanced Error Handling?

Advanced error handling allows your workflows to continue operating even when certain steps fail. Instead of causing a workflow to stop entirely, **n8n** enables you to **define specific actions for errors** (e.g., retrying the failed operation, logging the error, or sending notifications to administrators).

Types of Error Handling in n8n:

- **Retry Logic**: Automatically retrying a failed operation.
- **Error Nodes**: Defining what should happen when a node encounters an error.
- **Error Alerts and Notifications**: Sending alerts or notifications to relevant stakeholders when something goes wrong.
- **Fallback Actions**: Executing a different action when the primary action fails.

5.7.2. Implementing Retry Logic

The **Retry Logic** feature in **n8n** allows nodes to automatically **retry** an action if it fails. This is particularly useful for actions that are prone to transient issues, such as network requests or API calls.

Steps to Implement Retry Logic:

1. **Add the Action Node**: Begin by adding an action node (e.g., **HTTP Request, Send Email**) to your workflow.
2. **Enable Retry Settings**: In the **Node Properties Panel** of the action node, you'll find the **Retry Settings**. You can configure:
    -   **Max Retries**: The number of times to retry a failed action.
    -   **Retry Delay**: The time between retries (e.g., 5 minutes).
3. **Configure Conditions for Retries**: You can set retry logic for specific error conditions. For example, only retry if the error is related to a **timeout** or **temporary failure**.

Example: For an **HTTP Request** node, you can configure it to retry up to 3 times with a delay of 10 seconds between attempts. This ensures that temporary connectivity issues won't cause the entire workflow to fail.

Using Retry Logic for API Requests:

If an API call fails due to a timeout or temporary issue, you can configure **retry logic** to retry the call:

json

```
{
  "retries": 3,
  "retryDelay": 10
}
```

This configuration retries the request up to 3 times, waiting 10 seconds between each attempt.

5.7.3. Using Error Nodes

Error Nodes are a powerful tool in **n8n** that allows you to define specific actions when an error occurs in your workflow. You can use these nodes to capture errors and redirect the workflow, send notifications, or log them for later investigation.

Steps to Use Error Nodes:

1. **Add the Error Node**: Drag the **Error Trigger** node into your workflow.
2. **Define the Error Action**: Configure the error node to take specific actions, such as:
   - **Send an alert**: Send an email or Slack message to notify administrators.
   - **Retry the action**: Redirect the workflow to another part that retries the task.
   - **Log the error**: Record the error in a database or file for later review.

Example: If an **API request** fails, you can configure the **Error Node** to send a Slack notification to your development team, so they can investigate the issue.

5.7.4. Error Alerts and Notifications

Setting up **alerts** and **notifications** is an essential part of error handling, especially for critical workflows. These notifications ensure that you're aware of issues as soon as they occur and can take immediate action.

Steps to Set Up Error Notifications:

1. **Add a Slack or Email Node**: If you want to send a notification, you can use the **Send Slack Message** node or the **Send Email** node.
2. **Connect the Error Node**: After defining your **Error Node**, connect it to the notification node.
3. **Configure the Notification**:
   - For **Slack**, provide the channel and message content.
   - For **Email**, provide the recipient's address, subject, and body content.

Example: Set up the **Send Email** node to send a detailed error report if the workflow fails:

- **To**: admin@example.com
- **Subject**: "Error in n8n Workflow"
- **Body**: "An error occurred during the execution of the workflow. Please check the logs for details."

5.7.5. Fallback Actions

Fallback actions are a way to ensure that when a critical task fails, there is a predefined alternative action. Fallbacks can include retrying the task, logging the error, or performing a simpler task instead.

Setting Up Fallback Actions:

1. **Create a Conditional Check**: Use the **If Node** or **Switch Node** to check if an error has occurred.
2. **Define Alternative Action**: Set up an alternative action in case the primary action fails. For example, if an API request fails, you can set the fallback to send a default message.

Example: If a **payment processing node** fails, you can set the fallback action to **send a failure notification** or **log the failure** for later analysis.

5.8. Performance Optimization for Large Workflows

As your workflows grow in complexity and size, optimizing their performance becomes increasingly important. Poorly designed workflows can lead to delays, timeouts, and inefficient execution. In this section, we'll explore strategies for **optimizing the performance** of your **n8n workflows**, ensuring they run efficiently even with large amounts of data.

5.8.1. Best Practices for Optimizing n8n Workflows

1. Minimize Unnecessary Nodes

Each node in **n8n** executes a specific task, and every additional node can increase the execution time. To optimize your workflows:

- **Remove Unnecessary Nodes**: Ensure that each node serves a purpose and eliminate any redundant nodes that don't contribute to the process.
- **Combine Nodes When Possible**: Some tasks can be combined into a single node (e.g., data transformations can be done in the **Set node** instead of using multiple action nodes).

2. Use the Wait and Delay Nodes

If your workflow interacts with external services (like APIs), consider using **Wait** or **Delay** nodes to manage timing:

- **Wait Node**: Pauses the workflow for a specified duration, helping you avoid overwhelming external systems with too many requests at once.
- **Delay Node**: Similar to the wait node but can be more granular with configurable time intervals.

3. Use Efficient Data Structures

- **Batch Data Processing**: When dealing with large datasets, process the data in **batches** instead of handling everything at once. This can prevent timeouts and reduce the load on your systems.
  - For example, use the **SplitInBatches node** to process large sets of data in smaller chunks.
- **Limit Data Retrieval**: When fetching data from external systems, only retrieve the data you need (e.g., limit the number of rows returned by a database query or API request). This reduces unnecessary data processing and speeds up execution.

4. Leverage Parallel Execution

For workflows with tasks that can run independently, you can use **parallel execution** to perform multiple actions simultaneously rather than sequentially. This significantly reduces the total execution time.

- **Use the Execute Workflow Node**: You can trigger different workflows to run in parallel by using the **Execute Workflow node**.
- **Parallel Node Execution**: Connect nodes to run simultaneously instead of sequentially, ensuring tasks that don't depend on each other run concurrently.

5. Optimize API Calls

Interacting with external APIs can slow down workflows. To optimize API calls:

- **Limit the Number of API Requests**: If your workflow involves multiple API calls, batch the requests together if possible. Some APIs support batch processing for multiple operations in one request.
- **Cache Results**: If you frequently call the same API, consider caching the results locally in a **database** or a **Set node** to avoid repeated requests.

6. Monitor Workflow Execution

Keep an eye on the **execution log** to monitor how long each node takes to execute. Identify slow nodes and optimize them accordingly, either by refactoring the workflow or optimizing the services being called.

5.8.2. Optimizing Large Workflows in n8n

1. Use Efficient Data Flow Management

- **Minimize Data Transfer**: Keep data flow within the workflow efficient. Use **expressions** to pass only the necessary data from one node to another instead of sending large datasets.
- **Filter Data Early**: If you're working with large datasets, use a **filtering node** as early as possible to limit the amount of data passed through the workflow.

2. Manage External Integrations

- **API Rate Limits**: Be mindful of **API rate limits** when interacting with external services. Use the **Wait node** or **Delay node** to pace API requests and avoid hitting rate limits.

- **Optimize Database Queries**: If you're querying databases, ensure your queries are efficient. Use indexed fields in SQL queries, limit the number of results returned, and avoid unnecessary joins or complex operations.

3. Clean Workflow Design

- **Organize Workflows for Clarity**: Cleanly separate different parts of the workflow into logical sections. This can help you identify bottlenecks and optimize them more effectively.

In this chapter, we've covered **advanced error handling**, including **retry logic**, **error nodes**, and **fallback actions** to ensure that your workflows continue to function reliably even in the face of issues. Additionally, we explored **performance optimization** techniques to help improve the efficiency and scalability of your **n8n workflows**, especially as they grow in complexity.

By following these best practices, you can create robust, efficient workflows that handle errors gracefully and execute quickly, even with large datasets or complex tasks.

Chapter 6: Integrating External Systems with n8n Agents

6.1. Connecting to APIs and Web Services

Integrating external APIs and web services into **n8n agents** is a powerful way to extend the capabilities of your workflows. APIs allow you to interact with external systems, retrieve data, send data, and trigger actions in other applications. This section will explore how to **connect to APIs** and **web services** using **n8n agents**.

6.1.1. What is an API?

An **API** (Application Programming Interface) allows two software applications to communicate with each other. APIs are used to access the functionality of external systems, retrieve data, and send data.

- **REST APIs**: Most modern web services use REST (Representational State Transfer) architecture, which is lightweight and operates over HTTP. RESTful APIs use methods such as **GET**, **POST**, **PUT**, and **DELETE** to perform actions.
- **SOAP APIs**: Some legacy systems use SOAP (Simple Object Access Protocol) for web services, which relies on XML messaging.

6.1.2. Using n8n to Connect to APIs

n8n provides the **HTTP Request node** for connecting to APIs and web services. This node allows you to make HTTP requests (GET, POST, PUT, DELETE) to external services and retrieve or send data.

Steps to Connect to an API:

1. **Add the HTTP Request Node**:
   - In the **Nodes Panel**, search for **HTTP Request** and drag it onto the canvas.
2. **Configure the HTTP Request Node**:
   - **URL**: Enter the API endpoint you wish to interact with. For example, to fetch weather data from OpenWeather, the URL would look like:

```
url

https://api.openweathermap.org/data/2.5/w
eather?q=London&appid=YOUR_API_KEY
```

- o **Method**: Choose the appropriate HTTP method (GET, POST, etc.).
- o **Headers**: If the API requires authentication, you will need to set the appropriate headers (e.g., **Authorization** token, **Content-Type**, etc.).
- o **Body**: For methods like **POST** or **PUT**, you will need to define the data you want to send (e.g., JSON data or form fields).

3. **Test the API Request**:
   - o Click **Execute Workflow** to test the API request. **n8n** will make the request to the external service, retrieve the data, and display it in the **Execution Log**.

Example: Fetching Data from an API

For example, let's say we want to fetch user data from a **JSONPlaceholder** API:

- **URL**:
  `https://jsonplaceholder.typicode.com/users/1`
- **Method**: GET

In the **HTTP Request node**, you would enter the URL and method, then connect it to the next action, such as processing the response data.

4. **Handling API Responses**:
   - o The response from the API can be used in subsequent nodes. For example, after retrieving user data from an API, you can use the **Set node** to store the data, or pass it to another node for further processing.

Working with API Authentication:

- **OAuth Authentication**: Many APIs (e.g., Google, Microsoft) use **OAuth** for authentication. In n8n, you can use the **OAuth2** credentials manager to authenticate with services that require OAuth.

- **API Keys**: Some APIs require an API key in the **Authorization** header or as a query parameter. For example:

```json
{
  "Authorization": "Bearer YOUR_API_KEY"
}
```

6.1.3. Handling API Errors

When interacting with APIs, errors can occur (e.g., rate limits, invalid API keys, or data not found). **n8n** provides error handling capabilities to gracefully manage these situations.

- **Retry Logic**: Use the **retry settings** in the **HTTP Request node** to automatically retry failed API calls.
- **Error Nodes**: You can configure **error nodes** to alert you or log the failure when an API request fails.

6.2. Integrating with Databases (SQL, NoSQL, and REST APIs)

Integrating with databases is a common requirement for many workflows, especially when you need to store, retrieve, or process data dynamically. **n8n** supports integration with **SQL databases**, **NoSQL databases**, and **REST APIs** for database interactions.

6.2.1. SQL Database Integration (MySQL, PostgreSQL, etc.)

n8n provides built-in nodes to interact with **SQL databases** like MySQL, PostgreSQL, and SQLite. These nodes allow you to run SQL queries to fetch or manipulate data in a relational database.

Steps to Connect to a SQL Database:

1. **Add the SQL Database Node**:
   - For MySQL, drag the **MySQL node** from the **Nodes Panel** onto the canvas.

- o Similarly, you can use the **PostgreSQL** node for PostgreSQL databases.
2. **Configure Database Connection**:
   - o In the **Node Properties Panel**, enter the necessary connection details such as **host**, **username**, **password**, and **database name**.
3. **Write SQL Queries**:
   - o You can write SQL queries directly in the **SQL Query** field to interact with the database.

   Example: Retrieving all active users from a MySQL database:

   sql

   ```
   SELECT * FROM users WHERE status = 'active';
   ```

4. **Test the Database Query**:
   - o Click **Execute Workflow** to run the query and check the **Execution Log** for the results.
   - o You can then use the retrieved data in subsequent nodes (e.g., sending emails, updating records).

Using SQL to Insert Data:

You can also use the SQL nodes to insert, update, or delete records in the database. Example: Inserting a new user record:

sql

```
INSERT INTO users (name, email, status) VALUES
('John Doe', 'john@example.com', 'active');
```

6.2.2. NoSQL Database Integration (MongoDB, Redis, etc.)

For **NoSQL databases** like MongoDB or Redis, **n8n** provides dedicated nodes to interact with these systems. NoSQL databases are ideal for handling unstructured or semi-structured data.

Steps to Connect to a NoSQL Database:

1. **Add the NoSQL Database Node**:
   - o For MongoDB, drag the **MongoDB node** onto the canvas.

o   Similarly, you can use the **Redis node** for Redis integrations.
2. **Configure the NoSQL Database Connection**:
    o   Provide connection details such as the database **URL**, **username**, **password**, and **collection name** (for MongoDB).
3. **Write Queries**:
    o   For MongoDB, you can use MongoDB queries to interact with collections (e.g., finding, inserting, or updating documents).

Example: Finding a user by email:

```json
```

```json
{ "email": "john@example.com" }
```

4. **Test the NoSQL Query**:
    o   Click **Execute Workflow** to verify the query and inspect the results in the **Execution Log**.

6.2.3. Integrating with REST APIs for Data Storage

In addition to traditional databases, **n8n** allows you to integrate with services that provide **RESTful data storage**. For example, you could interact with services like **Airtable** or **Google Sheets**, where data is stored in a **table format** but managed through an API.

Steps to Integrate with a REST API for Data Storage:

1. **Add the API Node**: For services like **Google Sheets** or **Airtable**, you can use the corresponding nodes to integrate with these services.
2. **Configure API Authentication**: For API-based services, you will typically need to configure **API keys** or **OAuth** authentication.
3. **Define Data Operations**: Depending on the service, you can define operations like **Create**, **Read**, **Update**, or **Delete** data in the API.

6.2.4. Combining Databases with Web APIs

Sometimes, you may need to combine **database operations** with **API calls** to get data from external sources and store it in a database. For example:

- **Fetch data from an API** (e.g., customer details from a CRM).
- **Process or filter the data**.
- **Store the processed data** in a **SQL or NoSQL database** for future use or reporting.

Example Workflow:

1. **Webhook Trigger**: Receive an API request containing customer data.
2. **HTTP Request Node**: Fetch additional data from an external service (e.g., customer social media activity).
3. **SQL Node**: Store the customer and social media data in a **PostgreSQL database**.
4. **Send Notification**: Send an email or Slack message confirming the data has been saved.

Integrating **external systems** like **APIs, SQL databases,** and **NoSQL databases** with **n8n agents** greatly extends the power of your workflows. By using the **HTTP Request node, SQL/NoSQL nodes**, and other integration nodes, you can build sophisticated workflows that interact with external services, retrieve and store data, and automate complex tasks.

This chapter covered the essentials of connecting to APIs and databases, providing you with the foundation to build workflows that work with real-world data. In the next chapters, we will dive deeper into scaling and optimizing workflows for large-scale systems.

6.3. Authentication and Security in External System Integrations

When integrating with **external systems** (e.g., APIs, databases, third-party services), **authentication** and **security** are paramount to ensure that your data is protected and that only authorized actions are performed. **n8n** provides various mechanisms for authenticating and securing your connections, from **OAuth** to **API keys** and **basic authentication**.

This section will explore the best practices for handling authentication and ensuring **secure connections** in your **n8n agent workflows**.

6.3.1. Why is Authentication and Security Important?

Authentication ensures that your **n8n agents** can securely interact with **external systems** by verifying their identity. Without proper authentication, unauthorized users or services could access your systems, potentially exposing sensitive data or performing unauthorized actions.

Key Security Risks:

- **Data Breaches**: If credentials (e.g., API keys or OAuth tokens) are exposed or mishandled, malicious actors could access your systems.
- **Unauthorized Actions**: Without proper authentication, external services could perform unintended actions, such as modifying or deleting data.

6.3.2. Types of Authentication Methods in n8n

n8n supports several methods of authentication to integrate securely with **external systems**. Let's explore the most commonly used methods:

1. API Keys

API keys are a common and simple authentication mechanism where a unique **key** is used to authenticate an API request.

- **Usage**: API keys are typically passed in the request **header** or **URL** as part of the query string.
- **Example**:
  - **API Key in URL**:

    ```url
    https://api.example.com/v1/data?api_key=YOUR_API_KEY
    ```

  - **API Key in Header**:

    ```json
    {
    ```

```
        "Authorization": "Bearer YOUR_API_KEY"
    }
```

2. Basic Authentication

Basic Authentication involves sending the **username** and **password** in the HTTP request header. The credentials are encoded in **Base64** and sent in the **Authorization** header.

- **Usage**: This method is simple but less secure, as the credentials are base64-encoded (not encrypted). It's suitable for systems where encryption is handled over **HTTPS**.
- **Example**:

```json
json

{
    "Authorization": "Basic
BASE64_ENCODED_USERNAME_PASSWORD"
}
```

3. OAuth 2.0 Authentication

OAuth 2.0 is a more secure and flexible authentication method that enables access without sharing your **username** and **password**. OAuth allows a user to authenticate an application by granting permission without exposing their credentials.

- **Usage**: OAuth is commonly used by large services like **Google**, **Microsoft**, and **GitHub**, providing **access tokens** that are used to authenticate API calls.

4. Bearer Token Authentication

A **Bearer Token** is often used alongside OAuth to authenticate API requests. This token is usually obtained after successful OAuth authentication and is used in the request header to authenticate further API calls.

- **Example**:

```json
json
```

```
{
    "Authorization": "Bearer YOUR_ACCESS_TOKEN"
}
```

5. JWT (JSON Web Token)

JWT is a compact, URL-safe means of representing claims to be transferred between two parties. It is often used for securing API requests, especially in modern web applications.

- **Usage**: After user authentication, the server sends a JWT, which is used in subsequent requests to verify the user's identity.
- **Example**:

```json
json

{
    "Authorization": "Bearer YOUR_JWT_TOKEN"
}
```

6.3.3. Securing API Keys and Credentials in n8n

Proper handling of sensitive data, such as **API keys**, **OAuth tokens**, and **passwords**, is essential to ensure the security of your workflows.

1. Use n8n's Credentials Manager

n8n offers a **Credentials Manager** where you can securely store sensitive information like API keys, tokens, and other credentials. You can reference these credentials in your nodes instead of hardcoding them into the workflow.

- **Steps to Add Credentials**:
    1. In the **Credentials** tab in **n8n**, click **Create New** to add credentials for a service (e.g., Google Sheets, Slack).
    2. Enter the required details (API key, OAuth token, etc.).
    3. Once added, you can link these credentials to the appropriate nodes in your workflow.

2. Use Environment Variables for Credentials

You can store sensitive credentials in environment variables to keep them separate from the workflow configuration. This is especially useful when deploying **n8n** to production environments, such as on a **server** or **cloud**.

- **Example**: Set your credentials in the `.env` file:

```ini

N8N_GOOGLE_API_KEY=your-api-key
```

3. Encrypt Credentials

To enhance security, ensure that your credentials are encrypted. **n8n** automatically encrypts stored credentials, but when transmitting sensitive data (e.g., via **webhooks**), always use **HTTPS** to prevent **Man-in-the-Middle (MITM)** attacks.

6.4. Working with OAuth and API Keys for Secure Connections

Many modern APIs and services require **OAuth** or **API keys** to authenticate requests. This section will explore how to work with both **OAuth** and **API keys** in **n8n** to establish secure connections to external systems.

6.4.1. Working with OAuth in n8n

OAuth 2.0 is a secure, token-based authentication system widely used by services like **Google**, **Facebook**, **GitHub**, and others. In **n8n**, you can integrate OAuth by using the **OAuth2 credentials** manager.

Steps to Authenticate with OAuth2:

1. **Add OAuth2 Credentials**:
   - In the **Credentials Manager**, create a new set of **OAuth2** credentials for the service you want to integrate with (e.g., Google Drive, GitHub).
   - Enter the necessary **client ID** and **client secret**, which you can obtain by registering your app with the service.
   - Configure **OAuth2 scopes** if needed (e.g., access to user files, email, etc.).

2. **Configure OAuth2 in Workflow**:
   o After setting up OAuth2 credentials, use the appropriate **OAuth2-enabled nodes** (e.g., **Google Sheets, GitHub, Slack**) in the workflow.
   o The credentials are automatically referenced, and **n8n** will handle the token exchange process for you.

Example: Connecting to Google Sheets via OAuth2:

1. In **n8n**, create **OAuth2 credentials** for Google Sheets.
2. Configure the **Google Sheets node** to use the credentials you just created.
3. The **Google Sheets node** will automatically authenticate using OAuth2, and you can start interacting with Google Sheets directly in your workflows.

Handling OAuth2 Refresh Tokens:

OAuth tokens have an expiration time, and you may need to refresh them. **n8n** handles **refresh tokens** automatically, refreshing the access token when it expires, so your workflows won't break due to expired tokens.

6.4.2. Working with API Keys

API keys are a simpler authentication method, commonly used for accessing public APIs. API keys are often passed in the request **header** or **URL** to authenticate the request.

Steps to Use API Keys in n8n:

1. **Add API Key Credentials**:
   o In **n8n's Credentials Manager**, create a new **API Key** set of credentials for the external service you want to connect to (e.g., Airtable, OpenWeather).
   o Enter the required **API key** and associate it with the corresponding service.
2. **Use API Keys in Nodes**:
   o Once API credentials are stored, you can reference them in the relevant **n8n nodes** (e.g., **HTTP Request, Airtable, SendGrid**).

o **n8n** will use the stored API key automatically when making requests to the external service.

Example: Sending Data with an API Key:

If you are using **Airtable** to store data, you would:

1. Add **Airtable API credentials** in the **Credentials Manager**.
2. Add an **Airtable node** and configure it to use the API key.
3. **n8n** will authenticate the request using the API key, and you can retrieve or send data to Airtable as part of the workflow.

In this chapter, we've covered the various ways to securely **authenticate** and **connect** to external systems using **API keys**, **OAuth2**, and **Bearer tokens**. We also discussed how to securely store and manage credentials within **n8n**, using the **Credentials Manager** and **environment variables**. By following the security best practices outlined in this chapter, you can ensure that your integrations are secure and protected from unauthorized access.

By leveraging **OAuth2** for secure authentication and **API keys** for simple access, you can integrate **n8n agents** with a wide range of external services, enabling seamless automation across different platforms.

6.5. Using File Systems: Importing and Exporting Data

File system integration allows you to **import** and **export** data to and from your **n8n workflows**. By leveraging **local file systems** or **network drives**, you can manage files, process them, and interact with external systems. In this section, we will explore how to **import data from files**, **process it**, and **export data** in various formats using **n8n agents**.

6.5.1. Importing Data from Files

In many workflows, the first step is to **import data** from external files, such as **CSV**, **JSON**, or **Excel** files. n8n provides several nodes to facilitate file importation, such as the **Read Binary File** and **CSV File Read** nodes.

Steps to Import Data from Files:

1. **Add a File Read Node**:
   - In the **Nodes Panel**, search for the **Read Binary File** node if you are working with binary files (e.g., images or PDFs).
   - For structured data files, such as **CSV** or **Excel**, use the **Read CSV File** or **Read Binary File (for Excel)** node.
2. **Configure the Node**:
   - **For CSV File**: Set the **File Path** to the location of your CSV file and configure any delimiters or headers if required.
   - **For Binary Files**: Use the **Read Binary File** node to read binary files and pass them as binary data in the workflow.

   Example configuration for reading a CSV file:

   ```json
   json

   {
     "file_path": "/path/to/your/file.csv",
     "delimiter": ",",
     "header": true
   }
   ```

3. **Test the File Import**: After configuring the file import node, click **Execute Workflow** to test the data import. The data will be available in the **Execution Log** or passed as variables for further processing.
4. **Process the Imported Data**: After importing, you can use other **n8n nodes** (such as **Set**, **Function**, or **Filter** nodes) to process and manipulate the data before it's exported, saved to a database, or passed to another system.

Use Case for Importing Data:

- **Importing Customer Data from a CSV**: For example, you might import customer information stored in a CSV file into your workflow, process the data (e.g., clean it, transform it), and then use it for further actions like sending email newsletters or adding to a database.

6.5.2. Exporting Data to Files

Once your data has been processed, you may need to **export** it to a file format for external use, such as creating a report, storing data for backup, or integrating with another system.

Steps to Export Data to Files:

1. **Add a File Export Node**:
   - Use the **Write Binary File** node for binary data export (e.g., PDFs or images).
   - For structured data (e.g., CSV, JSON), use the **Write JSON File** or **Write CSV File** node.
2. **Configure the Export Node**:
   - Set the **File Path** and ensure the appropriate file format (e.g., `.json`, `.csv`) is selected.
   - For **CSV Export**:
     - Configure whether to include headers, how to handle row delimiters, and any other relevant settings.
   - For **JSON Export**, specify the data to be written to the file.

Example configuration for exporting data as CSV:

```json
json

{
  "file_path": "/path/to/output/file.csv",
  "delimiter": ",",
  "include_headers": true
}
```

3. **Test the Export**: Run the workflow and check that the exported file is created and contains the expected data.

Use Case for Exporting Data:

- **Exporting Processed Data to CSV**: After processing a dataset, you might export the results to a CSV file for reporting or archiving purposes.

6.5.3. Handling Large Files

When working with **large files**, performance and memory management become essential considerations. Here are a few tips to manage large file imports and exports efficiently:

- **Chunking**: Instead of loading entire files into memory, use **batch processing** to read or write data in chunks. This ensures that your workflows don't run out of memory.
- **Optimize File Formats**: If possible, use file formats that are efficient in size and speed, such as **JSON** or **CSV**, as these formats are easier to work with than binary formats (like images or PDFs) when dealing with large amounts of data.
- **Async Handling**: For long-running file operations, consider using asynchronous operations to ensure that the workflow doesn't block execution while waiting for a file operation to complete.

6.6. Integrating with Cloud Storage (Google Drive, AWS S3, etc.)

Integrating with cloud storage platforms like **Google Drive**, **AWS S3**, and others enables you to manage files in the cloud and trigger actions based on file uploads or changes. This section will guide you through integrating cloud storage into your **n8n agent workflows**, allowing for seamless file management and automation.

6.6.1. Google Drive Integration

Google Drive is a widely used cloud storage service that allows you to store, retrieve, and manage files. **n8n** provides a node specifically for integrating with Google Drive, which allows you to automate tasks like uploading, downloading, and organizing files.

Steps to Connect Google Drive to n8n:

1. **Create Google Drive Credentials**:
   - In the **n8n dashboard**, navigate to **Credentials Manager** and create new credentials for **Google Drive** using **OAuth2**.

- You'll need to set up **Google API credentials** by creating a project in the **Google Developer Console** and enabling the **Google Drive API**.
2. **Add Google Drive Node**:
   - Drag the **Google Drive node** from the **Nodes Panel** and configure it to use the credentials you just created.
3. **Set Up File Operations**:
   - You can configure the node to perform various operations on Google Drive, such as:
     - **Upload a file**: Upload files from your local system or other workflows to Google Drive.
     - **Download a file**: Retrieve a file from your Google Drive account.
     - **Delete or Rename a file**: Manage the files in your Google Drive account.

Example: Uploading a file to Google Drive:

```json
{
  "operation": "upload",
  "file_name": "report.csv",
  "file_data": "{{ $node['Set'].json['file_data']
}}"
}
```

4. **Test the Google Drive Integration**:
   - Click **Execute Workflow** to ensure that the workflow correctly interacts with your **Google Drive** account.

Use Case for Google Drive:

- **Automating File Uploads**: Automatically upload generated reports, logs, or backup files to Google Drive at specified intervals.

6.6.2. AWS S3 Integration

AWS S3 (Simple Storage Service) is a popular cloud storage service provided by **Amazon Web Services**. It's widely used for storing large amounts of data, such as backups, logs, and media files. **n8n** offers a dedicated node for **AWS S3** integration, enabling you to automate file uploads, downloads, and management tasks.

Steps to Connect AWS S3 to n8n:

1. **Create AWS S3 Credentials**:
   - In **n8n**, navigate to the **Credentials Manager** and create a new set of **AWS S3 credentials**.
   - You'll need your **AWS Access Key ID** and **AWS Secret Access Key**, which can be obtained from the **AWS IAM Console**.
2. **Add the AWS S3 Node**:
   - Drag the **AWS S3 node** onto the canvas and configure it with the credentials you just created.
3. **Set Up S3 Operations**:
   - Use the **AWS S3 node** to perform various file operations:
     - **Upload**: Upload files from your local system or workflow to a specific S3 bucket.
     - **Download**: Download files from an S3 bucket to your local system or to another workflow.
     - **Delete or List**: Manage and list files in your S3 bucket.

Example: Uploading a file to AWS S3:

json

```
{
  "operation": "upload",
  "bucket": "my-bucket-name",
  "file_name": "image.jpg",
  "file_data": "{{ $node['Set'].json['file_data']
}}"
}
```

4. **Test the AWS S3 Integration**:
   - Execute the workflow and check the **Execution Log** to ensure that the file operations with **AWS S3** are successful.

Use Case for AWS S3:

- **Automated Backup**: Automatically back up generated reports or logs to AWS S3 on a regular schedule.

6.6.3. Other Cloud Storage Integrations

In addition to **Google Drive** and **AWS S3**, **n8n** supports integrations with several other cloud storage services, such as **Dropbox**, **OneDrive**, and **Box**. The general setup process for these services is similar:

- **Create credentials** for the cloud service in **n8n's Credentials Manager**.
- **Configure the relevant cloud storage node** (e.g., **Dropbox** node).
- **Define file operations** such as upload, download, or listing files.

In this chapter, we've explored how to integrate with both local and cloud-based storage systems, enabling your **n8n agents** to interact with **files** seamlessly. By using **file system nodes**, you can **import** and **export** data from files and automate tasks like generating reports, saving logs, or interacting with cloud storage platforms like **Google Drive** and **AWS S3**.

By connecting to cloud storage services, you can create more flexible workflows that leverage cloud-based file storage, enhancing your automation capabilities even further. With these integrations, you can automate file management tasks and keep your data accessible across different platforms.

6.7. Hands-on Example: Building a Data Transfer Agent Using APIs

In this hands-on example, we will walk through the process of building a **Data Transfer Agent** using **APIs** in **n8n**. This agent will be designed to retrieve data from one external API and transfer it to another system via a different API. This is a common use case for integrating disparate systems or syncing data across platforms.

Scenario:

We will create an agent that:

1. Fetches **user data** from a **public API** (e.g., JSONPlaceholder).
2. **Transforms the data** (e.g., extract user information).
3. **Sends the transformed data** to a **Google Sheets API** for storage.

By following this example, you'll learn how to integrate with external APIs, manipulate data, and automate data transfer between services.

Step 1: Create a New Workflow

1. In the **n8n Dashboard**, click the **"Create New Workflow"** button to open the **Workflow Editor**.
2. You should see an empty canvas where we will begin building the agent.

Step 2: Fetch Data from an External API

For this example, we will use the **JSONPlaceholder** API, which provides fake user data. You can replace this with any external API that provides the necessary data for your workflow.

1. **Add the HTTP Request Node**:
    - In the **Nodes Panel**, search for the **HTTP Request** node and drag it onto the canvas.
    - This node will be used to fetch user data from the JSONPlaceholder API.
2. **Configure the HTTP Request Node**:
    - **URL**: `https://jsonplaceholder.typicode.com/user s`
    - **Method**: GET (to retrieve the data).

    Here's how the configuration looks:

    `json`

```
{
  "URL":
"https://jsonplaceholder.typicode.com/users",
  "Method": "GET"
}
```

3. **Test the API Request**:
   o Click on **Execute Workflow** to test the API call. You should see a list of user data returned from the API in the **Execution Log**.

Example response (simplified):

json

```
[
  {
    "id": 1,
    "name": "Leanne Graham",
    "username": "Bret",
    "email": "Sincere@april.biz",
    "address": {
      "street": "Kulas Light",
      "suite": "Apt. 556",
      "city": "Gwenborough"
    }
  },
  ...
]
```

Step 3: Transform Data Using the Set Node

Now that we have the data from the API, we need to transform it. Specifically, we want to extract and restructure the data before sending it to **Google Sheets**.

1. **Add the Set Node**:
   o Drag the **Set node** onto the canvas and connect it to the **HTTP Request node**.

- The **Set node** will be used to extract and restructure the user data.
2. **Configure the Set Node**:
   - In the **Node Properties Panel**, define the fields you want to extract and pass forward.

For instance, you may want to pass only the **user's name, email, and address** to the next step. You can do this by mapping the fields from the API response to new keys:

```json
json

{
  "user_name": "{{$json['name']}}",
  "user_email": "{{$json['email']}}",
  "user_address":
"{{$json['address']['city']}}"
}
```

This will create new keys in the output data, such as:

- `user_name`: Leanne Graham
- `user_email`: Sincere@april.biz
- `user_address`: Gwenborough

Step 4: Send Data to Google Sheets

Next, we will send the transformed user data to **Google Sheets**.

1. **Set Up Google Sheets Integration**:
   - Before proceeding, you need to set up **Google Sheets credentials** in **n8n** using **OAuth2**.
   - In **n8n**, navigate to **Credentials Manager** and create **Google Sheets credentials**. Follow the prompts to authenticate with your Google account.
2. **Add the Google Sheets Node**:
   - In the **Nodes Panel**, search for **Google Sheets** and drag it onto the canvas.
   - Configure the **Google Sheets node** to use the credentials you just created.

3. **Configure the Google Sheets Node**:
   - **Action**: Select the **Append** option, as we want to add new rows to the sheet.
   - **Spreadsheet**: Select the specific Google Sheet you want to use (ensure the Google Sheets API has been authorized and the sheet is accessible).
   - **Sheet Name**: Select the sheet within the spreadsheet where you want the data to be stored (e.g., `Users`).
4. **Map Data to Google Sheets**:
   - Map the fields you want to send to Google Sheets (e.g., **user_name**, **user_email**, **user_address**) to the corresponding columns in the sheet.

Example mapping:

   - **user_name** → Column 1
   - **user_email** → Column 2
   - **user_address** → Column 3

The data will now be appended to the selected sheet as a new row for each user.

Step 5: Test the Data Transfer Workflow

1. **Execute the Workflow**:
   - Click **Execute Workflow** to run the entire process. The workflow will:
     - Fetch user data from the API.
     - Transform the data using the **Set node**.
     - Send the data to **Google Sheets**.
2. **Verify the Results**:
   - Check your Google Sheet to ensure the data has been correctly appended in the appropriate columns.

Example of Google Sheets after execution:

user_name	user_email	user_address
Leanne Graham	Sincere@april.biz	Gwenborough
Ervin Howell	Shanna@melissa.tv	Wisokyburgh

user_name	user_email	user_address
...	...	...

Step 6: Automating the Process

Once you've verified that the workflow works as expected, you can automate the process by configuring a **trigger**. For instance:

- Use a **Webhook Trigger** to initiate the workflow whenever new data is available.
- Use a **Cron Trigger** to run the workflow at scheduled intervals (e.g., daily or hourly).

By doing this, your **n8n agent** will continuously fetch data, transform it, and send it to Google Sheets automatically.

In this chapter, we demonstrated how to build a **Data Transfer Agent** in **n8n** using **APIs**. We walked through the following steps:

1. **Fetching data** from an external API (JSONPlaceholder).
2. **Transforming the data** using the **Set node**.
3. **Sending the transformed data** to Google Sheets via the Google Sheets node.

This hands-on example showcased how to **integrate external systems**, **process data**, and **automate data transfer** between platforms, all within **n8n**.

By following these steps, you can easily extend the workflow to integrate other services or APIs, creating powerful automation solutions for various use cases.

Chapter 7: Managing Complex Workflows with Multiple Agents

7.1. Organizing Large Workflows Using Multiple Agents

As workflows grow in complexity, it becomes essential to manage them effectively. One way to do this is by using **multiple agents** to break down large workflows into smaller, more manageable components. **n8n** provides several features to handle complex workflows, and **multiple agents** can help you organize tasks, improve performance, and maintain scalability.

In this section, we'll explore how to effectively organize large workflows using multiple agents and how to break workflows into smaller, reusable components.

7.1.1. What Are Multiple Agents in n8n?

In **n8n**, an **agent** refers to a specific set of tasks or operations that are managed within a workflow. These agents can be used to handle individual processes or parts of a larger workflow. **Multiple agents** can work in parallel or sequentially to accomplish a complex task.

Why Use Multiple Agents?

- **Modularity**: Break large workflows into smaller, reusable agents.
- **Separation of Concerns**: Each agent handles a specific task or function, making it easier to maintain.
- **Parallelism**: Run agents in parallel for improved performance and efficiency.

7.1.2. Breaking Down Complex Workflows Using Multiple Agents

When dealing with large workflows, breaking them down into **agents** allows for cleaner, easier-to-manage automation. For example, if you are building an order processing system, you could break the workflow into several agents:

1. **Order Validation Agent**: Validates the order details (e.g., checking if the payment was successful).
2. **Shipping Agent**: Handles the shipping process, including generating shipping labels.
3. **Notification Agent**: Sends notifications to the customer about the order status.

Steps to Organize Workflows Using Multiple Agents:

1. **Create Separate Workflows**: Design each **agent** (i.e., each smaller workflow) to handle a specific task.
2. **Use the Execute Workflow Node**: The **Execute Workflow node** in n8n lets you call one workflow from another, enabling you to link multiple agents together.
3. **Modularize Tasks**: For tasks that are used repeatedly, consider creating **sub-workflows**. This allows you to reuse the same set of steps across multiple workflows without redundancy.

Example: Creating Separate Agents for Order Processing

1. **Order Validation Agent**: Validates the order data (e.g., checking inventory, payment confirmation).
2. **Shipping Agent**: Manages the shipment, including creating a shipping label and notifying the shipping department.
3. **Notification Agent**: Sends out confirmation emails and order status updates to the customer.

By using **multiple agents**, each workflow is smaller and more manageable, making it easier to debug and maintain.

7.1.3. Best Practices for Using Multiple Agents

- **Reusability**: Build agents to be modular and reusable. This will save you time when creating new workflows that require similar tasks.
- **Decouple Dependencies**: Try to design workflows where agents can function independently of each other. This reduces the risk of cascading failures and simplifies testing.

- **Logging and Monitoring**: Implement logging and monitoring in each agent to track the performance and success of tasks. This helps you catch issues early and ensure smooth operation.

7.2. Managing Agent Dependencies and Sequence

When working with multiple agents, managing their **dependencies** and ensuring they run in the correct **sequence** is crucial for maintaining a smooth workflow. **n8n** provides features like **Execute Workflow nodes** and **Wait nodes** to help manage dependencies and ensure that tasks are executed in the correct order.

In this section, we will explore how to manage agent dependencies and control their execution sequence to ensure optimal workflow execution.

7.2.1. What are Agent Dependencies?

Agent dependencies refer to the relationships between agents where one agent's output becomes another agent's input. This is common when the result of one agent influences the operation of subsequent agents.

Managing Dependencies:

- **Input/Output Variables**: Use the output of one agent as the input to another agent. This ensures that data flows in a logical sequence.
- **Conditional Logic**: In some cases, the execution of an agent depends on a condition. For example, if an order is valid, the next agent in the sequence (e.g., payment processing) will execute; otherwise, it might terminate the workflow.

Steps to Manage Agent Dependencies:

1. **Use Execute Workflow Node**: To call one agent from another, use the **Execute Workflow** node. This node will execute another workflow as part of the current workflow.
2. **Use Conditional Logic**: If an agent is only executed under certain conditions, use nodes like **If**, **Switch**, or **Wait** to control the sequence.

3. **Define Input/Output**: When creating multiple agents, pass relevant data between agents using **JSON objects** or **variables**.

Example: Managing Dependencies in an Order Processing System

1. **Order Validation Agent** (Agent 1) checks if the order is valid. If the validation fails, the workflow stops.
2. If the order is valid, the **Payment Processing Agent** (Agent 2) is triggered, which checks if the payment has been processed successfully.
3. If payment is successful, the **Shipping Agent** (Agent 3) handles the shipment.

Each agent depends on the completion of the previous one, so managing the sequence ensures that the workflow runs in the correct order.

7.2.2. Controlling Execution Order with Wait and Delay Nodes

In cases where you need to **control the timing** of agent execution (e.g., waiting for external data or delays between tasks), **n8n** provides nodes like **Wait** and **Delay** to manage timing.

Using the Wait Node:

- The **Wait node** allows you to pause the workflow until a specific event or condition occurs.
- **Example**: If your workflow depends on the completion of an external API request, you can use the **Wait node** to pause the workflow until the request is complete.

Using the Delay Node:

- The **Delay node** allows you to delay the execution of a task by a specified amount of time.
- **Example**: If you want to delay sending an email for a specific number of minutes after an action, you can use the **Delay node** to schedule that email.

7.2.3. Using Execute Workflow Nodes for Sequential Execution

The **Execute Workflow node** is crucial when you want to run multiple workflows in a specific order.

Steps for Sequential Execution:

1. **Create Independent Workflows**: Create separate workflows for each agent, such as one for order validation, another for payment processing, and so on.
2. **Add Execute Workflow Node**: Use the **Execute Workflow node** to call the next workflow in the sequence.
3. **Configure Node Sequencing**: Ensure that the workflows are connected in the correct order to maintain the sequence. You can control dependencies using **If** nodes or **Wait nodes** between the workflows.

Example:

- Workflow 1 (Order Validation) → Workflow 2 (Payment Processing) → Workflow 3 (Shipping)

7.2.4. Using Conditional Logic for Flexible Execution

To ensure that workflows run only when necessary, you can use **conditional logic** (e.g., **If nodes, Switch nodes**) to create more flexible workflows.

Steps to Implement Conditional Execution:

1. **Add an If Node**: After completing the first agent (e.g., order validation), use the **If node** to check if the order meets the required conditions (e.g., the payment is approved).
2. **Branch the Workflow**: Depending on the condition, you can either:
   o Execute the next agent in the workflow.
   o Skip the agent or send an error notification if the condition isn't met.

In this chapter, we explored how to manage **complex workflows** by using **multiple agents** and controlling **agent dependencies** and **execution sequence**. By breaking workflows into smaller, modular agents, you can manage large workflows more effectively and ensure that each agent performs its designated task without causing issues.

We also covered how to **organize workflows** into independent agents, control **execution order** using the **Execute Workflow node**, and leverage **conditional logic** to create flexible workflows that handle different scenarios.

Using these best practices, you can create scalable, maintainable workflows that efficiently handle a wide variety of tasks and processes

7.3. Best Practices for Managing Workflow Complexity

As workflows grow in size and complexity, it becomes crucial to implement strategies to ensure that they remain **manageable, scalable**, and **efficient**. **n8n agents** provide powerful automation capabilities, but with large or intricate workflows, it's easy to introduce unnecessary complexity or performance bottlenecks. In this section, we will explore best practices for managing **workflow complexity** to maintain clean, efficient, and reliable automation systems.

7.3.1. Modularize Workflows with Multiple Agents

One of the most effective ways to manage **workflow complexity** is by breaking large workflows into smaller, **modular agents**. Each agent should focus on a specific task or function. By keeping workflows modular, you make them easier to understand, maintain, and scale.

Best Practices for Modularization:

- **Create Reusable Agents**: Design workflows (or agents) that can be reused across different parts of your automation system. For example, an agent for **sending emails** can be reused across multiple workflows.
- **Use the Execute Workflow Node**: The **Execute Workflow node** allows you to call other workflows from within the main workflow,

creating a clear hierarchy and modular structure. This keeps the main workflow clean and focused while delegating specialized tasks to sub-workflows.

- **Break Down Tasks into Independent Units**: For example, an e-commerce system may have separate agents for validating orders, processing payments, and managing inventory. Each agent can operate independently, simplifying the overall system.

7.3.2. Use Conditional Logic to Simplify Execution Paths

When building workflows with multiple paths or conditions, it's easy to overcomplicate things. To keep your workflows manageable, use **conditional logic** wisely.

Best Practices for Conditional Logic:

- **Use If and Switch Nodes**: Use the **If** and **Switch nodes** to handle decisions and branches within the workflow. This allows for **conditional paths** based on the data passed through the workflow.
- **Avoid Deeply Nested Logic**: While **n8n** allows you to create deeply nested conditions, try to keep the logic as flat as possible. Deep nesting can make the workflow difficult to understand and debug.
- **Test Each Branch Separately**: When building conditional logic, test each condition and branch independently to ensure the expected behavior. This minimizes debugging time and makes workflows easier to manage.

7.3.3. Use Descriptive Naming and Comments

As workflows become more complex, it's essential to keep everything organized. Use **descriptive naming conventions** for nodes and workflows, and add **comments** to explain the logic behind more complex parts of the workflow.

Best Practices for Naming and Commenting:

- **Node Naming**: Use meaningful and clear names for each node (e.g., **Order Validation, Payment Processing, Send Confirmation Email**). Avoid generic names like **Node 1** or **Action 2**.
- **Add Comments**: Use the **Comment node** in **n8n** to annotate parts of the workflow that may not be immediately clear. This is particularly important for complex logic or calculations.

  Example:

  ```plaintext

  // This node checks if the payment is
  successful before proceeding
  ```

- **Organize Your Workflow Layout**: Keep the layout organized by arranging nodes in a logical sequence. Avoid clutter by grouping related nodes together, using **spacers** or **color-coding** if needed.

7.3.4. Optimize Workflow Performance

Complex workflows, especially those with large datasets or multiple API calls, can introduce performance bottlenecks. Optimizing these workflows ensures they run smoothly without unnecessary delays or timeouts.

Best Practices for Performance Optimization:

- **Minimize API Calls**: API calls are often the most time-consuming part of a workflow. Reduce the number of API calls by caching responses, batching requests, or retrieving only the data you need.
- **Limit Data Passed Between Nodes**: Only pass the essential data from one node to the next. Avoid sending unnecessary large data sets across nodes, as this can increase memory usage and slow down the workflow.
- **Use Batch Processing**: If you're working with large datasets (e.g., customer records), use the **SplitInBatches** node to process them in smaller chunks. This avoids overloading your system and allows for better resource management.

7.3.5. Monitor and Log Workflow Performance

Monitoring and logging workflow performance is crucial to identify
potential issues early on. **n8n** provides tools to track workflow execution, log
errors, and analyze performance bottlenecks.

Best Practices for Monitoring:

- **Use the Execution Log**: Regularly check the **Execution Log** to track
  how long each node takes to execute and identify any slow-
  performing parts of the workflow.
- **Enable Error Handling**: Implement error handling by using the
  Error Trigger and **Error Workflow** nodes. These allow you to
  monitor and respond to errors in real-time.
- **Use Metrics and Dashboards**: If you're deploying workflows in
  production, consider integrating with monitoring tools or setting up
  dashboards to track the performance of your workflows.

7.4. Version Control and CI/CD for Workflows

Managing the versioning and deployment of **n8n workflows** is essential for
maintaining control over changes, ensuring quality, and automating the
deployment process. **Version Control** and **Continuous
Integration/Continuous Deployment (CI/CD)** practices can be applied to
workflows just as they are for software development.

In this section, we'll explore best practices for implementing **version control**
and **CI/CD** in your **n8n agent workflows**.

7.4.1. Why Version Control and CI/CD for Workflows?

As workflows grow and evolve, keeping track of changes becomes
increasingly important. Version control helps track changes, roll back to
previous versions, and collaborate with team members. **CI/CD** ensures that
new versions of workflows can be automatically tested and deployed without
manual intervention, streamlining the deployment process.

Benefits:

- **Track Changes**: Keep a history of changes made to workflows, nodes, and configurations.
- **Collaborate Effectively**: Multiple team members can work on workflows simultaneously without conflicts, with proper versioning and review.
- **Automated Deployment**: Automatically deploy workflows to production, ensuring consistency and reducing human error.

7.4.2. Implementing Version Control for n8n Workflows

Currently, **n8n** does not have built-in version control, but you can integrate **version control systems** like **Git** into your workflow management by exporting workflows as JSON files and storing them in a Git repository.

Steps to Implement Version Control:

1. **Export Workflow as JSON**: You can export an **n8n workflow** as a **JSON file** by clicking the **Export** button in the workflow editor.
2. **Store in a Git Repository**: Once exported, store the **JSON file** in a Git repository. This allows you to track changes over time.
3. **Commit Changes**: Whenever you make changes to your workflow, export it again, and commit the changes to the repository. This keeps track of each change, including updates to nodes and logic.
4. **Collaborate with Team**: Share the Git repository with your team members to collaborate on workflows. Use branches for feature development, and merge them into the main workflow once tested.

Example Git Workflow:

- **Main Branch**: Store the stable, production-ready version of your workflows.
- **Feature Branches**: Developers can work on separate branches for different features or improvements.
- **Merge Requests**: Once a feature is complete, create a merge request to review and merge it into the main branch.

7.4.3. Implementing CI/CD for n8n Workflows

By integrating **CI/CD** tools like **Jenkins**, **GitLab CI**, or **GitHub Actions**, you can automate the deployment of workflows and ensure that they are properly tested before being pushed to production.

Steps to Set Up CI/CD for n8n Workflows:

1. **Store Workflows in a Git Repository**: As mentioned in the version control section, keep workflows in a Git repository.
2. **Automate Testing**: Set up automated tests to verify that the workflow logic works as expected. These tests can be executed on the CI server whenever changes are made.
3. **Automate Deployment**: Use **CI/CD tools** to automatically deploy the workflow to the **n8n server** once it passes the tests.
4. **Automate Rollback**: In case something goes wrong with the deployment, have an automated process in place to roll back to the previous stable version of the workflow.

Example CI/CD Pipeline:

1. **Commit Workflow to GitHub**: Developers commit the updated workflow JSON to the repository.
2. **GitHub Actions** triggers on commit, running tests to ensure no errors in the workflow logic.
3. **Successful Tests**: Once the tests pass, the workflow is deployed to the production **n8n server** using an API or command-line interface.

7.4.4. Best Practices for CI/CD and Version Control

- **Use Descriptive Commit Messages**: Each commit should clearly explain the change or feature added to the workflow.
- **Test Changes Before Deployment**: Use staging environments or testing servers to test changes before deploying them to production.
- **Automate Backup**: Ensure that you have automated backups of the current stable version before deploying new changes.
- **Document Changes**: Keep a changelog or documentation of each version of the workflow to track what changes were made over time.

In this chapter, we explored best practices for **managing workflow complexity** and **version control** in **n8n** workflows. By breaking large workflows into **modular agents**, using **conditional logic**, and optimizing performance, you can ensure your workflows remain efficient, maintainable, and scalable.

Additionally, we discussed how to implement **version control** and **CI/CD** for workflows, enabling you to automate deployment processes and maintain workflow integrity across environments.

By following these best practices, you can manage complex workflows, collaborate effectively with team members, and ensure that your workflows are stable and up-to-date.

7.5. Optimizing for Scalability: Best Practices

As workflows in **n8n** grow in complexity and usage, optimizing for **scalability** becomes crucial. Scalability ensures that your workflows can handle increasing data volumes, concurrent executions, and expanding automation requirements without sacrificing performance or stability. In this section, we'll cover key best practices to optimize **n8n workflows** for scalability, ensuring they can grow as your business or system demands increase.

7.5.1. Design Workflows for Parallelism

One of the most effective ways to optimize workflows for scalability is by leveraging **parallelism**. Instead of executing tasks sequentially, you can design workflows that run multiple tasks simultaneously, significantly improving execution speed.

Best Practices for Parallel Execution:

- **Use Execute Workflow Node**: You can break large workflows into smaller sub-workflows and run them in parallel using the **Execute Workflow node**. This helps divide the work across multiple independent agents, reducing the overall execution time.

Example: A workflow that processes customer orders can use parallel execution to validate orders, process payments, and generate shipping labels concurrently.

- **Split in Batches**: For tasks that require processing large datasets (e.g., customer records or product inventories), use the **SplitInBatches node** to break the data into smaller chunks and process them in parallel.

    Example: If you have a list of 1000 customer records to process, splitting them into batches of 100 records ensures that each batch is processed in parallel, reducing overall processing time.

Considerations for Parallelism:

- **Resource Management**: Ensure your system can handle the increased resource demand from running tasks in parallel. If running workflows on a server, ensure that your server has sufficient CPU and memory resources.
- **Concurrency Limits**: Some external systems may have concurrency or rate limits (e.g., APIs with request limits). Be mindful of these when designing workflows that make external API calls in parallel.

7.5.2. Minimize Redundant API Calls

API calls can be a major bottleneck in workflows, especially when interacting with external services. Reducing the number of API calls can significantly improve performance and scalability.

Best Practices to Minimize API Calls:

- **Cache API Responses**: For data that doesn't change frequently (e.g., user details, pricing information), implement caching mechanisms to store API responses and avoid redundant requests.

    Example: Use a **Set node** to store the response from an API call in a variable, and then reuse that data in subsequent nodes instead of making the same API request repeatedly.

- **Use Bulk API Endpoints**: Many APIs offer bulk endpoints to handle multiple requests in a single API call. Use these bulk endpoints whenever possible to reduce the number of requests.

  Example: Instead of making separate API requests to update multiple records, use a bulk update API endpoint that can handle updates for all records in one request.

- **Rate Limit Management**: If you're calling APIs with rate limits, implement **retry logic** and **backoff strategies** to handle rate limit issues gracefully.

7.5.3. Optimize Data Flow and Node Efficiency

Efficient data handling and optimizing node execution can lead to a significant performance boost, especially when workflows grow in complexity.

Best Practices for Optimizing Data Flow:

- **Pass Only Required Data**: Minimize the amount of data passed between nodes. Only send necessary data from one node to another to reduce memory usage and improve performance.

  Example: If you're processing customer data, only pass the customer name, email, and purchase details to the next node, and avoid passing unnecessary information like their address or historical order data.

- **Use Function Node for Complex Logic**: Instead of using multiple nodes for data transformations, consider using the **Function node** to handle complex logic within a single node. This reduces overhead and speeds up processing by consolidating logic into one location.
- **Avoid Excessive Node Connections**: In complex workflows, try to reduce the number of direct node connections. When too many nodes are connected directly, it can create a heavy processing load. Instead, try using **sub-workflows** to divide the tasks into separate, independent processes.

Best Practices for Node Efficiency:

- **Optimize Node Settings**: For nodes that interact with external systems (like APIs or databases), review their settings and ensure that you're not overloading them with unnecessary operations. Use **pagination** or **limit results** wherever applicable.
- **Use Built-in n8n Features**: Take advantage of n8n's built-in features like **Error Handling** and **Retry Logic** to avoid repetitive work and handle failures more efficiently.

7.5.4. Horizontal Scaling for Increased Load

As workflows and data grow, **horizontal scaling** becomes essential to handle higher loads. Horizontal scaling involves adding more instances of n8n to distribute the processing load across multiple servers.

Steps for Horizontal Scaling:

1. **Docker and Kubernetes**: Deploy **n8n** in a **Docker container** and manage it with **Kubernetes** to enable horizontal scaling. With **Kubernetes**, you can easily manage multiple n8n instances, load balancing, and scaling based on demand.
2. **Cloud Platforms**: If you're deploying n8n in the cloud (e.g., AWS, GCP, or Azure), use their auto-scaling features to automatically spin up additional n8n instances when demand increases.
3. **Distributed Databases**: Use distributed databases (e.g., **PostgreSQL** with replication) to handle large-scale data storage and ensure high availability and load balancing.

7.5.5. Monitoring and Tuning Workflow Performance

Finally, to ensure that your workflows are performing optimally, you need to monitor their execution and **fine-tune** based on performance metrics.

Best Practices for Monitoring:

- **Execution Logs**: Use the **Execution Log** to monitor workflow performance, check for bottlenecks, and identify slow-performing nodes.
- **Metrics Dashboard**: Set up a **metrics dashboard** (e.g., using tools like **Prometheus** and **Grafana**) to monitor the health and performance of your n8n instance. This can include CPU, memory usage, execution times, and error rates.
- **Profiling and Optimization**: Periodically run profiling on your workflows to identify areas for optimization, such as excessive API calls, redundant operations, or long-running nodes.

7.6. Monitoring Workflow Execution with n8n

Monitoring is crucial for ensuring that workflows are running smoothly and errors are detected early. n8n offers several tools and strategies for monitoring the execution of your workflows, helping you maintain a reliable automation system.

7.6.1. Execution Logs for Workflow Monitoring

n8n automatically logs the execution of every workflow. The **Execution Log** provides a detailed history of how each node in the workflow was executed, including any errors or issues that occurred.

How to Use the Execution Log:

1. **Access the Execution Log**:
   - From the **n8n Dashboard**, navigate to the **Execution History** tab to view logs for past workflows.
2. **Analyze Workflow Execution**:
   - Each entry in the execution log will show the node name, execution time, and the data passed between nodes.
   - Errors and warnings are highlighted in the log, making it easy to identify and troubleshoot issues.
3. **Troubleshooting Failures**:
   - If a workflow fails, the **Execution Log** will show which node caused the failure and the error message returned by the node. This allows you to quickly debug and fix the issue.

Example of Execution Log Entry:

```plaintext
2023-05-01 12:45:01 - HTTP Request Node - Success
(200 OK)
2023-05-01 12:45:05 - Set Node - Data
transformation complete
2023-05-01 12:45:10 - Google Sheets Node - Error:
API rate limit exceeded
```

7.6.2. Alerts and Notifications for Workflow Failures

In addition to using the **Execution Log** for manual monitoring, you can set up **alerts and notifications** to be notified whenever a workflow fails or encounters issues.

Best Practices for Alerts:

1. **Email Notifications**:
   o Use the **Send Email** node to send an email notification to administrators when a workflow fails or encounters an error.
2. **Slack Notifications**:
   o Set up **Slack** notifications to alert a designated channel when a workflow fails or encounters a specific condition.
3. **Error Workflow**:
   o Use the **Error Trigger** node to automatically trigger a notification or logging action when a workflow fails.

Example Setup:

- Configure an **Error Trigger** to listen for any errors during the workflow execution.
- Connect it to a **Send Email** node to send an alert to administrators if a critical task fails.

7.6.3. Monitoring Performance Metrics with External Tools

For larger workflows, you may want to integrate **n8n** with external monitoring tools to track performance metrics such as execution times, resource usage, and node performance.

Tools for Monitoring:

- **Prometheus & Grafana**: Use **Prometheus** to collect performance metrics and **Grafana** to visualize them in a dashboard. This gives you insights into resource usage, slow nodes, and workflow execution times.
- **New Relic**: Integrate **New Relic** for advanced performance monitoring and alerting. It provides real-time insights into workflow performance and allows for deep analysis of any bottlenecks.

7.6.4. Logging and Auditing

For compliance and troubleshooting purposes, it's important to keep track of the entire workflow lifecycle, including changes, errors, and successful executions. **n8n** allows you to implement comprehensive **logging** and **auditing** practices.

Best Practices for Logging:

- **Store Logs in a Centralized Location**: Use a **logging service** like **Elasticsearch** or **Loggly** to store and search logs across different workflows and systems.
- **Audit Trail**: Ensure that critical actions (e.g., data writes, external API calls) are logged for auditing purposes.

In this chapter, we explored how to manage **workflow complexity** and ensure scalability by following best practices for workflow design, parallelism, performance optimization, and horizontal scaling. We also covered how to **monitor workflow execution** using **execution logs**, **alerts**, and **external monitoring tools** to ensure workflows run smoothly and to catch any issues early.

By following these best practices, you can create **scalable workflows**, monitor their execution, and ensure reliability even as workflows become more complex and demanding. Let me know if you need more information on any of these topics or examples on how to implement them in your workflows!

7.7. Managing Agent State and Persistence

Managing the state and persistence of **n8n agents** is a key part of building reliable workflows, especially when dealing with long-running processes, complex logic, or workflows that need to maintain data across multiple executions. **State management** ensures that the workflow knows what data it has processed, and **persistence** ensures that critical data or context isn't lost between workflow runs.

In this section, we will explore how to manage **agent state**, how to persist data across workflow executions, and best practices for handling complex workflows that require state retention.

7.7.1. What is Agent State and Why is it Important?

The **state** of an agent refers to the data and context that an agent maintains during its execution. Managing the agent's state is critical for workflows that involve conditional logic, loops, or processes that take time to complete.

For example:

- In an **e-commerce workflow**, the state might include the current status of the order (e.g., "order placed," "payment confirmed," "shipped").
- In a **data processing workflow**, the state might involve the current step or stage in processing a batch of records.

Why State Management is Important:

- **Persistence**: Ensures that data is available across multiple executions of an agent, preventing the loss of critical context.
- **Consistency**: Keeps track of workflow progress and decisions, preventing actions from being repeated unnecessarily.

- **Efficiency**: Allows workflows to resume from the last known state, saving time and resources by not needing to start from scratch.

7.7.2. Managing State in n8n Workflows

n8n allows you to manage and maintain the state of workflows through several mechanisms, such as **variables, database storage**, and **external storage**. Let's look at some ways to manage the state of workflows and agents.

Using Variables for Temporary State

In **n8n**, you can use the built-in **Set node** or **Function node** to store variables for the current state of the workflow. These variables can hold context-specific data such as customer details, order status, or progress information.

- **Set Node**: Stores values from previous steps and makes them available for the next node in the workflow.
- **Function Node**: Allows for more advanced logic, where you can process and store variables programmatically in JavaScript.

Example: Storing Customer Order State

You can use the **Set node** to store and pass customer order data throughout the workflow. If the order passes validation, the workflow can store the status in the `order_status` field:

```json
json

{
  "order_status": "validated",
  "customer_name": "John Doe",
  "order_id": "12345"
}
```

These variables can be passed between nodes and used for further processing or conditional logic.

7.7.3. Persisting State Across Workflow Runs

For long-running processes or workflows that span multiple executions, it is crucial to persist state data between runs. **n8n** provides several ways to achieve this, such as storing the state in an external database or **cloud storage**.

Using External Databases for Persistence

You can use external databases (e.g., **MySQL**, **PostgreSQL**, **MongoDB**) to store workflow state and maintain consistency between executions. For example, you can store the current status of an order or task in the database so that the workflow can pick up where it left off during the next execution.

1. **Store State in a Database**:
   - After processing a part of the workflow (e.g., order validation), save the current state in the database.
   - On the next workflow execution, retrieve the state from the database and continue from where it left off.
2. **Example**:
   - **Store Order Data**: If you're working with a large number of orders, you could store the **order status**, **payment status**, and **shipment progress** in a database.
   - **Retrieve Order State**: On each execution, retrieve the order data from the database and check its status. If the order has been shipped, move to the next stage.

Using Files for Persistence

For simpler workflows, you can use **file storage** (e.g., local files or **cloud storage**) to store state data. This is useful for smaller workflows or workflows that don't require heavy database integrations.

- Store data in **JSON**, **CSV**, or **XML** files.
- For example, you could store workflow state data in a **JSON file** on Google Drive or AWS S3 to persist between executions.

7.7.4. Best Practices for Managing Agent State and Persistence

- **Avoid Overloading State**: Only store essential data that's required for workflow continuity. Overloading workflows with unnecessary state data can lead to inefficiencies.
- **Use Databases for Long-Term Persistence**: If your workflow needs to handle a large volume of data or require persistent state across multiple runs, use a relational or NoSQL database.
- **Use Files for Short-Term Persistence**: For less complex workflows or temporary data, use **files** for persistence. Ensure that the file system is reliable and accessible.
- **State Cleanup**: Periodically clean up stored state data that is no longer needed. For example, once an order is fully processed, remove its state from the database to free up resources.

7.8. Collaborative Workflow Development in Teams

When building workflows in **n8n**, collaboration is often necessary, especially in larger teams or organizations. Effective collaboration helps ensure that workflows are well-designed, tested, and maintained.

In this section, we'll explore strategies for **collaborative workflow development**, including best practices for teamwork, version control, and working with external contributors.

7.8.1. Best Practices for Collaborative Workflow Development

1. Use Version Control (Git)

Although **n8n** doesn't have built-in version control, you can still use **Git** to track changes to your workflows. This allows multiple developers to collaborate on the same workflows, keep track of changes, and revert to previous versions when necessary.

- **How to Use Git with n8n**:
    1. **Export Workflows**: Periodically export workflows as **JSON files**.

2. **Store in Git Repository**: Commit the exported workflows to a **Git repository** (e.g., GitHub, GitLab).
3. **Track Changes**: Collaborators can push and pull changes to/from the repository and resolve conflicts using Git.

2. Modular Workflow Design

As workflows become more complex, breaking them down into **modular agents** can make it easier for multiple team members to work on different parts of the project simultaneously. You can design each workflow or agent to perform a specific task (e.g., order validation, payment processing), and then use the **Execute Workflow node** to call them in sequence.

3. Document Workflows Clearly

Documenting workflows clearly ensures that all team members understand the purpose and functionality of each workflow and node. Use **n8n's Comment Node** to add inline documentation explaining complex logic or key decisions in the workflow.

- **Inline Comments**: Use comments to explain the **why** behind decisions in the workflow (e.g., why specific nodes are used or why certain conditions are checked).
- **Workflow Descriptions**: Provide an overview of what the workflow does, the expected input/output, and any dependencies on other workflows or systems.

7.8.2. Collaboration Tools for Teams

1. n8n's User Management and Permissions

n8n provides role-based access control (RBAC) for teams. This feature allows you to grant specific team members access to view, edit, or execute workflows based on their role.

- **Roles**: Define roles like **Admin**, **User**, or **Viewer**, each with different levels of access.
- **Permissions**: Control permissions at the **workflow** or **node** level to ensure that users can only interact with specific parts of the system.

2. Collaborative Tools Integration

To improve collaboration, you can integrate **n8n** with tools that facilitate teamwork and communication:

- **Slack**: Send workflow updates or alerts to specific channels.
- **Trello** or **Asana**: Use n8n to automate project management tasks, such as creating tasks or updating statuses based on workflow progress.
- **GitHub/GitLab**: Integrate version control into your workflows to allow developers to track changes and collaborate on workflow updates.

7.8.3. Using GitOps for Version Control and Deployment

GitOps is a set of practices that uses **Git repositories** as the source of truth for defining workflows and infrastructure. With **n8n**, GitOps can be used to manage the workflow development lifecycle.

Steps for Using GitOps:

1. **Store Workflows in Git**: Export **n8n workflows** to JSON files and commit them to a Git repository.
2. **Automate Deployment**: Set up CI/CD pipelines to deploy workflows automatically from the repository to your **n8n instance** whenever changes are made.
3. **Audit Workflow Changes**: Use **Git** to track changes to workflows, so you can easily revert to a previous version if something goes wrong.

In this chapter, we've explored how to effectively **manage agent state and persistence**, ensuring that your workflows can track progress and maintain context over time. We also covered best practices for **collaborative workflow development**, allowing multiple team members to work together efficiently on **n8n agents**.

By modularizing workflows, implementing version control, and using collaboration tools like **Git** and **GitOps**, you can streamline the development, deployment, and management of complex workflows, ensuring consistency and scalability as your system grows.

Chapter 8: Deploying and Scaling n8n Agents in Production

8.1. Deploying n8n Agents in Cloud Environments (AWS, Azure, GCP)

When moving **n8n agents** into production, scalability, reliability, and accessibility are paramount. Cloud environments such as **AWS, Azure**, and **Google Cloud Platform (GCP)** provide robust infrastructure solutions that can support and scale your **n8n agents** as demand increases. In this section, we will discuss the best practices for deploying **n8n agents** in cloud environments to ensure a smooth production deployment.

8.1.1. Why Use Cloud Environments for n8n Deployment?

Cloud environments offer several advantages for deploying **n8n agents**:

- **Scalability**: Easily scale resources up or down based on workload.
- **High Availability**: Use cloud-native features to ensure that your workflows are highly available and resilient.
- **Flexibility**: Cloud platforms support a wide range of configurations and services to meet your specific needs.

Benefits of Cloud Deployment:

- **Managed Services**: Cloud providers offer fully managed services for databases, storage, and networking, which simplifies the deployment of **n8n**.
- **Cost Efficiency**: Pay for only the resources you use, and scale up or down as needed.
- **Security**: Cloud providers offer built-in security measures such as encryption, firewalls, and identity management systems.

8.1.2. Deploying n8n on AWS (Amazon Web Services)

AWS offers flexible and scalable infrastructure to deploy **n8n agents**. The most common method is deploying **n8n** on an EC2 instance or using containerized solutions like **ECS** (Elastic Container Service) or **EKS** (Elastic Kubernetes Service).

Steps to Deploy n8n on AWS EC2:

1. **Launch an EC2 Instance**:
   - Use the AWS Management Console to launch an EC2 instance with your desired specifications (e.g., `t2.micro` for small workloads).
   - Select an appropriate **Amazon Machine Image (AMI)**, such as an Ubuntu server.
2. **Install Docker on EC2**:
   - Connect to the EC2 instance using SSH and install Docker:

```bash
sudo apt-get update
sudo apt-get install docker.io
```

3. **Install n8n Using Docker**:
   - Pull the **n8n Docker image** from Docker Hub and run it:

```bash
docker run -d --name n8n -p 5678:5678
n8nio/n8n
```

4. **Configure n8n**:
   - Set up any necessary environment variables for database connections, authentication, etc.
   - Optionally, use a **reverse proxy** (like **Nginx**) to secure **n8n** with **SSL**.
5. **Test the Deployment**:
   - Access **n8n** through the public IP address of the EC2 instance (`http://<EC2-PUBLIC-IP>:5678`).

Scaling on AWS:

- **Auto Scaling**: You can configure auto-scaling groups to scale EC2 instances based on traffic.
- **Elastic Load Balancer (ELB)**: Use an ELB to distribute traffic across multiple EC2 instances to ensure high availability.

8.1.3. Deploying n8n on Microsoft Azure

Azure provides a highly scalable environment for **n8n deployment**, and the process is similar to AWS. You can deploy **n8n** on a **virtual machine (VM)** or use **Azure Kubernetes Service (AKS)** for containerized workloads.

Steps to Deploy n8n on Azure VM:

1. **Create a Virtual Machine**:
   - In the **Azure portal**, create a new **VM** instance running Ubuntu or any other preferred Linux distribution.
   - Choose a VM size based on your needs (e.g., **Standard B1ms** for smaller workloads).
2. **Install Docker**:
   - SSH into the Azure VM and install Docker:

   bash

   ```
   sudo apt-get update
   sudo apt-get install docker.io
   ```

3. **Deploy n8n with Docker**:
   - Run the n8n Docker container:

   bash

   ```
   docker run -d --name n8n -p 5678:5678
   n8nio/n8n
   ```

4. **Secure the Deployment**:
   - You can use **Nginx** or **Azure Application Gateway** to set up an SSL-secured endpoint for **n8n**.

5. **Test the Deployment**:
   - o Access **n8n** via the public IP or domain name configured in your Azure VM.

Scaling on Azure:

- **Azure Load Balancer**: Use Azure's **Load Balancer** to distribute traffic across multiple VMs.
- **Azure Scale Sets**: Implement **Azure VM Scale Sets** to automatically scale VMs based on load.

8.1.4. Deploying n8n on Google Cloud Platform (GCP)

Google Cloud offers several ways to deploy **n8n**, including using **Google Compute Engine (GCE)** or **Google Kubernetes Engine (GKE)** for containerized solutions.

Steps to Deploy n8n on GCP Compute Engine:

1. **Create a GCE VM Instance**:
   - o In the **Google Cloud Console**, create a new **Compute Engine VM** running your preferred Linux distribution (e.g., Ubuntu).
   - o Configure the instance with sufficient resources based on the expected workload.
2. **Install Docker**:
   - o SSH into your instance and install Docker:

bash

```
sudo apt-get update
sudo apt-get install docker.io
```

3. **Run n8n in Docker**:
   - o Pull the **n8n Docker image** and run it:

bash

```
docker run -d --name n8n -p 5678:5678
n8nio/n8n
```

4. **Configure Firewall**:
    o   Ensure the necessary firewall rules are in place to allow
        HTTP/HTTPS traffic to **n8n**.
5. **Test the Deployment**:
    o   Visit your GCE VM's **external IP** (`http://<GCE-`
        `PUBLIC-IP>:5678`) to verify **n8n** is running.

Scaling on GCP:

*   **Google Cloud Load Balancer**: Distribute traffic across multiple
    instances of **n8n** using **Google Cloud Load Balancer**.
*   **GKE (Google Kubernetes Engine)**: For large-scale deployments,
    consider using **Google Kubernetes Engine (GKE)** to manage
    containers and scale **n8n** seamlessly.

8.2. Setting Up n8n on Docker and Kubernetes

For production deployments, containerization offers flexibility, scalability,
and ease of management. **Docker** and **Kubernetes** are the two most
commonly used containerization technologies for deploying **n8n** at scale.

8.2.1. Setting Up n8n on Docker

Docker allows you to package **n8n** and its dependencies into a portable
container, making it easy to deploy and manage across different
environments.

Steps to Set Up n8n on Docker:

1. **Install Docker**:
    o   Follow the official Docker installation guide for your
        operating system (Linux, macOS, or Windows).
2. **Run n8n in Docker**:
    o   Once Docker is installed, run the following command to pull
        and run the **n8n** container:

bash

```bash
docker run -d --name n8n -p 5678:5678
n8nio/n8n
```

3. **Configure Persistence**:
   - o To persist data, mount external volumes for **n8n**'s configuration files and database:

bash

```bash
docker run -d --name n8n -p 5678:5678 -v
/path/to/data:/root/.n8n n8nio/n8n
```

4. **Secure Deployment**:
   - o Use a **reverse proxy** (e.g., **Nginx**) to set up **SSL** for securing **n8n**.
5. **Monitor n8n with Docker**:
   - o Use Docker monitoring tools like **Docker stats** or **Prometheus** to monitor the performance of the **n8n** container.

8.2.2. Setting Up n8n on Kubernetes (K8s)

Kubernetes provides a powerful platform for managing containerized applications and automating their deployment, scaling, and operations. Deploying **n8n** on Kubernetes allows you to manage large-scale workflows efficiently.

Steps to Set Up n8n on Kubernetes:

1. **Install Kubernetes**:
   - o Set up a **Kubernetes cluster** using your preferred platform (e.g., **GKE, EKS, AKS**, or self-hosted Kubernetes).
2. **Create a Deployment for n8n**:
   - o Create a **deployment.yaml** file to define the n8n deployment:

yaml

```yaml
apiVersion: apps/v1
kind: Deployment
```

```
metadata:
  name: n8n
spec:
  replicas: 2
  selector:
    matchLabels:
      app: n8n
  template:
    metadata:
      labels:
        app: n8n
    spec:
      containers:
        - name: n8n
          image: n8nio/n8n
          ports:
            - containerPort: 5678
```

3. **Deploy to Kubernetes**:
   - Use the `kubectl` command to deploy the **n8n** container to Kubernetes:

bash

```
kubectl apply -f deployment.yaml
```

4. **Set Up Services and Ingress**:
   - Expose the **n8n** service using a **Kubernetes service** and set up **Ingress** to route traffic to **n8n**.
   - Use **Let's Encrypt** or another SSL provider to secure traffic with HTTPS.
5. **Monitor and Scale**:
   - Use **Kubernetes autoscaling** to automatically scale **n8n** based on resource usage or traffic demand.
   - Monitor Kubernetes pods and containers with tools like **Prometheus** and **Grafana**.

8.2.3. Best Practices for Docker and Kubernetes Deployments

- **Persistent Storage**: Always use persistent volumes for important data and configurations (e.g., workflow data, database storage).
- **Scaling**: Both **Docker** and **Kubernetes** support scaling. Set up **replica sets** or **pods** to scale horizontally as your workload increases.
- **Security**: Use **SSL** for secure connections to n8n, and secure your containers with best practices for secrets management and environment variable handling.

In this chapter, we covered the **deployment** and **scaling** of **n8n agents** in cloud environments such as **AWS**, **Azure**, and **Google Cloud**. We also explored containerized deployments using **Docker** and **Kubernetes** to ensure your workflows are scalable, secure, and highly available in production environments.

By following these deployment strategies and best practices, you can ensure that your **n8n agents** are efficiently deployed and capable of handling increasing traffic and workload demands.

8.3. Scheduling Agent Runs with Cron Jobs

Scheduling agent runs at specific intervals is essential for automating tasks that need to run periodically or at specific times. **Cron jobs** are a reliable way to automate tasks based on time, and **n8n** provides built-in support for scheduling workflows. In this section, we'll cover how to schedule **n8n agents** using **Cron Jobs** and **n8n's Cron Trigger Node** to run workflows at predefined times or intervals.

8.3.1. What are Cron Jobs?

A **Cron job** is a time-based job scheduler in Unix-like operating systems. It allows you to run commands or scripts at specified times, making it ideal for automating routine tasks. Cron jobs are configured by writing expressions in a format known as **cron syntax**.

- **Cron Syntax Format**:

```
pgsql

* * * * * /path/to/script
- - - - -
| | | | |
| | | | | +---- Day of the week (0 - 6) (Sunday
= 0)
| | | +------ Month (1 - 12)
| | +-------- Day of the month (1 - 31)
| +---------- Hour (0 - 23)
+------------ Minute (0 - 59)
```

Cron jobs are typically used for tasks such as:

- Backups
- Data synchronization
- Sending periodic reports or notifications

8.3.2. Scheduling n8n Agents with Cron Trigger Node

In **n8n**, you can easily schedule workflows using the **Cron Trigger node**, which allows you to configure workflows to run based on cron-like expressions directly within **n8n** without relying on an external cron service.

Steps to Schedule n8n Workflows Using Cron Trigger:

1. **Add the Cron Trigger Node**:
   o In the **Nodes Panel**, search for **Cron Trigger** and drag it onto the canvas.
2. **Configure Cron Trigger**:
   o Set up the schedule in the **Cron Trigger node** by specifying the minute, hour, day, month, and day of the week. These parameters will define when the workflow should run.

   Example: To schedule a workflow to run **every day at 8:00 AM**:

   o **Minute**: 0
   o **Hour**: 8
   o **Day of Month**: *
   o **Month**: *

o **Day of Week**: *

The cron expression would look like this:

```
0 8 * * *
```

3. **Test the Cron Trigger**:
   o After configuring the trigger, click **Execute Workflow**. The workflow will run based on the cron schedule you've set.
4. **Use in Complex Workflows**:
   o You can combine **Cron Trigger** with other workflow nodes to automate more complex tasks, such as checking for new data, sending periodic reports, or performing backups.

8.3.3. Example: Daily Data Backup Workflow

Imagine you need to create a daily backup of a database. You can use the **Cron Trigger node** to schedule the task, with the following workflow:

1. **Cron Trigger Node**: Set to run at midnight every day.
2. **Database Query Node**: To fetch the data that needs to be backed up.
3. **File System Node**: To store the backup on a cloud drive or local file system.

Cron expression: 0 0 * * * (run at midnight every day)

8.3.4. Best Practices for Cron Jobs in n8n

- **Timezone Management**: Ensure that the timezone used by the **Cron Trigger node** aligns with your server or local timezone to avoid confusion. **n8n** uses the server's timezone, so if you're using **n8n** in the cloud, double-check the time settings.
- **Run in Off-Peak Hours**: Schedule resource-heavy tasks (e.g., backups, data syncing) during off-peak hours to minimize the impact on performance.

- **Monitor Cron Jobs**: Use **n8n's Execution Log** to track whether scheduled workflows are running as expected. You can set up alerts to notify you if the workflow fails.

8.4. Managing Agent Workloads and Scaling n8n

When deploying **n8n agents** in production, managing workloads and scaling is essential to ensure that the system performs well under varying loads. **n8n** supports both **horizontal** and **vertical scaling**, allowing you to scale based on demand and ensure that workflows continue to execute smoothly.

In this section, we'll explore how to manage **n8n agent workloads** and scale **n8n** effectively to handle increasing traffic, more complex workflows, and large data volumes.

8.4.1. Scaling n8n for Increased Workloads

Scaling is crucial when the number of workflows or the complexity of your workflows grows. You can scale **n8n** using **vertical scaling** (adding more resources to the existing server) or **horizontal scaling** (adding more instances of n8n to distribute the load).

1. Vertical Scaling (Scaling Up)

Vertical scaling involves increasing the resources (CPU, memory, disk space) of your existing **n8n instance** to handle higher workloads. This can be done by upgrading your **server's** hardware or resizing your cloud instance.

Steps for Vertical Scaling:

- **Increase CPU or RAM**: If you're running **n8n** on a cloud service (e.g., AWS, Azure, GCP), you can resize the instance to add more **CPU** and **RAM**.
- **Increase Disk Space**: If your workflows involve large datasets, ensure you have sufficient disk space to handle data storage needs.
- **Optimize Performance**: Adjust system configurations (e.g., caching, database optimizations) to make the most of your available resources.

2. Horizontal Scaling (Scaling Out)

Horizontal scaling involves adding more instances of **n8n** to distribute the load and handle more concurrent workflows. This is particularly useful when workflows experience high concurrency or need to process large amounts of data in parallel.

Steps for Horizontal Scaling:

- **Use Docker and Kubernetes**: Deploy **n8n** using **Docker** containers and **Kubernetes** to scale out by adding multiple containers or pods to handle increased traffic.

  Example: With **Kubernetes**, you can automatically scale the number of pods running the **n8n** container based on CPU or memory usage.

- **Load Balancing**: Use a **load balancer** to distribute incoming requests across multiple **n8n** instances. This ensures that no single instance gets overwhelmed with too many requests.

8.4.2. Configuring Distributed n8n Workflows

When scaling **n8n** horizontally, it's important to ensure that workflows are distributed efficiently across multiple instances.

1. Distributed Workflows with Shared Storage:

- **Use Shared Databases**: Store workflow data and logs in a **centralized database** so that multiple **n8n instances** can access the same data. For example, use **PostgreSQL** or **MongoDB** to store workflow execution results and credentials.
- **Shared File Storage**: If workflows involve file handling, use **cloud storage services** like **AWS S3** or **Google Cloud Storage** to ensure that files are accessible from all instances.

2. Using Redis for Queue Management:

- For large workflows or workflows that involve long-running processes, use **Redis** as a queue system to manage tasks across multiple **n8n agents**.

Example: If you're processing multiple tasks in parallel, **Redis** can queue the tasks, allowing multiple **n8n agents** to work independently and retrieve tasks from the queue.

3. Load Balancer for Efficient Distribution:

- Set up a **load balancer** to distribute incoming HTTP requests or webhook triggers across multiple **n8n instances**. This ensures that no single instance is overwhelmed with traffic.

8.4.3. Auto-Scaling n8n for Dynamic Workloads

To handle dynamic workloads that fluctuate based on time of day or external triggers, **auto-scaling** is a great solution. Many cloud platforms provide **auto-scaling** features that allow you to automatically scale your **n8n instances** up or down based on predefined metrics, such as **CPU usage** or **request count**.

Steps for Auto-Scaling:

1. **Set Up Auto-Scaling on Cloud Providers**:
   - On **AWS**, use **Auto Scaling Groups** to automatically add or remove **n8n instances** based on load.
   - On **Azure**, use **Virtual Machine Scale Sets** to scale your **n8n** deployment based on demand.
2. **Configure Scaling Policies**:
   - Define the metrics that trigger auto-scaling, such as **CPU utilization** (e.g., scale up when CPU usage exceeds 70%).
   - Set a maximum and minimum number of instances to ensure you don't exceed your resource budget.
3. **Monitor Performance and Scaling**:
   - Regularly monitor performance metrics to ensure that your auto-scaling policies are working as expected. Tools like **CloudWatch** (AWS) or **Stackdriver** (GCP) can help you track performance and adjust scaling policies if necessary.

8.4.4. Cost Optimization for Scalable Deployments

As you scale **n8n** to handle increased traffic and workloads, it's important to keep an eye on costs. **Cloud environments** offer flexibility but can also become costly if not properly managed.

Best Practices for Cost Optimization:

- **Right-size Resources**: Ensure that your **n8n instances** are appropriately sized for the workloads they handle. Use cloud monitoring tools to adjust instance sizes based on actual usage.
- **Spot Instances**: If your workflows can tolerate interruptions, consider using **spot instances** (AWS, GCP) to reduce costs.
- **Storage Management**: Use **object storage** (e.g., AWS S3) for file storage to minimize costs compared to traditional block storage.

In this chapter, we covered how to deploy and scale **n8n agents** in **cloud environments** like **AWS**, **Azure**, and **GCP**. We also discussed how to scale **n8n** using **Docker** and **Kubernetes** for containerized deployments, ensuring that your workflows are highly available, scalable, and efficient.

By using techniques like **Cron Jobs** for scheduling, **horizontal and vertical scaling** for increased workloads, and **auto-scaling** for dynamic demands, you can ensure that your **n8n agents** perform well under high traffic and large-scale environments.

8.5. Securing Your Workflows and Agents in Production

When deploying **n8n agents** in production, security should be a top priority. Exposing workflows to external systems, APIs, and user inputs can introduce potential vulnerabilities. This section will discuss best practices for securing **n8n workflows** and agents, including strategies for **authentication**, **authorization**, **data encryption**, and **network security**.

8.5.1. Securing Access to n8n

By default, **n8n** workflows can be accessed via the **web interface**, which is ideal for development and testing but can be a security risk in production. To ensure your workflows and agents are secure in a production environment, you need to restrict unauthorized access.

Best Practices for Securing n8n Access:

1. **Enable Authentication**:
    - **Basic Authentication**: Use **Basic Authentication** for simple user verification (username and password) for the **n8n web interface**.
    - **OAuth2 Authentication**: For more secure and flexible authentication, implement **OAuth2** for managing user access, particularly if multiple users or services interact with the **n8n** interface.
    - **API Keys**: Use **API keys** to authenticate calls to workflows and agents, ensuring that only authorized services can trigger or interact with workflows.
2. **Restrict Web Interface Access**:
    - **Firewall Rules**: Use **firewall rules** to restrict access to the **n8n web interface** to only trusted IP addresses or networks.
    - **VPNs**: For additional security, deploy **n8n** behind a **VPN**, ensuring that only authenticated users within the VPN network can access the workflows.
3. **Use HTTPS (SSL/TLS)**:
    - **Encrypt Traffic**: Always use **HTTPS** to encrypt traffic between clients and your **n8n instance**. This ensures that sensitive data, such as API keys, passwords, and user data, is protected during transmission.
    - **SSL Certificates**: Obtain an **SSL certificate** from a trusted provider (e.g., **Let's Encrypt**) or use cloud services like **AWS Certificate Manager** or **Google Cloud SSL** for automatic certificate management.

8.5.2. Securing Workflow Data

Workflow data, such as sensitive user information or transactional data, should be encrypted to prevent unauthorized access. Securing data at rest and in transit is essential for protecting privacy and ensuring compliance with regulations such as **GDPR** or **HIPAA**.

Best Practices for Securing Workflow Data:

1. **Data Encryption in Transit**:
   - **TLS/SSL Encryption**: Ensure that all external communication (e.g., between **n8n** and APIs, databases, or third-party services) is encrypted using **TLS/SSL**. This prevents **man-in-the-middle (MITM)** attacks.
   - **Secure Webhooks**: If your workflows use **webhooks**, ensure that they are secured with **HTTPS** and require **authentication** via API keys or OAuth tokens.
2. **Data Encryption at Rest**:
   - **Database Encryption**: Encrypt sensitive data stored in databases (e.g., using **AES** encryption). Many cloud services (e.g., **AWS RDS**, **Google Cloud SQL**) provide automatic encryption at rest.
   - **Encrypt Workflow Variables**: When handling sensitive data within workflows, consider encrypting sensitive variables before passing them between nodes.
3. **Token Management**:
   - **Rotate API Keys**: Regularly rotate API keys and tokens used in workflows to minimize the risk of token theft. Consider using **environment variables** to manage tokens securely.
   - **Secret Management Services**: Use **secret management systems** such as **AWS Secrets Manager**, **HashiCorp Vault**, or **Azure Key Vault** to store and manage credentials securely.

8.5.3. Authorization and Permissions for Workflow Access

It's important to manage who can access and execute workflows and agents, particularly in a team-based or multi-user environment.

Best Practices for Authorization:

1. **Role-Based Access Control (RBAC)**:
   - **n8n** allows you to set up **role-based access control (RBAC)**, enabling you to define what different users can and cannot do within the system. For instance, you may have separate roles

for **admins**, **editors**, and **viewers** with varying levels of permissions.

2. **Limit Access to Sensitive Data**:
   o When designing workflows, only grant access to sensitive data based on the user's role. For example, ensure that only admins have access to the full database or private API keys.

3. **Audit Trails**:
   o Enable **logging and auditing** for workflow access and execution. Keep track of who triggered workflows, what data was accessed, and the results of the workflow. This helps identify and resolve security incidents quickly.

8.5.4. Network Security for Production Workflows

Securing the **network layer** is essential to ensure that your **n8n agents** and workflows are protected from external threats.

Best Practices for Network Security:

1. **Use a Virtual Private Cloud (VPC)**:
   o Deploy **n8n** inside a **VPC** in cloud environments like **AWS**, **Azure**, or **Google Cloud** to isolate your workflow infrastructure from the public internet.

2. **Private Networking**:
   o Use private IP addresses for communication between internal services and ensure that they are not accessible from the internet.

3. **Load Balancers and Reverse Proxies**:
   o Use **load balancers** and **reverse proxies** (e.g., **Nginx**) to route traffic securely and manage SSL certificates. This allows you to separate public-facing interfaces from the internal infrastructure.

4. **Security Groups and Firewalls**:
   o Configure **security groups** or **firewall rules** to only allow traffic from trusted IP addresses or networks. This minimizes the attack surface.

8.6. Best Practices for Versioning and Continuous Deployment

Versioning and continuous deployment (CI/CD) practices help ensure that changes to **n8n agents** are reliable, repeatable, and easy to manage. This section will discuss best practices for implementing **version control** and **CI/CD** for **n8n workflows** to automate updates and ensure smooth production deployments.

8.6.1. Version Control for n8n Workflows

Managing versions of **n8n workflows** is crucial to maintain consistency, collaboration, and rollback capabilities. While **n8n** doesn't have built-in version control, you can integrate **Git** to store, track, and manage workflow versions.

Steps for Versioning n8n Workflows:

1. **Export Workflows as JSON**:
   - Regularly export your workflows as **JSON files** using the **Export Workflow** feature in **n8n**.
2. **Store in a Git Repository**:
   - Create a **Git repository** (e.g., on **GitHub** or **GitLab**) and store the exported workflow JSON files there.
   - Commit and push changes whenever workflows are updated.
3. **Tag Versions**:
   - Use **tags** in Git to create versioned releases of your workflows. For example, tag versions like **v1.0.0**, **v1.1.0**, etc.

Example:

1. **Commit Workflow to Git**:
   - After making changes to a workflow, export the JSON, and commit it to the Git repository.
2. **Collaborate**:
   - Use **Git branches** to work on different features or updates to workflows. Merge these changes into the main branch once they are reviewed and tested.

8.6.2. Continuous Integration and Deployment (CI/CD)

Automating the deployment of **n8n workflows** can greatly reduce manual intervention and ensure that workflows are tested and deployed consistently.

Steps for Setting Up CI/CD for n8n Workflows:

1. **Set Up a Git Repository**:
   o Store your workflows as **JSON files** in a Git repository, as described above.
2. **Integrate with CI/CD Tools**:
   o Use tools like **GitHub Actions**, **GitLab CI**, or **Jenkins** to automate the deployment process.
   o Set up pipelines to trigger deployment whenever changes are pushed to the repository.
3. **Automate Workflow Testing**:
   o Implement automated testing for your workflows using testing frameworks that can simulate workflow execution.
   o This can include checking whether workflows execute without errors and validating that they produce the expected outputs.
4. **Automated Deployment to n8n**:
   o Use CI/CD tools to automatically deploy updated workflows to the **n8n** instance once tests pass. This can be done via APIs or by pulling the latest version from Git and updating the n8n instance.

8.6.3. Rollback and Backup Strategies

It's important to have a **rollback** strategy in place to restore previous versions of workflows if something goes wrong. By keeping backups and using **version control**, you can easily revert to earlier versions.

Best Practices:

- **Back Up Workflows Regularly**: Schedule regular exports of workflows to keep up-to-date backups.

- **Version Control**: Use **Git tags** to track versions and make it easy to revert to a previous version of a workflow.
- **Monitor Deployment**: Use tools like **Prometheus** or **Grafana** to monitor workflows in production, ensuring that they run as expected and trigger alerts if something goes wrong.

In this chapter, we discussed essential practices for securing **n8n workflows** in a production environment, including **authentication**, **data encryption**, and **network security**. We also explored **version control** and **continuous deployment (CI/CD)** for workflows, ensuring reliable and automated deployment processes.

By following these best practices, you can ensure that your **n8n agents** are secure, scalable, and maintainable, while also enabling efficient collaboration and version control for your team.

8.7. Setting Up Automated Backups and Monitoring

Ensuring that your **n8n agents** are protected from data loss and monitored for performance issues is essential when deploying workflows to production. Automated backups and monitoring systems are crucial for maintaining uptime, data integrity, and workflow reliability. This section will cover best practices for **automated backups** and **monitoring** for **n8n agents**.

8.7.1. Why Automated Backups Are Important

Automated backups are necessary to prevent data loss in case of system failures, accidental deletions, or corruption. **n8n workflows** often involve sensitive or critical data (e.g., user data, logs, process records) that must be preserved. Regularly backing up your data ensures that you can recover it when needed.

Benefits of Automated Backups:

- **Data Protection**: Safeguard important workflow data, execution logs, and configurations.

- **Recovery from Failures**: Quickly recover workflows or data in the event of system crashes or data corruption.
- **Compliance**: Automated backups ensure that your systems meet **regulatory compliance** for data retention.

8.7.2. Setting Up Automated Backups for n8n

To implement automated backups for **n8n agents**, you can use several strategies, such as backing up workflows, database configurations, and execution logs.

Best Practices for Automated Backups:

1. **Backing Up n8n Workflows**:
   - **n8n Workflow Exports**: Regularly export workflows as **JSON files** and store them in a backup location. You can automate this process using **n8n workflows** or external cron jobs.
   - **Backup Script**: Write a script that periodically exports your workflows using the **n8n API** or manually through the interface, and then saves them to a secure storage location (e.g., AWS S3, Google Cloud Storage, or an on-premises server).

   Example Cron Job for Automated Workflow Backups:

   - Set a cron job to export workflows every day at midnight:

   ```ruby
   0 0 * * * curl -X GET https://your-n8n-
   instance.com/api/workflows/export >
   /path/to/backup/workflow-backup.json
   ```

2. **Database Backups**:
   - If you are using an external database (e.g., **MySQL**, **PostgreSQL**), ensure that you regularly back up the database that stores the state, credentials, and other essential workflow data.

- o Many cloud platforms provide **automated database backups** (e.g., **AWS RDS, Google Cloud SQL**) that you can enable for daily or weekly backups.

    Example: Automate **PostgreSQL backups** using the following command:

    bash

    ```
    pg_dump your_database_name >
    /path/to/backup/backup_$(date +%Y%m%d).sql
    ```

3. **Backup Workflow Execution Logs**:
   - o Backing up **n8n execution logs** is important for tracking and debugging workflows. Use a file storage solution or cloud storage to store the logs.
   - o Consider exporting logs periodically using **cron jobs** or **API calls** to store them in **Google Cloud Storage** or **AWS S3** for long-term retention.
4. **Cloud-Based Backup**:
   - o Use cloud storage services like **AWS S3, Google Cloud Storage**, or **Azure Blob Storage** to store your backups securely. Cloud storage provides high availability and easy recovery options.
   - o **AWS Lambda** or **Google Cloud Functions** can be used to trigger backup processes automatically at scheduled intervals.

8.7.3. Monitoring n8n Workflows in Production

Monitoring is critical to ensure that your **n8n agents** are performing as expected and to catch potential issues before they impact production workflows. Effective monitoring can help you identify and address performance bottlenecks, failures, or slow workflows.

Best Practices for Monitoring n8n:

1. **Use n8n's Execution Log**:
   - o **n8n** provides an **Execution Log** that records all executions of workflows, including details of each node's execution. This

log can help you identify failures, performance issues, and other anomalies.

- o Regularly check the **Execution Log** to see if workflows are running smoothly and identify errors quickly.

2. **Integrate Monitoring Tools**:
   - o **Prometheus** and **Grafana** are popular tools for **monitoring performance** and **visualizing metrics**. You can integrate **n8n** with these tools to monitor resource utilization, execution times, error rates, and other critical metrics.
   - o **New Relic**, **Datadog**, or **AWS CloudWatch** can also be used to monitor performance and resource usage.

   Example of Prometheus Integration:

   - o Set up **Prometheus** to scrape metrics from your **n8n instance**, and use **Grafana** to visualize them. Monitor key metrics like **CPU usage**, **memory usage**, and **response times**.

3. **Set Up Alerts**:
   - o Use **alerts** to notify you when a workflow fails or when resource usage exceeds predefined thresholds. For example, you can set up alerts in **Slack**, **email**, or **SMS** whenever a workflow fails or a performance metric is breached.

   Example: Send a **Slack notification** when an error occurs in a workflow:

   - o Add a **Slack node** after the **Error Trigger node** to send an immediate notification to a channel.

4. **Health Checks**:
   - o Implement regular **health checks** to ensure that **n8n** is running smoothly. For example, you can set up an endpoint that pings your **n8n** instance to check its availability and respond with a healthy status.

   Example: Use **AWS CloudWatch** or **Google Cloud Monitoring** to check the health of your **n8n instance** and trigger alerts if the service becomes unavailable.

8.8. Real-World Deployment Example: Deploying a Customer Notification Agent

In this section, we'll walk through a real-world example of deploying a **Customer Notification Agent** in **n8n** to send notifications to customers based on certain triggers (e.g., order status updates).

8.8.1. Scenario

We are building an automated system to notify customers when their order status changes (e.g., from **"Processing"** to **"Shipped"**). The workflow will:

1. **Fetch order status** from an external API.
2. **Process the order status**.
3. **Send a notification** (via **email** or **SMS**) to the customer.

8.8.2. Workflow Steps

1. **Trigger Workflow**:
   - We will use the **Webhook Trigger node** to initiate the workflow whenever a new order status is updated in our system.
2. **Get Order Details**:
   - Use the **HTTP Request node** to fetch order details from an external API (e.g., an e-commerce platform's API).
3. **Process Order Data**:
   - Use a **Set node** to extract the relevant order data, such as **customer name, order number**, and **order status**.
   - Use **If nodes** to determine if the order status is **"Shipped"**, and proceed to send a notification.
4. **Send Customer Notification**:
   - If the order status is **"Shipped"**, use a **Send Email node** to send an email notification to the customer with the order details and tracking information.
   - Alternatively, use a **Twilio node** to send an **SMS** if preferred.
5. **Log the Notification**:
   - Optionally, use a **Database node** to log the notification in a **PostgreSQL** or **MySQL** database for audit purposes.

8.8.3. Deploying the Workflow

1. **Deploy the Workflow to Production**:
   - Once the workflow is tested and working in the **n8n editor**, deploy it to a production environment (e.g., **AWS EC2, Google Cloud VM**).
2. **Set Up Cron Jobs or Webhook Triggers**:
   - For periodic checks, set up a **Cron Trigger node** to run the workflow at regular intervals (e.g., every hour).
   - If you're integrating with an external system (e.g., an e-commerce platform), use a **Webhook Trigger node** to listen for status updates.
3. **Monitoring and Alerts**:
   - Set up monitoring using the **Execution Log** or external tools like **Prometheus** and **Grafana**.
   - Set up **alerts** to notify the team in case the workflow fails (e.g., **Slack, Email**).

8.8.4. Scaling the Workflow

As the number of orders grows, it may be necessary to scale the system to handle the increased load. Here are some tips for scaling the **Customer Notification Agent**:

1. **Horizontal Scaling**: Use multiple instances of **n8n** to handle concurrent workflows by deploying **n8n** on **Docker** or **Kubernetes** with a **load balancer**.
2. **API Rate Limits**: Use **rate limiting** and **pagination** when interacting with external APIs to avoid overloading the system and ensure smooth performance.
3. **Batch Processing**: If you have a large number of orders to process, break them into batches using the **SplitInBatches node** to process them more efficiently.

In this chapter, we discussed best practices for **automated backups** and **workflow monitoring** to ensure that your **n8n agents** are secure, resilient, and highly available in production. We also walked through a real-world example of deploying a **Customer Notification Agent**, which sends automated notifications to customers based on order status changes.

By following these deployment strategies, you can ensure that your **n8n agents** run reliably, scale as needed, and handle increasing workloads without compromising performance.

Chapter 9: Real-World Use Cases of n8n Agents

In this chapter, we will explore how **n8n agents** can be used to automate real-world workflows across various business functions. The flexibility of **n8n** makes it suitable for a wide range of use cases, from **business automation** to **data analysis and reporting**. We'll look at specific examples of how **n8n agents** can streamline operations, improve productivity, and provide valuable insights into business data.

9.1. Automating Business Workflows

Automating business workflows is one of the most common and powerful use cases of **n8n agents**. Many business processes are repetitive and time-consuming, involving multiple systems or manual intervention. **n8n** allows organizations to automate these processes, improving efficiency, reducing human error, and freeing up time for more valuable tasks.

9.1.1. What is Business Workflow Automation?

Business workflow automation involves automating tasks and processes that flow across departments, systems, or teams. These workflows often span across multiple systems (CRM, email, accounting, etc.) and may require human input at various stages.

For example, a business workflow might involve:

- **Lead capture and nurturing**
- **Order processing and invoicing**
- **Employee onboarding**
- **Customer support ticket management**

9.1.2. Real-World Example 1: Automating Lead Generation and Follow-Up

In a typical sales funnel, leads are captured from various sources (e.g., website forms, social media, or ads), and they need to be nurtured with follow-up emails or notifications. With **n8n**, you can automate this entire process, ensuring that leads are properly followed up without manual intervention.

Steps:

1. **Capture Leads**: Use a **Webhook Trigger node** to capture leads from forms on the website or social media platforms.
2. **Store Leads**: Use a **Google Sheets node** or **CRM API node** (e.g., **HubSpot**, **Salesforce**) to store lead data.
3. **Send Follow-Up Emails**: Use an **Email node** to automatically send a series of personalized follow-up emails to each lead at predefined intervals.
4. **Track and Update**: Monitor the responses (e.g., if the lead clicks on the email) and update the lead status in the CRM system or database.

This fully automated workflow can significantly improve response times and ensure that no leads are overlooked.

9.1.3. Real-World Example 2: Automating Order Processing

In an e-commerce setup, order processing is a critical workflow that often involves multiple steps: order verification, payment processing, shipment tracking, and customer notifications. Automating this workflow ensures quick order fulfillment and enhances customer satisfaction.

Steps:

1. **Capture Order Details**: Use a **Webhook Trigger node** to capture order details from an e-commerce platform (e.g., Shopify, WooCommerce).
2. **Verify Payment**: Use an **HTTP Request node** to check payment status via a payment gateway API (e.g., Stripe, PayPal).
3. **Generate Shipping Label**: Use a **Shipping API node** (e.g., UPS, FedEx) to generate shipping labels and tracking numbers.
4. **Send Customer Notification**: Use a **Send Email node** to notify customers about their order status, including tracking details.

This ensures orders are processed swiftly and customers are kept informed at every stage.

9.1.4. Real-World Example 3: Employee Onboarding Workflow

Onboarding new employees can be a time-consuming process, often involving multiple manual tasks: collecting documents, setting up accounts, and sending welcome emails. Automating this process ensures consistency and reduces the time spent on administrative tasks.

Steps:

1. **New Employee Registration**: Use a **Google Forms node** or **Webhook Trigger node** to capture new employee information.
2. **Create Accounts**: Use an **Active Directory API node** or **Google Workspace node** to create employee accounts in internal systems (e.g., email, file sharing).
3. **Send Onboarding Documents**: Automatically send a welcome email with the necessary documents (using an **Email node**).
4. **Track Progress**: Use a **Google Sheets node** to track the status of onboarding tasks (e.g., document submission, account creation).

By automating these tasks, HR teams can focus on high-value tasks, like mentoring new employees, rather than administrative overhead.

9.2. Agent-Driven Data Analysis and Reporting

Data analysis and reporting are essential functions in modern businesses, providing insights into performance, customer behavior, financial health, and much more. **n8n agents** can automate data collection, transformation, analysis, and reporting, freeing up analysts from repetitive tasks and enabling them to focus on deeper insights.

9.2.1. What is Agent-Driven Data Analysis?

Agent-driven data analysis refers to using **n8n agents** to automatically collect, process, and analyze data from various sources (e.g., databases, APIs, social media). This data can then be transformed into meaningful reports and visualizations.

For example, a sales team might want a daily report on total sales, customer demographics, and product performance. Instead of manually gathering this data from multiple sources, an **n8n agent** can do it automatically and generate the report.

9.2.2. Real-World Example 1: Sales and Revenue Reporting

Businesses often need to track key metrics such as daily sales, revenue growth, and profit margins. **n8n** can automate this process by pulling data from a **Sales Database** (e.g., **PostgreSQL**), processing it, and generating a report in a tool like **Google Sheets** or **Excel**.

Steps:

1. **Query Sales Data**: Use a **Database Query node** (e.g., **PostgreSQL, MySQL**) to pull sales data from the database.
2. **Data Transformation**: Use a **Set node** or **Function node** to clean, filter, and transform the data into a format suitable for reporting (e.g., calculate revenue, total sales, or profit margin).
3. **Generate Report**: Use a **Google Sheets node** or **Excel node** to generate a report with the sales data and key metrics.
4. **Send Report**: Use a **Send Email node** to email the sales report to relevant stakeholders (e.g., sales managers, executives).

This workflow automates the entire reporting process, ensuring that stakeholders have the latest data without manual intervention.

9.2.3. Real-World Example 2: Social Media Analytics

Social media marketing campaigns often require tracking engagement metrics such as likes, shares, comments, and followers. Instead of manually pulling data from multiple platforms (e.g., Facebook, Twitter, Instagram), an **n8n agent** can automate this process and compile a detailed social media performance report.

Steps:

1. **Fetch Data from Social Media APIs**: Use the **HTTP Request node** to connect to the APIs of various social media platforms (e.g., **Facebook Graph API, Twitter API, Instagram API**).
2. **Transform Data**: Use the **Function node** to process and analyze the data (e.g., count total likes, shares, and comments for each post).
3. **Create a Report**: Use a **Google Sheets node** to compile the data into a report, highlighting the best-performing posts and engagement metrics.
4. **Email the Report**: Use a **Send Email node** to send the report to marketing teams.

By automating the data collection and reporting process, social media teams can focus on strategy rather than manual data aggregation.

9.2.4. Real-World Example 3: Financial Dashboard and KPI Reporting

Financial reporting often involves pulling data from multiple systems (e.g., **accounting software**, **payment gateways**, **bank accounts**) to create a comprehensive view of the business's financial health. **n8n** agents can automate this process by pulling data from various sources, calculating key financial metrics (e.g., cash flow, expenses, profit margins), and generating a comprehensive dashboard or report.

Steps:

1. **Fetch Financial Data**: Use **API nodes** or **Database Query nodes** to pull financial data from sources like **QuickBooks**, **Stripe**, or **Bank APIs**.
2. **Analyze Data**: Use **Function nodes** to calculate key financial metrics (e.g., net profit, revenue growth, expenses).
3. **Generate Dashboard**: Use a **Google Sheets node** or **Excel node** to generate a financial dashboard with visualizations (e.g., bar charts, line graphs).
4. **Send Dashboard**: Use a **Send Email node** to distribute the dashboard to relevant stakeholders.

This process ensures that the finance team has up-to-date insights into the company's financial status without the need for manual report generation.

9.2.5. Best Practices for Agent-Driven Data Analysis

- **Data Validation**: Before processing data, ensure it is accurate and clean. Use **n8n's Function node** to implement validation rules (e.g., checking for missing or inconsistent data).
- **Use APIs Efficiently**: Many APIs, especially social media and CRM APIs, have rate limits. Be sure to implement **rate limiting** or use **pagination** to manage large datasets efficiently.
- **Automate Report Distribution**: Use **n8n agents** to send automated reports to stakeholders on a regular basis (e.g., daily, weekly).

- **Keep Reports Interactive**: For reports involving multiple KPIs or metrics, ensure the generated files (e.g., Google Sheets) are easy to filter, analyze, and share.

In this chapter, we explored two critical use cases for **n8n agents** in real-world business applications:

1. **Automating Business Workflows**: We discussed how **n8n** can automate various business processes such as lead generation, order processing, and employee onboarding.
2. **Agent-Driven Data Analysis and Reporting**: We examined how **n8n** can automate data collection, processing, and reporting, helping businesses gain insights from their data efficiently.

By automating routine business tasks and leveraging **n8n agents** for data-driven insights, organizations can improve operational efficiency, reduce errors, and make better-informed decisions. Let me know if you need more details or additional examples!

9.3. Automating Customer Support Systems with Agents

Customer support systems can be complex, often requiring multiple touchpoints, communication channels, and integrations with various tools. Automating these processes with **n8n agents** can streamline support workflows, improve response times, and enhance customer satisfaction. In this section, we'll explore how to use **n8n agents** to automate **customer support systems**, including ticket management, communication, and follow-ups.

9.3.1. What is Customer Support System Automation?

Customer support systems typically involve tasks such as:

- **Ticket creation** and management.
- **Customer inquiries** (via email, chat, social media).
- **Response management** (e.g., sending automated replies).
- **Escalation** of critical issues to support agents.

- **Follow-ups** after the issue has been resolved.

By automating these processes, you can improve efficiency, ensure consistency, and enable support teams to focus on more complex issues while ensuring that customers receive timely and accurate responses.

9.3.2. Real-World Example 1: Automating Ticket Creation and Management

Imagine an e-commerce company that receives customer inquiries via email, web forms, or social media. Instead of manually creating support tickets for each customer issue, **n8n** can automate this process by creating tickets based on incoming data, tracking their status, and sending notifications.

Steps:

1. **Capture Customer Inquiry**:
   - Use the **Webhook Trigger node** to capture customer inquiry data from **contact forms** or emails.
   - You could integrate with an **email service** like **Gmail** or **Mailgun** to automatically parse incoming emails and extract relevant data (e.g., issue description, customer contact details).
2. **Create a Support Ticket**:
   - Use the **Create Item** node (e.g., **Trello, Zendesk, Jira Service Desk**) to create a new ticket in a ticket management system.
   - Store the customer inquiry details (e.g., name, issue description, contact info) in the ticket.
3. **Automated Ticket Acknowledgment**:
   - Use a **Send Email node** or **Send SMS node** to send an automated acknowledgment to the customer, informing them that their ticket has been created and providing an estimated resolution time.
4. **Escalation Process**:
   - Use **If nodes** to escalate tickets that meet certain criteria (e.g., high-priority issues or tickets that have been open for too long). You can escalate the issue to a senior agent or assign it to a specific department.
5. **Track Ticket Status**:

o   Use the **Update Item** node to update the ticket's status based on the workflow's progress (e.g., "resolved," "awaiting response").

This automated workflow ensures that customer inquiries are handled promptly, without requiring manual intervention to create and track tickets.

9.3.3. Real-World Example 2: Automating Customer Feedback Collection and Follow-up

Collecting feedback from customers after a support interaction is vital for improving customer service. Automating this process ensures that feedback is collected consistently and timely.

Steps:

1. **Trigger Feedback Request**:
   o   Use the **Webhook Trigger node** to detect when a support case is closed, either manually by a support agent or automatically based on certain criteria (e.g., ticket status updates).
2. **Send Feedback Survey**:
   o   Use a **Send Email node** to automatically send a feedback survey (e.g., via Google Forms, Typeform) to the customer after their issue is resolved.
   o   Include questions like **"How satisfied are you with the service?"** and **"What can we do better?"**
3. **Process Feedback**:
   o   Use the **HTTP Request node** to capture the feedback from the survey responses. This can be integrated with **Typeform** or **Google Sheets** to store the results.
4. **Customer Follow-up**:
   o   Based on the feedback, automatically send a **follow-up email**. For example, if a customer is dissatisfied, send a follow-up email with an apology and offer additional support.

By automating the feedback collection and follow-up process, support teams can gain insights into customer satisfaction while reducing manual work.

9.3.4. Best Practices for Automating Customer Support Systems

1. **Use Conditional Logic**: Implement conditional logic (e.g., using **If nodes**) to route tickets based on issue type, customer priority, or urgency.
2. **Integrate with Existing Systems**: **n8n** can be integrated with popular customer support tools such as **Zendesk, Freshdesk, HubSpot Service Hub**, and **Jira Service Desk** to automate ticket creation and management seamlessly.
3. **Track SLA Compliance**: Use automated reminders and notifications to ensure support tickets are resolved within **Service Level Agreement (SLA)** guidelines.
4. **Maintain Personalization**: Although workflows are automated, ensure that communication with customers feels personalized by incorporating dynamic content (e.g., customer name, ticket number) into emails or SMS.

9.4. Integration with CRM Tools (Salesforce, HubSpot, etc.)

CRM tools like **Salesforce, HubSpot**, and **Zoho CRM** are essential for managing customer relationships, tracking sales leads, and nurturing prospects. **n8n agents** can be used to automate the flow of data between CRM systems and other business tools, improving efficiency and ensuring that customer interactions are tracked and followed up promptly.

9.4.1. What is CRM Integration?

CRM integration involves connecting your **n8n workflows** with a **CRM system** to streamline data flow between customer-facing teams (e.g., sales, marketing, support) and backend systems. By automating the process of updating contact records, adding leads, and following up with customers, businesses can ensure that no opportunity is missed and no customer is overlooked.

Benefits of CRM Integration:

- **Improved Data Accuracy**: Automatically sync data between various platforms, ensuring consistency across systems.

- **Streamlined Processes**: Automate routine tasks, such as updating contact details, logging interactions, and assigning leads.
- **Enhanced Customer Experience**: Provide a more personalized experience by tracking customer interactions and maintaining up-to-date records.

9.4.2. Real-World Example 1: Syncing Leads Between Web Forms and CRM

When capturing leads from your website (e.g., via a contact form), you want to automatically create a new record in your CRM to track the lead's status and follow-up actions. **n8n** can be used to integrate form submissions with a CRM like **Salesforce** or **HubSpot**.

Steps:

1. **Capture Lead Data**:
   o Use a **Webhook Trigger node** to capture lead data from a web form (e.g., customer name, email, message).
2. **Store Lead in CRM**:
   o Use a **Salesforce node** or **HubSpot node** to create a new lead or contact record in the CRM system.
3. **Follow-Up with the Lead**:
   o Use the **Send Email node** or **SMS node** to send an automated thank-you message or follow-up email to the lead.
4. **Track Lead Status**:
   o Update the lead status in the CRM system (e.g., from **New** to **Contacted** or **Qualified**).

By automating the process of adding leads and tracking their status, your sales team can focus on engaging with high-priority leads rather than manually entering data.

9.4.3. Real-World Example 2: Automating Customer Support Ticket Creation in CRM

When a customer submits a support ticket through a form, it's essential to track that interaction in the CRM system for follow-up and customer relationship management. **n8n** can automate this by creating a ticket in your CRM system whenever a new support request is submitted.

Steps:

1. **Capture Support Ticket**:
   - Use a **Webhook Trigger node** to capture support ticket submissions (e.g., via a contact form or email).
2. **Create a Case or Ticket in CRM**:
   - Use a **Salesforce Case node** or **HubSpot Tickets node** to create a new case or ticket in the CRM system, including relevant customer data (e.g., ticket subject, issue description, customer details).
3. **Automated Follow-up**:
   - Use a **Send Email node** to send an acknowledgment to the customer that their ticket has been created.
4. **Escalation and Updates**:
   - Use **If nodes** to escalate tickets based on priority or issue type, updating the CRM system accordingly.

9.4.4. Best Practices for CRM Integration

1. **Data Mapping**: Ensure that the data from external sources (e.g., web forms, emails) is correctly mapped to the relevant fields in the CRM (e.g., lead name, email address, phone number).
2. **Real-Time Syncing**: For more dynamic workflows, use real-time syncing between **n8n** and CRM systems. This ensures that CRM records are always up to date, without delay.
3. **Lead Scoring and Prioritization**: Automate the process of scoring leads based on predefined criteria (e.g., how many times they've engaged with the website or how many pages they've visited).
4. **Centralized Communication**: Use CRM systems as a hub to track all customer communication (e.g., tickets, emails, calls) to ensure that customer support or sales teams can access the full history of customer interactions.

In this chapter, we explored how **n8n agents** can be used in **real-world use cases**, including automating **customer support systems** and integrating with

CRM tools like **Salesforce** and **HubSpot**. By automating repetitive tasks such as ticket creation, lead management, and follow-up communications, businesses can improve efficiency, ensure no customer is overlooked, and enhance the overall customer experience.

These real-world examples show how powerful **n8n agents** can be when applied to everyday business processes.

9.5. Social Media Automation with Agents

Social media platforms like **Twitter, Facebook, Instagram**, and **LinkedIn** are vital tools for businesses to engage with customers, promote products, and gather feedback. **n8n agents** provide a powerful way to automate social media tasks such as posting updates, responding to comments, and managing social media interactions.

In this section, we'll explore how to automate social media activities using **n8n agents** for platforms like **Twitter** and **Facebook**, enabling businesses to engage more effectively and efficiently.

9.5.1. What is Social Media Automation?

Social media automation refers to using tools like **n8n** to schedule, post, and respond to content across social media platforms without manual intervention. By automating these tasks, businesses can:

- **Increase engagement** by posting regularly.
- **Respond to customer inquiries** quickly.
- **Track social media mentions** and keywords.

For example, you could automatically:

- Post daily promotions to your **Facebook page**.
- Tweet new blog posts on **Twitter**.
- Send welcome messages to users who follow your **Instagram** account.

Benefits of Social Media Automation:

- **Time-saving**: Automates repetitive tasks like posting and responding to comments, saving valuable time for social media managers.
- **Consistency**: Ensures your business maintains a consistent presence on social media by automating posts.
- **Engagement**: Quickly respond to customer comments or messages to enhance customer service and engagement.

9.5.2. Real-World Example 1: Automated Tweeting with Twitter API

Let's say you want to automatically tweet the latest blog posts from your website every time a new article is published. Using **n8n**, you can integrate **Twitter's API** to automate this process.

Steps:

1. **Trigger**: Use the **Webhook Trigger node** or **Cron Trigger node** to detect new blog posts from your website's **RSS feed** or **content management system**.
2. **Format Tweet**: Use the **Set node** or **Function node** to format the tweet, including the blog post title, URL, and hashtags.
3. **Post to Twitter**: Use the **Twitter node** to automatically post the tweet with the content from the new blog post.
4. **Log and Track**: Optionally, you can store the details of each tweet in a **Google Sheets** or **Database** node for reporting and tracking purposes.

Example Cron Trigger:

- Schedule the tweet to be posted every **hour**, fetching the latest blog posts and tweeting them to Twitter.

bash

```
0 * * * * curl -X POST https://your-n8n-
instance.com/webhook/new-post > /dev/null
```

9.5.3. Real-World Example 2: Automatically Posting to Facebook Page

If your business uses **Facebook** to engage with customers, you can automate posting promotional content or event announcements. **n8n** can integrate with **Facebook's Graph API** to automatically create and post content to a Facebook page.

Steps:

1. **Capture Data**: Use the **HTTP Request node** to fetch the data (e.g., new blog posts, promotions, or event details) from your website or external content sources.
2. **Create Facebook Post**: Use the **Facebook node** in **n8n** to create a new post on your Facebook page.
3. **Send Confirmation**: Use the **Send Email node** or **Slack node** to notify the social media team that the post has been successfully published.

Example: You can automate weekly updates about your latest promotions or upcoming events by using n8n's Cron Trigger to post on Facebook every Monday at 10 AM.

9.5.4. Best Practices for Social Media Automation

1. **Use Conditional Logic**: Use **If nodes** or **Switch nodes** to filter content and ensure only relevant posts are published. For example, only post product promotions if the inventory is above a certain threshold.
2. **Engage with Comments**: Set up workflows that automatically respond to common customer queries or messages, ensuring fast responses.
3. **Monitor Social Media Mentions**: Set up workflows that trigger when specific keywords or mentions are detected on social media, allowing you to monitor and respond to brand mentions.
4. **Track Social Media Performance**: Use **n8n** to automatically gather performance metrics (e.g., likes, shares, comments) from platforms like **Twitter** or **Facebook** and log them into a **Google Sheet** for reporting and analysis.

9.6. Email and SMS Automation for Marketing Campaigns

Email and **SMS marketing** are powerful tools for engaging customers, sending promotions, and nurturing leads. With **n8n agents**, you can automate these processes, ensuring timely and personalized communication at scale.

In this section, we'll explore how **n8n agents** can be used to automate **email** and **SMS marketing campaigns**, including scheduling emails, sending bulk messages, and managing subscriber lists.

9.6.1. What is Email and SMS Automation?

Email and **SMS automation** involves sending pre-designed messages automatically based on specific triggers or schedules. For instance:

- **Email automation** can be used for sending welcome emails, newsletters, or promotional offers.
- **SMS automation** can notify customers about their order status, shipping details, or new offers.

Automating these campaigns ensures that your business can reach customers with relevant messages at the right time without manual intervention.

Benefits of Email and SMS Automation:

- **Personalized Communication**: Automate personalized emails or SMS messages based on customer behavior or preferences (e.g., abandoned cart reminders).
- **Time Efficiency**: Save time by automating repetitive tasks like sending promotional emails or SMS reminders.
- **Increased Engagement**: Ensure timely delivery of marketing content to increase customer engagement and conversions.

9.6.2. Real-World Example 1: Automating Email Marketing Campaigns

Automating email marketing campaigns helps ensure that customers receive timely, personalized content without manual effort. Let's say you want to send out a **monthly newsletter** to subscribers with the latest product updates.

Steps:

1. **Capture Subscriber Data**: Use an **email list** stored in a **Google Sheets node** or **CRM** system to capture email addresses and customer details.
2. **Personalize Email Content**: Use the **Set node** or **Function node** to dynamically insert personalized content into the email (e.g., the customer's name or recent purchases).
3. **Send Email**: Use the **Send Email node** (e.g., **Gmail**, **Mailgun**) to automatically send the newsletter to your email list.
4. **Track Email Opens**: Use the **HTTP Request node** to integrate with services like **Mailgun** or **SendGrid** to track open rates and click-through rates.

Example Cron Trigger:

- Schedule the email campaign to be sent every **first day of the month**:

```bash
0 0 1 * * curl -X POST https://your-n8n-
instance.com/webhook/send-newsletter >
/dev/null
```

9.6.3. Real-World Example 2: SMS Campaigns for Promotional Offers

SMS campaigns can be a great way to reach customers with time-sensitive offers, such as flash sales or limited-time promotions. **n8n** can automate this process by sending **SMS messages** to customers via services like **Twilio**.

Steps:

1. **Create SMS List**: Capture customer phone numbers in a **Google Sheets node** or a **CRM system**.
2. **Define the Offer**: Use the **Set node** to create a personalized promotional message, including product details, discount codes, and expiry dates.
3. **Send SMS**: Use the **Twilio node** to send SMS messages to customers with the defined offer.
4. **Track Responses**: Use the **Twilio node** to track SMS replies, enabling you to follow up or offer additional assistance.

Example: Send a flash sale SMS to all customers with an active subscription to your service, promoting discounts or exclusive offers.

9.6.4. Real-World Example 3: Automated Abandoned Cart Email and SMS Reminders

One of the most effective ways to boost conversions is by automating abandoned cart reminders. When a customer adds items to their cart but doesn't complete the purchase, **n8n agents** can send reminders via email or SMS.

Steps:

1. **Capture Abandoned Cart Data**: Use a **Webhook Trigger node** to capture cart abandonment events from your e-commerce platform (e.g., **Shopify**, **WooCommerce**).
2. **Personalized Reminder**: Use the **Set node** or **Function node** to personalize the reminder (e.g., item names, images, discounts).
3. **Send Email or SMS**: Use either the **Send Email node** for email reminders or the **Twilio node** for SMS reminders.
4. **Follow-Up**: After a set time, send a follow-up reminder to customers who still haven't completed their purchase.

By automating this process, you can recover sales that might otherwise have been lost.

9.6.5. Best Practices for Email and SMS Automation

1. **Personalization**: Ensure that messages are personalized by dynamically inserting customer details such as their name, recent purchases, or abandoned cart items.
2. **Segmentation**: Segment your audience based on behavior, demographics, or preferences. Use conditional logic in **n8n** to send targeted campaigns.
3. **Frequency**: Avoid overwhelming customers with too many messages. Use **n8n's Cron Trigger** to schedule messages at appropriate times and intervals.
4. **Track Performance**: Monitor the success of your campaigns using **open rates**, **click-through rates**, and **conversion rates**. Use this data to fine-tune future campaigns.

In this chapter, we explored how **n8n agents** can automate **social media**, **email**, and **SMS marketing campaigns**. By automating repetitive tasks like posting updates on social media, sending marketing emails, and reminding customers about abandoned carts, businesses can significantly improve efficiency and customer engagement.

Using **n8n's powerful automation capabilities**, businesses can streamline marketing workflows, enhance personalization, and ultimately increase conversion rates while saving time and resources.

9.7. Custom Business Solutions: Tailored Workflow Examples

Every business has unique requirements, and **n8n** provides a flexible platform that can be used to create **custom workflows** tailored to specific business needs. From **inventory management** to **customer relationship management (CRM)**, **n8n agents** can be customized to solve specific challenges faced by businesses across various industries.

In this section, we'll explore several **tailored workflow examples** that demonstrate how **n8n agents** can be adapted to meet the diverse needs of businesses.

9.7.1. Custom Business Solutions with n8n

n8n agents are incredibly versatile and can be configured to perform a wide range of tasks in different areas of business. Whether it's **order management**, **inventory tracking**, **customer engagement**, or **automating manual tasks**, the flexibility of **n8n** allows businesses to develop highly customized workflows.

Examples of Tailored Workflow Solutions:

1. **Automated Invoice Generation and Emailing**
   - **Scenario**: A business needs to automatically generate invoices based on customer orders and send them to customers.
   - **Workflow**:
     - **Capture order data** from an e-commerce platform (e.g., WooCommerce, Shopify) using a **Webhook Trigger node**.
     - **Generate invoices** using data from the order (e.g., product list, pricing, shipping address) using the **Set node**.
     - **Generate PDF invoice** with the **PDF generator node**.
     - **Email the invoice** using the **Send Email node** and attach the generated PDF.

   This workflow ensures that invoices are automatically generated and sent to customers immediately after purchase, saving time and reducing the risk of errors.

2. **Automated Data Entry into CRM Systems**
   - **Scenario**: A business wants to automatically add leads from various channels (e.g., website forms, social media) into its CRM system.
   - **Workflow**:
     - Use **Webhook Trigger node** to capture form submissions or new leads.
     - **Process and clean the data** using the **Set node** to extract relevant information (e.g., name, email, company).
     - **Create a new lead in the CRM** (e.g., Salesforce, HubSpot) using the appropriate API node.

- **Send a confirmation email** to the new lead using the **Send Email node**.

Automating data entry into the CRM ensures that leads are properly tracked and followed up on without manual intervention.

3. **Inventory Management and Low Stock Alerts**
   - **Scenario**: A business needs to track inventory levels and send alerts when stock levels fall below a certain threshold.
   - **Workflow**:
     - **Monitor inventory data** using an API connection to the inventory management system.
     - **Check stock levels** using the **If node** to trigger actions if the stock level is below the threshold.
     - **Send an email alert** to the purchasing team when stock is low using the **Send Email node**.
     - **Update the inventory system** with new orders or stock updates using the **Update node**.

This workflow ensures that businesses never run out of stock or fail to replenish popular products in time.

4. **Automated Customer Feedback Collection**
   - **Scenario**: A business wants to collect customer feedback automatically after a product or service interaction.
   - **Workflow**:
     - **Trigger the workflow** using an **Order Completion Trigger** or **Service Completion Trigger** (e.g., after a service is marked as "complete").
     - **Send an automated feedback request** to the customer via email or SMS using the **Send Email** or **Twilio (SMS)** node.
     - **Collect responses** via a survey tool (e.g., Google Forms, Typeform).
     - **Store the feedback** in a **Google Sheets** or **CRM system** to analyze later.

Automating the feedback collection process allows businesses to consistently gather customer insights without additional effort from customer service teams.

9.7.2. Best Practices for Creating Custom Solutions

1. **Understand the Workflow**: Map out your business process before starting. Understanding each step in the process ensures the right steps are automated.
2. **Use Modular Design**: Break down complex workflows into smaller, reusable agents. This makes it easier to manage and debug your workflows.
3. **Use Conditional Logic**: Implement **If nodes** and **Switch nodes** to control the flow of tasks based on dynamic data. This allows workflows to adapt to different conditions (e.g., different email content for different customer segments).
4. **Leverage External APIs**: **n8n** can connect to a wide range of **third-party tools**. Use **API nodes** to extend your workflow's functionality.
5. **Test and Monitor**: Always test your workflows thoroughly to ensure they function as expected. Use **execution logs** and **alerts** to monitor workflow performance and catch errors early.

9.8. Hands-on Example: Building an E-commerce Automation Agent

In this section, we'll walk through a hands-on example of building an **E-commerce Automation Agent** using **n8n**. This agent will automate common tasks in an e-commerce business, such as order processing, inventory updates, and customer notifications.

9.8.1. Scenario: E-commerce Order Processing and Notifications

The goal is to create an automated agent that:

1. **Processes new orders**.
2. **Updates inventory levels** based on the order.
3. **Sends confirmation emails** to customers.
4. **Notifies the warehouse team** about the new order.

Step 1: Trigger the Workflow on New Order

1. Use a **Webhook Trigger node** to capture new orders from an **e-commerce platform** (e.g., **WooCommerce, Shopify**).
2. This could be a **POST request** from the platform, containing order data such as product name, quantity, customer details, etc.

Step 2: Process Order Data

1. Use a **Set node** to extract and map relevant order details, such as:
   o **Customer name**
   o **Shipping address**
   o **Order items (products and quantities)**
2. If there are any discounts or promotions, use an **If node** to apply them to the order total.

Step 3: Update Inventory

1. Use a **Database Query node** (e.g., **PostgreSQL, MySQL**) to update the inventory based on the products ordered.
2. The inventory count for each product should decrease according to the quantity ordered.

Step 4: Send Confirmation Email to Customer

1. Use the **Send Email node** (e.g., via **SMTP, Mailgun**, or **SendGrid**) to send an email to the customer confirming their order.
2. The email should include order details, estimated delivery time, and tracking information (if available).

Step 5: Notify Warehouse Team

1. Use a **Slack node** or **Send Email node** to notify the warehouse team of the new order.
2. Include relevant details, such as order items, customer shipping address, and expected fulfillment time.

Step 6: Log Order Details

1. Use a **Google Sheets node** or a **CRM node** (e.g., **Salesforce, HubSpot**) to log order details for further processing or analysis.

9.8.2. Workflow Overview

The **E-commerce Automation Agent** workflow will consist of the following nodes:

1. **Webhook Trigger**: Captures new order data.
2. **Set Node**: Extracts and processes order data.
3. **Database Query Node**: Updates inventory levels.
4. **Send Email Node**: Sends a confirmation email to the customer.
5. **Slack Node / Send Email Node**: Notifies the warehouse team.
6. **Google Sheets/CRM Node**: Logs the order data.

By automating this process, the e-commerce business can save time and reduce manual effort in handling orders, inventory, and customer communication.

9.8.3. Best Practices for E-commerce Automation

1. **Integration with Multiple Systems**: Ensure that your **n8n agent** integrates seamlessly with the various systems your business uses (e.g., payment gateways, inventory management, email services).
2. **Use Conditional Logic**: Add flexibility to the workflow by using **If nodes** for conditional actions, such as sending different types of emails based on customer segments or order size.
3. **Handle Errors Gracefully**: Implement **error handling** to catch issues in the workflow, such as failed payment processing or out-of-stock items.
4. **Optimize for Scalability**: As your e-commerce business grows, ensure your workflows can scale by using **batch processing**, **parallel execution**, and **horizontal scaling** (e.g., multiple n8n instances).

In this chapter, we explored **custom business solutions** by looking at tailored **n8n workflows** that automate business processes across various industries. We also walked through a **hands-on example** of building an **E-commerce Automation Agent** that automates order processing, inventory updates, customer notifications, and warehouse notifications.

By automating these key tasks, businesses can improve efficiency, reduce manual errors, and enhance customer satisfaction

Chapter 10: Troubleshooting and Optimization

In this chapter, we will explore best practices for troubleshooting and optimizing **n8n agents** to ensure your workflows run efficiently and without issues. Given that workflows in **n8n** may interact with multiple systems, APIs, and external services, it's important to identify and address common issues that can arise during execution. We'll cover some of the most common issues, debugging techniques, and optimization strategies to improve performance.

10.1. Common n8n Agent Issues and Their Fixes

Despite the power and flexibility of **n8n agents**, you may occasionally encounter issues that hinder workflow execution. Here we will explore some common problems that users face and provide practical solutions.

10.1.1. Workflow Execution Failures

Issue: Workflows may fail to execute due to configuration errors, missing data, or service unavailability.

Common Causes:

- **Incorrect node configuration**: Missing required fields, incorrect parameters, or misconfigured API credentials.
- **Missing data**: Nodes requiring data from previous steps may fail if the expected data is not passed correctly.
- **External service downtime**: If your workflow depends on an external API or service that is temporarily down, the workflow may fail.

Fix:

1. **Check Execution Logs**: Always check the **Execution Log** in **n8n** to get detailed information about the failure. The log will provide insights into which node failed and why.

2. **Verify Node Configuration**: Ensure that all nodes are correctly configured, and check the parameters for **required fields** (e.g., API keys, authentication credentials, or payload formats).
3. **Test API Connections**: If your workflow depends on an external service, test the connection to ensure the service is available and the credentials are valid.
4. **Handle Missing Data**: Use **If nodes** or **Set nodes** to handle missing data or optional fields. This ensures that workflows don't break if some data is missing but allows them to continue processing with defaults or empty values.

10.1.2. Data Formatting Errors

Issue: Workflow nodes may fail when data isn't formatted correctly, especially when dealing with APIs or external services that require specific formats.

Common Causes:

- **JSON vs. String Formatting**: Data being passed between nodes might be incorrectly formatted as a string when the receiving node expects a JSON object.
- **Data type mismatches**: Sometimes, workflows pass data in a format (e.g., number vs. string) that isn't compatible with the node's requirements.

Fix:

1. **Inspect Data Passed Between Nodes**: Use the **Set node** or **Function node** to inspect and format the data correctly before passing it to other nodes. Ensure the data structure aligns with the expected input type for each node.
2. **Use the JSON.parse() Function**: If the data is passed as a string but needs to be an object, use the **Function node** with **JSON.parse()** to convert the string into a valid JSON object.

```javascript
return JSON.parse($json["data"]);
```

3. **Use n8n's Built-in Data Conversion Nodes**: If necessary, use **Set nodes** to convert data types (e.g., turning a string into an integer or a date).

10.1.3. API Rate Limits and Timeouts

Issue: API calls may fail if the external service enforces rate limits or if the request takes too long, resulting in timeouts.

Common Causes:

- **API Rate Limits**: Many APIs enforce rate limits, meaning you can only send a certain number of requests within a given time period.
- **Timeouts**: When external services experience heavy traffic or are slow to respond, requests may time out, resulting in workflow failure.

Fix:

1. **Implement Retries**: Use **n8n's Retry node** to automatically retry failed API calls after a specified delay. This is useful when dealing with transient network or API issues.
2. **Respect Rate Limits**: When working with APIs that enforce rate limits (e.g., Twitter, GitHub), make sure your workflow includes mechanisms to wait between requests. Use **Delay nodes** or implement custom rate-limiting logic to control the frequency of requests.
3. **Handle Timeouts Gracefully**: Increase timeout settings where applicable (e.g., HTTP Request node). For instance, you may want to set a longer timeout period if you're working with APIs that take longer to process requests.
4. **Check API Status**: Before retrying, check the API status page to ensure there's no ongoing service disruption or maintenance.

10.1.4. Authentication Issues

Issue: Incorrect or expired API credentials often cause authentication failures, preventing successful connections to third-party services.

Common Causes:

- **Expired API keys or tokens**.
- **Incorrect OAuth credentials**.
- **Permission issues** (e.g., insufficient API access rights).

Fix:

1. **Verify API Keys**: Double-check the API keys, client secrets, and tokens being used in your workflow. Ensure they are correctly configured in the **n8n credentials manager**.
2. **Re-authenticate OAuth**: If you're using **OAuth2** to authenticate, ensure the credentials have not expired. You may need to refresh the access token or re-authenticate.
3. **Check Permissions**: Ensure the account used for API authentication has the appropriate permissions to access the data or perform the requested action.
4. **Test API Connections**: Use **n8n's HTTP Request node** to test the connection to the third-party API with the provided credentials.

10.1.5. Workflow Execution Delays

Issue: Workflows may run slower than expected, especially when dealing with large datasets or complex operations.

Common Causes:

- **Heavy data processing**: Workflows involving large datasets or complex data transformations can experience delays.
- **Overloaded n8n instance**: Insufficient system resources (e.g., CPU, RAM) can cause workflows to run slower than expected.

Fix:

1. **Optimize Workflow Design**: Break down large workflows into smaller, modular workflows that run independently and can be processed in parallel.
2. **Use Parallel Execution**: Leverage **n8n's parallel execution** capability to run independent tasks simultaneously, reducing total workflow runtime.

3. **Optimize Nodes**: For resource-intensive nodes (e.g., large database queries, API requests), consider using batch processing or paginated requests to reduce the load.

10.2. Debugging Tips for Agent Workflows

Debugging is an essential part of developing efficient **n8n agents**. When a workflow fails or behaves unexpectedly, you need to diagnose the issue quickly and efficiently. In this section, we will explore some useful debugging techniques that will help you troubleshoot and optimize your workflows.

10.2.1. Enable Debug Mode in n8n

n8n provides a **debug mode** that allows you to step through each node in a workflow and inspect the data being passed between them. This is an essential feature when debugging complex workflows.

How to Enable Debug Mode:

1. **Enable Debugging in the Workflow Settings**: In the **n8n editor**, select **Settings** from the top right corner and enable **Debugging**.
2. **Inspect Data in Nodes**: When debugging is enabled, you can click on each node to view its input and output data. This helps identify where the workflow is failing and why.

10.2.2. Use Execution Logs for Troubleshooting

Execution logs in **n8n** provide detailed information about each step of the workflow execution, including successes, failures, and the data passed between nodes.

How to Use Execution Logs:

1. **Access Execution Logs**: Go to the **Executions** tab in **n8n**, where you can view logs for each workflow execution.

2. **Review Detailed Logs**: For each execution, inspect the logs to see which node failed, the input data, and any error messages.

This is particularly useful when workflows are failing silently or behaving unexpectedly. The logs will provide error messages that can guide you toward fixing the issue.

10.2.3. Test Each Node Independently

When debugging, it's useful to test individual nodes to isolate the problem. This can help determine which node is causing the issue and allow you to focus your troubleshooting efforts on that node.

How to Test Nodes:

1. **Use the Execute Node Feature**: In the **n8n editor**, you can execute individual nodes by selecting them and clicking on the **Execute Node** button.
2. **Check Node Outputs**: After executing a node, inspect its output to ensure it's processing data correctly.

10.2.4. Use Conditional Logging

Sometimes, you may want to log specific data at certain points in the workflow, especially for conditional logic or error-handling scenarios.

How to Implement Conditional Logging:

1. **Use the Function Node for Logging**: You can use the **Function node** to create custom log messages based on specific conditions in your workflow.
2. **Store Logs in External Systems**: If you need to persist logs for auditing or further analysis, use a **Database node** or **Google Sheets node** to store custom logs.

Example:

javascript

```
if ($json["status"] === "error") {
  return [{ json: { log: "Error occurred during
processing." } }];
}
```

10.2.5. Check Resource Usage and Performance Metrics

If a workflow is slow or intermittently failing, it could be due to system resource constraints. Monitor your system's performance to see if CPU, memory, or disk usage is too high.

How to Check Resource Usage:

- **Monitor n8n Resources**: Use tools like **top** or **htop** (Linux) to monitor system resources in real-time.
- **Cloud Monitoring**: If deployed in the cloud, use **CloudWatch (AWS)**, **Google Cloud Monitoring**, or **Azure Monitor** to track system performance and resource usage.

In this chapter, we covered common issues that **n8n agents** might encounter, such as workflow failures, data formatting errors, API rate limits, and authentication issues. We also provided effective debugging techniques, including enabling debug mode, using execution logs, testing nodes independently, and conditional logging.

By following these troubleshooting tips and optimization strategies, you can ensure that your **n8n workflows** run smoothly and efficiently, even in complex production environments.

10.3. Performance Tuning for Large Workflows

As workflows grow in size and complexity, performance optimization becomes crucial. Large workflows with many nodes or high-volume data processing can lead to slow execution times, excessive memory usage, or failures due to timeouts or resource limitations. In this section, we'll explore how to optimize the performance of **n8n workflows** to ensure they run efficiently, even as their size or complexity increases.

10.3.1. Identifying Performance Bottlenecks

Before you can optimize performance, you first need to identify the bottlenecks that are slowing down your workflow. Common bottlenecks in **n8n workflows** include:

- **External API calls**: Requests to third-party services may take longer than expected, especially when the service is slow or the workflow makes too many requests.
- **Large data processing**: Workflows that process large datasets or perform complex transformations can consume a significant amount of memory and processing power.
- **Inefficient nodes**: Some nodes might be inefficient or not designed for large-scale processing.

How to Identify Bottlenecks:

1. **Execution Logs**: The **Execution Log** in **n8n** provides detailed information about each node's execution time. Look for nodes that take longer than expected or consistently delay the workflow.
2. **Test Node Performance**: Use the **Execute Node** feature to isolate and test specific nodes in the workflow. Measure the time each node takes to complete to identify any performance issues.
3. **Monitor System Resources**: Use system monitoring tools (e.g., **top**, **htop**) to check CPU, memory, and disk usage while workflows are running.

10.3.2. Optimizing Workflow Design

To improve performance, it's essential to design workflows in a way that minimizes inefficiencies and maximizes processing speed. Here are several strategies to optimize your workflows:

1. Minimize External API Calls

External API calls are often the most time-consuming part of a workflow. Reducing the number of API calls or optimizing their usage can drastically improve performance.

- **Batch API Requests**: Whenever possible, use bulk API endpoints to process multiple items at once rather than making individual requests for each item.
- **Use Caching**: Cache API responses to avoid making duplicate requests for the same data. This can be done by storing the responses in variables or a local database (e.g., **Redis, PostgreSQL**).
- **Rate Limiting**: Implement rate limiting to avoid hitting external APIs with too many requests in a short time. **n8n** provides nodes for controlling the rate at which API requests are made.

2. Use Parallel Execution

n8n allows workflows to be executed in parallel, meaning multiple nodes can run simultaneously instead of sequentially. This can significantly speed up workflows that have independent tasks.

- **Parallel Execution**: Use the **Execute Workflow node** to create parallel execution paths within your workflow. This allows you to break down large tasks into smaller, independent tasks that can run simultaneously.
- **Split in Batches**: Use the **SplitInBatches node** to process large datasets in smaller chunks, improving memory usage and processing speed.

3. Optimize Data Handling

Large datasets can slow down workflows if not handled efficiently. To optimize data handling:

- **Limit Data Passed Between Nodes**: Only pass the necessary data from one node to another. Avoid sending large datasets across nodes unless absolutely necessary.
- **Use Pagination**: If working with large datasets (e.g., from an API or database), use **pagination** to retrieve data in smaller chunks, reducing memory consumption and speeding up processing.

4. Efficient Node Usage

Some nodes can be inefficient, especially when processing large amounts of data or interacting with external systems.

- **Use Function Node**: If you need to perform complex data transformations, use the **Function node** instead of multiple individual nodes. The **Function node** allows you to write custom JavaScript, which can be more efficient than using multiple standard nodes.
- **Avoid Nested Loops**: Try to avoid deeply nested loops or conditions, as they can quickly increase workflow complexity and execution time.

10.3.3. Scaling Workflows with Horizontal Scaling

When workflows grow in size or traffic increases, it might be necessary to scale your **n8n instance** to handle the load. **Horizontal scaling** involves adding more instances of **n8n** to distribute the workload, ensuring that no single instance is overloaded.

Steps for Horizontal Scaling:

1. **Deploy Multiple Instances**: Use **Docker**, **Kubernetes**, or cloud services to deploy multiple instances of **n8n**.
2. **Load Balancer**: Use a **load balancer** to distribute incoming requests across the different **n8n** instances, ensuring even load distribution and preventing any instance from becoming a bottleneck.
3. **Shared Storage**: Use a centralized database or file storage solution to ensure that data (e.g., logs, workflow data, state) is accessible to all **n8n** instances.
4. **Auto-Scaling**: Set up auto-scaling based on resource usage (e.g., CPU or memory), so that more **n8n** instances are spun up automatically as needed.

10.3.4. Monitoring and Adjusting Performance

Regular monitoring and adjustment are key to ensuring that your **n8n workflows** continue to perform well as they evolve.

Best Practices for Monitoring:

1. **Use Performance Metrics**: Use monitoring tools like **Prometheus**, **Grafana**, or **CloudWatch** to track performance metrics, such as execution times, CPU, and memory usage.
2. **Monitor Workflow Logs**: Regularly review the **Execution Logs** to identify nodes that take longer than expected and investigate any issues.
3. **Review Resource Usage**: Monitor system resources while workflows are running to ensure that the instance is not overloaded and that resource usage is within expected limits.

10.4. Handling Failures and Retries in Complex Workflows

Failures in workflows are inevitable, especially when dealing with external services, unreliable APIs, or network issues. Implementing **failure handling** and **retry mechanisms** ensures that your workflows are robust and can recover from errors without manual intervention.

10.4.1. Why Failure Handling is Crucial

n8n agents often interact with external systems and APIs, which can fail for various reasons, such as:

- **API rate limits** being exceeded.
- **Network failures** or timeouts.
- **Authentication issues** with external services.

Handling failures gracefully and retrying failed tasks is crucial to maintaining workflow reliability and minimizing downtime.

10.4.2. Implementing Retry Mechanisms

n8n offers built-in features to help automate the retry process for failed workflows or nodes.

Best Practices for Retries:

1. **Use Retry Nodes**:
   - The **Retry node** in **n8n** can be used to automatically retry failed tasks after a specified delay. You can configure the retry attempt count and delay between retries to suit your use case.

   Example: Retry a failed HTTP request 3 times, with a 5-second delay between each attempt.

2. **Delay Between Retries**:
   - Use the **Delay node** to add a delay between retries, ensuring that the external system is given time to recover or stabilize. This is especially useful when interacting with rate-limited APIs or slow services.

3. **Backoff Strategy**:
   - Implement an exponential backoff strategy for retries. This means that the retry interval increases with each subsequent failure, preventing overwhelming the external service with repeated requests.
   - For example, retry every **1 minute** after the first failure, **5 minutes** after the second failure, and **15 minutes** after the third failure.

4. **Limit Retries**:
   - Set a **maximum retry limit** to avoid endless retry loops. After a certain number of retries, the workflow should either fail gracefully or trigger an alert for manual intervention.

   Example: Retry up to 5 times before sending an alert or logging the failure for further investigation.

10.4.3. Handling Failures Gracefully with Error Nodes

To ensure that failures do not stop the entire workflow, use **Error Trigger** and **Error Workflow** nodes to handle errors and failures without breaking the entire process.

Best Practices for Error Handling:

1. **Use the Error Trigger Node**:
   - The **Error Trigger node** can be used to capture errors that occur in other parts of the workflow. Once an error is detected, you can set up alternative flows to handle the error (e.g., send a notification to the admin, retry the task, or log the failure).
2. **Error Workflows**:
   - Create a dedicated **error handling workflow** that triggers whenever a failure occurs. This workflow can handle tasks such as notifying stakeholders, logging the error, or attempting recovery actions.
3. **Notification on Failure**:
   - Send a **Slack** or **Email notification** when a failure occurs. Use **Send Email** or **Slack** nodes to notify team members that manual intervention may be required.
4. **Graceful Degradation**:
   - In complex workflows, implement **graceful degradation**, where parts of the workflow continue to execute even if one part fails. For example, if an external API fails, the workflow can still process local data or move forward with the available information.

10.4.4. Logging Failures and Monitoring Recovery

It's important to log every failure and monitor recovery efforts to ensure that no issues are overlooked.

Best Practices:

1. **Centralized Error Logs**: Store errors and failure details in a **centralized database** or **cloud storage** for easy monitoring and future reference.
2. **Alerts**: Set up alerts to notify you immediately when a workflow fails after all retries, allowing you to address the issue promptly.
3. **Monitor Workflow Status**: Use monitoring tools like **Prometheus** or **Grafana** to keep track of workflow health and failure rates. Set up dashboards to visualize failure patterns and workflow performance over time.

In this chapter, we covered key techniques for optimizing the performance of **n8n agents** and handling failures in complex workflows. By identifying performance bottlenecks, optimizing data flow, and scaling workflows appropriately, you can ensure that workflows perform efficiently even as they grow in size. Additionally, implementing failure handling and retry mechanisms ensures that your workflows remain robust and can recover from errors without manual intervention.

By applying these optimization and failure management strategies, you can create workflows that are reliable, efficient, and resilient to unexpected issues.

10.5. Improving Efficiency in Data Processing with Agents

Efficient data processing is a critical aspect of building workflows with **n8n agents**, especially when working with large datasets or real-time data. Unoptimized workflows can consume excessive resources, leading to delays, timeouts, or even system failures. In this section, we'll explore strategies to improve the efficiency of data processing within **n8n workflows**, ensuring they run smoothly and handle large datasets effectively.

10.5.1. Why Efficiency Matters in Data Processing

When dealing with data-heavy workflows, inefficient data handling can significantly affect performance, causing the workflow to run slowly or use up too many system resources. For example:

- **Large datasets**: When workflows process large volumes of data (e.g., from APIs, databases, or files), they may take longer to complete, consuming more memory and CPU resources.
- **Real-time data processing**: If workflows need to handle data in real-time (e.g., processing incoming data from IoT devices or webhooks), delays or slow processing can negatively impact user experience or business operations.

By optimizing how **n8n agents** process data, you can:

- **Reduce processing time**.
- **Minimize resource consumption**.
- **Ensure timely execution** of workflows, even with large data sets.

10.5.2. Best Practices for Improving Efficiency in Data Processing

Here are some practical strategies to optimize the performance of data processing within **n8n workflows**:

1. Use Pagination for API Calls

Many APIs return large datasets that can be slow to process. Instead of fetching all the data in one go, use **pagination** to retrieve smaller chunks of data at a time, reducing memory usage and improving processing speed.

- **Example**: When using the **HTTP Request node** to retrieve data from an API, check if the API supports pagination. You can then loop through the results using the **Set node** and a **Loop node** to process each page of data individually.

2. Break Data into Chunks

For workflows that process large amounts of data (e.g., bulk data imports), **batch processing** can be highly effective. Instead of processing all the data in a single flow, break it into smaller chunks using the **SplitInBatches node**.

- **Example**: When dealing with a large dataset (e.g., a list of 10,000 records), break the dataset into smaller batches of 500 records. This prevents memory overload and ensures the workflow can run efficiently without hitting system resource limits.

3. Minimize Data Passing Between Nodes

When passing large datasets between nodes, ensure that only the necessary data is being transferred. Passing large data unnecessarily can slow down workflows and increase memory consumption.

- **Example**: Instead of passing the entire data payload from one node to another, use the **Set node** to extract only the required fields and pass only relevant data to subsequent nodes.

4. Use Caching for Repetitive Data

If your workflow processes data that doesn't change frequently, consider using **caching** to avoid redundant API calls or data fetches. This can significantly speed up workflows by reducing the need to fetch the same data multiple times.

- **Example**: Use **Redis** or a similar caching system to store frequently used data, such as customer profiles or inventory levels. You can retrieve the data from the cache instead of calling the external API every time the workflow runs.

5. Offload Heavy Computation to External Services

If your workflow requires heavy computation (e.g., complex mathematical calculations or data transformations), consider offloading the processing to an external service (e.g., a cloud function, microservice, or serverless function like **AWS Lambda** or **Google Cloud Functions**). This reduces the workload on **n8n** and speeds up execution.

- **Example**: Instead of performing data transformations directly within **n8n**, send the data to an external function that processes it and returns the result to the workflow.

6. Use Parallel Execution for Independent Tasks

If your workflow contains tasks that are independent of each other, you can improve efficiency by running these tasks in parallel. **n8n** supports parallel execution, allowing multiple tasks to be processed simultaneously.

- **Example**: If you need to fetch data from multiple APIs (e.g., weather data, stock prices, news articles), use the **Execute Workflow node** to trigger these tasks in parallel rather than sequentially. This reduces overall workflow runtime.

7. Optimize Node Configuration

Some **n8n nodes** (e.g., **HTTP Request**, **Database Query**) may have options for optimizing performance, such as configuring connection timeouts or adjusting batch sizes. Review the documentation for each node to identify options for improving performance.

- **Example**: Configure the **HTTP Request node** to use a **connection timeout** to avoid long waiting times if an external service is slow to respond.

10.5.3. Monitoring and Improving Performance

To ensure ongoing performance optimization, it's important to continuously monitor your workflows and adjust as necessary. Use the following strategies to maintain optimal performance:

1. Monitor Workflow Execution Times

Regularly check the **Execution Log** to identify any nodes that consistently take longer to execute. This will help you pinpoint any inefficiencies or bottlenecks.

- **Example**: If a node takes too long to process, consider breaking it down into smaller steps, optimizing the configuration, or implementing batch processing.

2. Use System Monitoring Tools

Use system monitoring tools like **Prometheus**, **Grafana**, or cloud-native monitoring solutions (e.g., **AWS CloudWatch**, **Google Cloud Monitoring**) to track resource usage, such as CPU, memory, and disk I/O, during workflow execution. These tools can alert you when a workflow is consuming excessive resources, allowing you to take corrective action.

10.6. Managing Workflow Timeout Issues

Timeouts can occur when workflows take too long to complete, either
because the data processing is resource-intensive or external services are
slow to respond. In this section, we'll cover best practices for managing
timeout issues in **n8n workflows**.

10.6.1. Why Timeout Issues Occur

Timeout issues are typically caused by:

- **External API or service latency**: Some services may take longer to
  respond than expected, especially during peak usage or with large
  datasets.
- **Long-running workflows**: Complex workflows with multiple nodes
  or heavy data processing may take longer than the system's timeout
  limit.
- **Limited resources**: Insufficient system resources (e.g., memory,
  CPU) may cause workflows to be terminated before they are
  completed.

10.6.2. Handling Timeout Issues in n8n

1. Increase Timeout Settings for External API Calls

If your workflow depends on external APIs or services, it's important to
ensure that the timeout settings for the **HTTP Request node** or similar
nodes are configured to allow enough time for the request to complete.

- **Adjust Timeout**: The **HTTP Request node** in **n8n** allows you to set
  a **timeout** parameter. Increase the timeout duration if you expect the
  API to take longer than the default timeout.

  ```json
  {
    "timeout": 120000
  }
  ```

This will give the workflow up to 2 minutes to complete the API request before it is considered a failure.

2. Use Retry Logic for Timeout Failures

If a node fails due to a timeout or temporary issue, use **retry logic** to automatically attempt the action again after a specified delay. The **Retry node** in **n8n** can be used to configure how many times the task should be retried, and the delay between retries.

- **Example**: If an **HTTP Request node** times out, set the **Retry node** to retry the request 3 times with a 10-second delay between attempts.

3. Split Long-Running Workflows into Smaller Parts

If workflows are consistently timing out due to their size or complexity, consider splitting the workflow into smaller, more manageable parts. This can reduce the time each part takes to execute and decrease the likelihood of timeouts.

- **Example**: Use **Execute Workflow nodes** to break the workflow into smaller sub-workflows that can be triggered independently.

4. Use the Delay Node to Manage Timeouts

For workflows that depend on external systems or APIs with rate limits or known latency, consider introducing a **Delay node** to space out requests and prevent timeouts due to resource overload or rate-limiting restrictions.

- **Example**: Add a **Delay node** to pause the workflow for a specified time (e.g., 1 minute) before proceeding with the next request. This prevents the system from being overwhelmed and helps avoid timeout issues.

5. Optimize Long-Running Nodes

Certain nodes, such as database queries or data processing nodes, may take a long time to execute, especially when working with large datasets. Try to optimize these nodes by:

- Using **indexed database queries** to improve performance.
- Implementing **pagination** or **batch processing** for large datasets.

- Simplifying complex data transformations by breaking them into smaller tasks or leveraging **external services** (e.g., cloud functions, serverless computing) to offload processing.

10.6.3. Using Monitoring and Alerts for Timeout Detection

Monitoring is a crucial part of preventing and managing timeout issues. By setting up monitoring and alerting systems, you can proactively detect workflow delays or failures before they affect your business processes.

Best Practices:

- **Use Cloud Monitoring Tools**: Set up alerts in cloud monitoring platforms like **AWS CloudWatch**, **Google Cloud Monitoring**, or **Azure Monitor** to detect when workflows exceed expected execution times.
- **Track Workflow Health**: Use **Prometheus** or **Grafana** to create custom dashboards that show workflow execution times, system resource usage, and potential timeout issues.
- **Set Up Email Alerts**: Use **n8n's Send Email node** to notify administrators when a workflow exceeds a specific execution time or fails due to a timeout.

In this chapter, we discussed strategies for improving the efficiency of data processing in **n8n workflows** and handling timeout issues. By using techniques like **pagination**, **batch processing**, **parallel execution**, and **retry mechanisms**, you can ensure that workflows perform efficiently and handle large datasets effectively. Additionally, understanding how to manage timeout issues by adjusting timeout settings, optimizing long-running workflows, and implementing proper monitoring and alerting systems will ensure the smooth execution of workflows in production.

10.7. Error Logging and Monitoring Tools for Production Environments

Ensuring the reliability and performance of **n8n agents** in a **production environment** requires effective **error logging** and **monitoring**. By capturing and analyzing errors in real-time, you can quickly identify and resolve issues, ensuring that workflows run smoothly and efficiently. In this section, we'll cover best practices for **error logging** and **monitoring**, and provide insights on useful tools and strategies to keep track of workflow performance in production.

10.7.1. Why Error Logging and Monitoring Are Crucial

In a **production environment**, workflows are often mission-critical. Failure to properly log and monitor errors can lead to:

- **Downtime**: Unattended errors can cause workflows to halt or behave unexpectedly.
- **Unresolved issues**: Without proper logging, issues might go undetected, leading to longer recovery times and a negative impact on user experience.
- **Lack of visibility**: Without monitoring, it's difficult to measure workflow performance and detect bottlenecks or inefficiencies.

By implementing **error logging** and **monitoring**, you can:

- **Track errors and failures** in real-time.
- **Respond quickly** to issues that may arise.
- **Optimize workflows** by identifying bottlenecks and performance issues.

10.7.2. Best Practices for Error Logging in n8n

To ensure that errors are tracked and resolved quickly, follow these best practices for error logging in **n8n**:

1. Enable Execution Logs

n8n provides an **Execution Log** feature that captures detailed information about each workflow execution, including successes, failures, and the data passed between nodes. This is crucial for debugging and understanding the root cause of any issues.

- **How to Use Execution Logs**:
    1. In the **n8n editor**, go to the **Executions** tab to view the logs.

2. For each execution, you can see the start and end time, execution status, and detailed logs for each node.
3. Review error messages to identify which node failed and why.

2. Centralized Error Logging

For large-scale workflows, consider storing **error logs** in a centralized logging service such as **ElasticSearch**, **AWS CloudWatch**, **Google Cloud Logging**, or **Loggly**. This provides a more organized and searchable way to track errors across multiple workflows and instances.

- **How to Implement Centralized Logging**:
  1. Set up an **HTTP Request node** or a **Webhook Trigger node** to send error logs to an external logging service.
  2. Include information such as workflow name, error message, and execution timestamp.
  3. Use **structured logging** (e.g., JSON format) to make logs easier to parse and search.

3. Use Node-Specific Error Handling

In **n8n**, you can define **error triggers** for specific nodes to handle errors gracefully. The **Error Trigger** node allows you to capture errors from other nodes and handle them separately (e.g., by sending notifications or retrying).

- **How to Set Up Error Triggers**:
  1. Add an **Error Trigger node** to your workflow.
  2. Configure it to capture errors from specific nodes or the entire workflow.
  3. Define actions, such as sending an alert, logging the error, or retrying the failed task.

4. Create Custom Error Messages

When building workflows, you may want to add custom error messages that provide more context about the failure. Use the **Function node** to generate custom error messages when certain conditions are met.

- **Example**: If a node fails due to missing data, you can use the **Function node** to log a custom error message like:

```javascript
javascript

if (!item.name) {
   throw new Error("Item name is missing.");
}
return items;
```

This ensures that the error message is more informative, which makes it easier to diagnose and resolve the issue.

10.7.3. Monitoring Tools for n8n Workflows

Monitoring allows you to track workflow performance, detect issues early, and optimize for efficiency. Here are some common tools and strategies for monitoring **n8n agents**:

1. Prometheus and Grafana

Prometheus is an open-source monitoring system that collects metrics from various sources, while **Grafana** is used to visualize the data. Integrating **n8n** with **Prometheus** allows you to monitor system performance, workflow execution times, and resource usage.

- **How to Integrate Prometheus with n8n**:
    1. Install **Prometheus** and configure it to scrape metrics from your **n8n** instance.
    2. Use the **Prometheus node** in **n8n** to gather performance metrics, such as execution time and error rates.
    3. Visualize the metrics using **Grafana** dashboards, which can help you monitor workflow performance and identify areas for optimization.

2. Cloud-Based Monitoring (AWS CloudWatch, Google Cloud Monitoring)

If you are hosting **n8n** on cloud platforms like **AWS** or **Google Cloud**, you can leverage their monitoring solutions to track resource usage (e.g., CPU, memory) and workflow execution performance.

- **How to Use CloudWatch**:
    1. Set up **CloudWatch metrics** to monitor the health of your **n8n instance**.
    2. Create **Alarms** that trigger when resource usage exceeds certain thresholds or when workflows fail.
    3. Use **AWS CloudWatch Logs** to capture detailed logs and errors for further analysis.

3. Use Datadog or New Relic

Datadog and **New Relic** are popular cloud monitoring platforms that provide real-time performance monitoring, alerting, and detailed analytics.

- **How to Integrate Datadog**:
    1. Install the **Datadog Agent** on your **n8n instance** to capture system metrics such as CPU and memory usage.
    2. Use **Datadog APM** (Application Performance Monitoring) to track the performance of **n8n workflows**, including execution times, errors, and throughput.

10.7.4. Setting Up Alerts for Workflow Failures

Set up **alerts** to be notified whenever a workflow fails or experiences performance issues. This allows you to take immediate action before the problem impacts business operations.

How to Set Up Alerts:

1. **Slack Alerts**: Use the **Slack node** in **n8n** to send a message to your team's Slack channel whenever a workflow fails or a specific error occurs.
2. **Email Alerts**: Use the **Send Email node** to send an email notification to admins when a workflow fails, including relevant error details for faster troubleshooting.
3. **Third-Party Alerts**: Integrate **n8n** with third-party services like **PagerDuty**, **Opsgenie**, or **VictorOps** to escalate critical issues to the appropriate team members.

10.8. Optimizing Workflow Execution Time and Cost

Optimizing workflow execution time and cost is essential for maintaining efficient, scalable **n8n workflows** in production. This section will explore strategies for improving workflow speed, reducing resource consumption, and controlling costs in cloud-based deployments.

10.8.1. Optimizing Workflow Execution Time

Reducing workflow execution time is crucial for maintaining efficient processes and minimizing resource usage. Here are several ways to speed up workflows:

1. Minimize Node Processing Time

- **Reduce Node Complexity**: Break down complex nodes into simpler tasks and use **Function nodes** where applicable. Custom code can sometimes run faster than using multiple nodes.
- **Use Batching and Parallel Execution**: Instead of running a process sequentially for each item, use the **SplitInBatches node** or **Execute Workflow node** to process items in parallel, reducing overall execution time.
- **Avoid Redundant Data Processing**: Avoid processing the same data multiple times. Use **Set nodes** to filter and pass only the necessary data between nodes, improving performance.

2. Use Efficient Data Handling

- **Data Pagination**: When working with APIs or databases that return large datasets, implement **pagination** to retrieve data in smaller chunks.
- **Database Query Optimization**: If your workflows rely on databases, ensure your queries are optimized (e.g., using indexes and limiting data retrieval).

3. Optimize External API Calls

- **Rate Limiting**: Use rate-limiting to avoid overloading external services and causing delays. Introduce **Delays** or manage the frequency of API requests.
- **Use Bulk API Endpoints**: Where possible, use **bulk API endpoints** to handle multiple records in a single request rather than making individual requests for each record.

10.8.2. Reducing Workflow Cost

While **n8n** is generally cost-effective, workflows that are inefficient or resource-intensive can increase operational costs, especially in cloud environments. Here's how to optimize costs:

1. Horizontal and Vertical Scaling

Scale your **n8n instance** appropriately to balance workload and resource usage:

- **Vertical Scaling**: Increase CPU or memory resources if workflows are resource-intensive.
- **Horizontal Scaling**: Distribute workloads across multiple instances (via **Docker** or **Kubernetes**) to balance the load and avoid overloading any single instance.

2. Efficient Resource Usage in Cloud Environments

Cloud providers often charge based on resource usage (e.g., CPU, memory, storage). To reduce costs:

- **Use Auto-Scaling**: Use cloud-based auto-scaling to dynamically adjust the number of **n8n instances** based on load, so you only pay for what you need.
- **Use Spot Instances or Reserved Instances**: Consider using **spot instances** (AWS, GCP) or **reserved instances** (Azure, GCP) for cost savings when running **n8n** in the cloud.

3. Storage Optimization

- **Use Object Storage**: For storing large files or data logs, use cloud object storage services (e.g., **AWS S3**, **Google Cloud Storage**)

instead of traditional block storage, as they tend to be more cost-effective.
- **Clean Up Old Data**: Regularly archive or delete old workflow logs, execution data, or backup files to keep storage costs low.

In this chapter, we discussed strategies for **error logging** and **monitoring** in **n8n workflows** to help you track, troubleshoot, and optimize workflows in production environments. We also covered ways to **optimize workflow execution time** and **reduce costs**, ensuring your workflows are both efficient and cost-effective, especially in cloud-based deployments.

By applying these best practices, you can ensure that your **n8n agents** perform at their best while maintaining reliable and cost-efficient operations in production.

Chapter 11: Extending n8n Agents

One of the great advantages of **n8n** is its extensibility. You can **extend n8n agents** by writing custom nodes to integrate with any service, API, or external system that isn't supported by default. Additionally, you can create reusable agent templates that can be shared and repurposed across workflows. In this chapter, we'll dive into **extending n8n agents** by writing **custom nodes** and building **reusable agent templates**.

11.1. Writing Custom Nodes for n8n

Custom nodes are an essential part of **n8n's extensibility**. They allow you to integrate **n8n agents** with external services and APIs that are not already built into the platform. Writing custom nodes is relatively straightforward and requires a basic understanding of **JavaScript** and **Node.js**. Custom nodes can either be standalone or part of larger workflows to enable complex integrations.

11.1.1. Overview of n8n Node Structure

Each **n8n node** typically consists of the following components:

- **Node Parameters**: The fields that the user interacts with to configure the node.
- **Execution Logic**: The code that executes when the node is triggered, typically written in JavaScript.
- **Input and Output Data**: The data passed between nodes in the workflow. Custom nodes will read input data, process it, and pass it along to the next node.

When you write a custom node, you define:

- **The input fields (parameters)** that the user will configure.
- **The behavior** of the node, such as making API requests or processing data.
- **The output data** that the node will pass on to other nodes.

11.1.2. Setting Up a Custom Node

To begin writing a custom node, you will need the following:

1. **n8n Local Development Environment**: You should have **n8n** set up locally for development purposes. If you haven't already, you can follow the n8n setup guide.
2. **Node.js Environment**: Custom nodes are written in **JavaScript** using **Node.js**, so make sure you have it installed.

11.1.3. Steps to Create a Custom Node

1. **Create a Custom Node Folder**:
   - Inside the n8n project directory, create a folder for your custom node under the packages/nodes-base/nodes directory. The folder should be named according to the integration it provides (e.g., MyCustomNode).
2. **Create the Node Files**: Inside your custom node folder, create two files:
   - MyCustomNode.node.ts (or .js if using JavaScript) – The core file defining your node's behavior.
   - MyCustomNode.credentials.ts – (Optional) This file stores authentication credentials if your node requires them.
3. **Define the Node's Parameters**: In the MyCustomNode.node.ts file, use **n8n's node structure** to define the parameters the user will interact with. Example:

```javascript
const { NodeOperationError } = require('n8n-
workflow');

module.exports = class MyCustomNode {
  constructor() {
    this.description = {
      displayName: 'My Custom Node',
      name: 'myCustomNode',
      icon: 'file:myCustomNode.svg',
      group: ['input'],
      version: 1,
      description: 'A custom node for my
workflow',
```

```
      defaults: {
        name: 'My Custom Node',
        color: '#1f77b4',
      },
      inputs: ['main'],
      outputs: ['main'],
      properties: [
        {
          displayName: 'API URL',
          name: 'apiUrl',
          type: 'string',
          default: '',
          description: 'The base URL of the
API',
        },
        // Add more parameters here
      ],
    };
  }

  async execute() {
    // The logic for the node (e.g., making an
API request)
    const response = await
this.helpers.request({
      url: this.getNodeParameter('apiUrl'),
      method: 'GET',
    });
    return this.prepareOutputData([response]);
  }
};
```

4. **Write Node Execution Logic**: In the `execute` function, you will define the main logic of the node, which will typically involve making an **API request**, processing data, or interacting with external systems.
5. **Register Your Custom Node**: After writing the node, you need to register it within the **n8n** system. This is done by adding your custom node to the `packages/nodes-base/nodes/index.ts` file.

   Example:

```javascript
const MyCustomNode =
require('./nodes/MyCustomNode');

module.exports = {
  nodes: [
    MyCustomNode,
    // Other nodes
  ],
};
```

6. **Test Your Custom Node**: After registering your custom node, restart **n8n**, and you should be able to see your custom node listed in the **n8n editor** under the nodes section. Test it by adding it to a workflow and configuring the parameters.

11.1.4. Handling Authentication in Custom Nodes

If your custom node requires authentication (e.g., API keys, OAuth), you can handle it using the **credentials system** built into **n8n**.

Steps to Add Authentication to Your Custom Node:

1. **Create a Credentials File**: In the same folder as your node, create a `MyCustomNode.credentials.ts` file.
2. **Define Authentication Parameters**:
   o Define the credentials needed (e.g., **API keys, OAuth tokens**).
3. **Integrate Credentials with Your Node**:
   o In your node's `execute` function, use the credentials to authenticate the request.

Example for **API key-based authentication**:

```javascript
module.exports = class MyCustomNode {
  async execute() {
```

```
    const apiKey =
this.getCredentials('myCustomApi').apiKey;
    const response = await this.helpers.request({
      url: 'https://api.example.com/data',
      method: 'GET',
      headers: {
        'Authorization': `Bearer ${apiKey}`,
      },
    });
    return this.prepareOutputData([response]);
  }
};
```

11.2. Building Reusable Agent Templates

n8n agents can be made more powerful and reusable by creating **agent templates**. These templates allow you to package and reuse a predefined set of actions or workflows that can be shared across different projects.

11.2.1. What is an Agent Template?

An **agent template** is a predefined **n8n workflow** or **set of nodes** that can be easily imported and reused in other workflows. Templates allow businesses to reuse common automation logic across different workflows or projects, reducing development time and improving consistency.

11.2.2. Steps to Create Reusable Agent Templates

1. **Design the Workflow**:
    o Create a workflow in **n8n** that you want to reuse across multiple projects.
    o This could be a **complex workflow** that integrates multiple systems or a **simple automation** like sending emails after a form submission.
2. **Export the Workflow**:

- o In the **n8n editor**, click the **Export** button to save the workflow as a JSON file. This file contains all the nodes, parameters, and logic associated with the workflow.
3. **Package the Template**:
   - o Once exported, you can share this JSON file with others or use it in other **n8n instances**.
   - o Optionally, you can create a custom **n8n template repository** on **GitHub** to store and share reusable templates.
4. **Import the Template**:
   - o To use the template in a different workflow, simply **import** the workflow JSON file into your **n8n editor** using the **Import** option.

11.2.3. Example: Creating a Customer Onboarding Template

Let's say you create a **customer onboarding workflow** that includes:

1. Sending a **welcome email**.
2. Adding the customer to a **CRM system**.
3. Assigning them to a **marketing segment**.

Once this workflow is designed and tested, you can export it as a template and reuse it for all new customer onboardings in different projects.

11.2.4. Sharing Templates with the n8n Community

To make your templates available to the **n8n community**, consider publishing them on **n8n's template marketplace** or sharing them on **GitHub**. You can also create **documentation** for your templates to help others understand how to configure and use them.

- **Steps for Sharing**:
  - o **Create a GitHub repository** for your templates and workflows.
  - o **Include documentation** on how to use and customize the template.
  - o **Share the repository** with the **n8n community** for feedback and contributions.

11.2.5. Best Practices for Building Reusable Templates

1. **Modular Design**: Break workflows into smaller, reusable parts. This allows you to reuse portions of workflows in different contexts.
2. **Configuration Flexibility**: Ensure that templates are flexible enough to be customized. Use **parameters** and **credentials** that can be easily configured without changing the core logic.
3. **Documentation**: Provide clear documentation on how to use the template, what each part of the workflow does, and any setup required.
4. **Versioning**: Maintain version control for your templates to track changes over time, especially if you're sharing them with a larger team or community.

In this chapter, we explored how to extend **n8n agents** by writing **custom nodes** and building **reusable agent templates**. By creating custom nodes, you can integrate any external service or API with **n8n**, while reusable templates help you quickly deploy common workflows across multiple projects. This extensibility makes **n8n** a powerful tool for automating complex business processes and integrating with various systems.

11.3. Using n8n's External Plugins and Community Extensions

n8n has a rich ecosystem of **external plugins** and **community extensions** that allow you to extend its functionality and integrate it with third-party services, APIs, and platforms. These plugins and extensions are created by the **n8n** community and can help you enhance the capabilities of your workflows without having to reinvent the wheel.

In this section, we'll explore how to use **n8n's external plugins** and **community extensions**, and provide some tips for integrating them into your workflows.

11.3.1. What are External Plugins and Community Extensions?

External plugins and **community extensions** are pre-built, reusable components that extend **n8n's** functionality. These can range from:

- **API integrations** with popular third-party services (e.g., **Slack, GitHub, Google Sheets**).
- **Custom nodes** that add new features or logic to workflows.
- **Extended triggers** that can listen for specific events from external systems.
- **Utilities** to handle common tasks like data processing, file handling, or notifications.

By using these plugins, you can:

- **Save time** by not having to build integrations from scratch.
- **Improve functionality** by leveraging solutions already tested and created by the community.
- **Customize workflows** by adding unique features or connecting to systems not natively supported by **n8n**.

11.3.2. Exploring the n8n Community Plugins

The **n8n Community Plugins** repository contains a collection of open-source plugins that extend the core functionality of **n8n**. These plugins are available through the **n8n community** and are built by contributors around the world.

How to Access and Install Plugins:

1. **Visit the n8n Plugin Repository**: You can explore the list of available community plugins on platforms like GitHub or the official **n8n website**.
2. **Install Plugins**: To install a plugin, you can either:
   - **Install directly from the n8n interface** if the plugin is available in the **n8n plugin marketplace**.
   - **Install via npm** if the plugin requires a custom installation:

   ```bash
   ```

```
npm install n8n-plugin-name
```

3. **Activate Plugins**: Once installed, the plugin should appear in the **n8n editor** and can be added to your workflows by simply dragging it onto the canvas.

Popular n8n Plugins to Consider:

- **Slack Node**: Send automated messages, alerts, or perform actions within Slack channels.
- **Google Sheets Node**: Automate tasks like adding rows to a sheet or reading data from Google Sheets.
- **GitHub Node**: Automate GitHub workflows, such as creating issues, monitoring repositories, or posting comments.
- **Trello Node**: Integrate **n8n** with **Trello** to create boards, lists, and cards automatically.

Community Extensions for AI and Automation:

- **OpenAI GPT-3 Integration**: Leverage the power of **GPT-3** by integrating it with **n8n** to generate content, answer questions, or analyze text data.
- **Zapier Webhooks**: Use **Zapier** to automate workflows between **n8n** and other platforms that **n8n** doesn't natively integrate with.

11.3.3. Contributing to the n8n Plugin Ecosystem

If you've developed your own plugins or extensions, you can contribute them back to the **n8n** community. Contributing to the **n8n plugin ecosystem** provides great benefits, such as:

- **Sharing your work** with other **n8n users**.
- **Getting feedback** and suggestions for improvement from the community.
- **Enhancing your professional profile** by contributing to an open-source project.

To contribute a plugin, follow the community guidelines outlined in the **n8n** documentation, including providing clear installation instructions, usage examples, and contributing code.

11.4. Integrating AI and Machine Learning with n8n Agents

Integrating **AI** and **machine learning** into **n8n agents** enables automation workflows that can perform complex tasks, such as text analysis, sentiment analysis, predictive analytics, and even image recognition. With the rise of AI-driven tools, businesses are increasingly looking to enhance their workflows with intelligent agents that can learn from data and make decisions autonomously.

In this section, we'll explore how to integrate **AI** and **machine learning** into **n8n agents** to enhance their capabilities.

11.4.1. Why Integrate AI and Machine Learning into n8n?

AI and machine learning can bring significant value to automation workflows by enabling **n8n agents** to:

- **Analyze large datasets** for trends, patterns, or insights.
- **Generate recommendations** for marketing campaigns, customer service, or inventory management.
- **Classify text** or **images** based on predefined models.
- **Predict outcomes** such as sales forecasts or customer churn.

For example, an **AI-powered n8n agent** could automate the process of categorizing customer feedback, predicting the next best product to offer, or even generating personalized marketing content.

11.4.2. Integrating AI Services with n8n

There are several **AI and machine learning services** that you can integrate into **n8n** workflows. Many of these services provide pre-built models for common tasks such as text analysis, sentiment detection, or image recognition.

Popular AI Integrations in n8n:

1. **OpenAI GPT-3**:
    o   **n8n** can integrate with **OpenAI's GPT-3** to generate text, answer questions, summarize information, or translate languages. By leveraging **GPT-3**, you can create workflows that automatically generate blog posts, email responses, or code snippets.
    o   Use the **OpenAI node** in **n8n** to send data to the GPT-3 API and process the response.

    Example Use Case: Automatically generate social media posts based on the latest news or blog content by using GPT-3.

2. **Google Cloud AI**:
    o   Google's **Cloud AI** suite offers powerful machine learning tools for image recognition, text analysis, and predictive analytics. Integrating **Google Cloud AI** with **n8n** allows you to easily incorporate **natural language processing (NLP)**, **vision API**, and **speech recognition** into your workflows.
    o   Use the **Google Cloud nodes** to make API requests for specific AI tasks (e.g., sentiment analysis, image labeling).
3. **IBM Watson**:
    o   IBM **Watson** provides several AI services, including **NLP**, **language translation**, **text-to-speech**, and **speech-to-text**. By integrating **n8n** with **Watson** services, you can perform tasks such as analyzing customer feedback or transcribing audio files into text.
    o   Use **IBM Watson nodes** in **n8n** to connect with their AI services and process data.
4. **Microsoft Azure AI**:
    o   **Azure Cognitive Services** offers a range of AI models for vision, language, speech, and decision-making. Integrating **Azure AI** with **n8n** enables automated workflows for tasks like **image classification**, **text analysis**, and **voice recognition**.
    o   Use the **Azure Cognitive Services node** in **n8n** to interact with these services and enhance your workflows.

11.4.3. Building Custom AI Models with n8n

If you require more advanced or custom machine learning models, you can use **n8n** to integrate with platforms such as **TensorFlow**, **PyTorch**, or **scikit-learn**.

Steps to Build Custom AI Models:

1. **Prepare Your Data**:
   o Use **n8n nodes** to gather and clean the data you need for training your machine learning model. This could include pulling data from APIs, databases, or spreadsheets.
2. **Train the Model**:
   o Use tools like **Google Colab**, **AWS SageMaker**, or a local environment to train your custom machine learning model. This could involve tasks such as classification, regression, or clustering based on the data you have.
3. **Integrate Model with n8n**:
   o Once your model is trained, expose it as an API or use a cloud-based service like **Google AI Platform** or **AWS Lambda** to deploy the model. Then, use **n8n** to send data to the model and process the results.

Example Use Case: Build a predictive model for customer churn based on customer behavior data, and then use n8n to automatically identify at-risk customers and send retention offers.

11.4.4. Example Use Case: AI-Powered Text Classification

Let's say you want to build an **AI-powered text classification agent** that automatically categorizes customer feedback into predefined categories (e.g., **Positive**, **Negative**, **Neutral**).

Steps:

1. **Collect Feedback Data**: Use a **Webhook Trigger node** to capture incoming customer feedback from a form or email.
2. **Send Data to AI Service**: Use the **OpenAI node** or **Google Cloud NLP node** to analyze the sentiment of the feedback text.

3. **Classify Feedback**: Based on the AI analysis, use an **If node** to categorize feedback into positive, negative, or neutral.
4. **Store Results**: Use a **Google Sheets node** or **Database node** to store the categorized feedback for further analysis or reporting.

This type of automation allows businesses to quickly sort and respond to customer feedback, improving customer experience and operational efficiency.

In this chapter, we explored how to extend **n8n agents** by using **external plugins** and **community extensions** to integrate with third-party services, APIs, and platforms. We also discussed how to integrate **AI and machine learning** into **n8n workflows** to automate complex tasks such as sentiment analysis, predictive analytics, and text classification.

By leveraging AI services like **OpenAI**, **Google Cloud AI**, and **IBM Watson**, you can enhance your **n8n agents** to make intelligent, data-driven decisions, automate customer interactions, and gain deeper insights into your business data.

11.5. Developing Custom Action Scripts in JavaScript

When extending **n8n agents**, one of the most powerful techniques is writing **custom action scripts** using **JavaScript**. These custom scripts enable you to define the behavior of a node more precisely and create more sophisticated logic for processing data or interacting with external services. This section will guide you through the process of writing custom action scripts in **JavaScript** to extend **n8n's** capabilities.

11.5.1. Why Write Custom Action Scripts in JavaScript?

Custom action scripts are used to execute complex logic that goes beyond the built-in functionality of **n8n** nodes. For instance:

- **Data transformations**: Performing complex calculations or reformatting data that can't be done using default nodes.

- **API integrations**: Making custom API calls that aren't supported by **n8n's built-in nodes**.
- **Advanced workflows**: Implementing business rules, custom validations, or decision-making logic that requires custom code.

JavaScript is an ideal choice for writing these custom action scripts because:

- **n8n's core engine is based on JavaScript**, so integrating custom scripts within workflows is seamless.
- **JavaScript is a flexible and widely-used language** for backend and automation tasks, making it a suitable option for defining complex behavior within **n8n** nodes.

11.5.2. Creating Custom Action Scripts in n8n

Custom action scripts are typically written inside the **Function node** or **Set node**, which are designed to allow custom JavaScript code to manipulate data. Below is a guide on how to write and use custom action scripts within **n8n**.

Steps to Create a Custom Action Script in n8n:

1. **Set Up the Node**:
   o Start by adding a **Set node** or **Function node** to your workflow, depending on the task at hand. The **Set node** is useful when you need to manipulate or add variables, while the **Function node** is better suited for more complex logic.
2. **Write JavaScript Code**:
   o Inside the node, you will write the JavaScript code that performs the custom actions. In the **Function node**, this code will execute during the workflow's execution.

Example 1: Data Transformation with Custom Script

Suppose you want to transform data from an API response. For example, you want to convert temperatures from Celsius to Fahrenheit.

1. **Set Up the Function Node**:
   o Add a **Function node** after an **HTTP Request node** that fetches weather data.

2. **Write the JavaScript Code**:

```javascript
// Example: Convert Celsius to Fahrenheit for the
fetched weather data
const temperatureCelsius = $json["main"]["temp"];
// Get the temperature in Celsius
const temperatureFahrenheit = (temperatureCelsius *
9/5) + 32;  // Convert to Fahrenheit

// Add the converted value to the output
return [
  {
    json: {
      temperatureFahrenheit: temperatureFahrenheit,
      temperatureCelsius: temperatureCelsius,
    },
  },
];
```

In this example, the **Function node** takes the temperature in Celsius and converts it to Fahrenheit before passing the data forward in the workflow.

Example 2: Custom API Call with Action Script

Another use case for custom JavaScript is when you need to make an API call that is not supported by default **n8n nodes**.

1. **Set Up the Function Node**:
   o Add a **Function node** to call an external API, such as fetching data from a third-party service.
2. **Write the Custom API Call Logic**:

```javascript
const axios = require('axios');  // Use axios for
making the HTTP request

// Define the API endpoint and parameters
const apiEndpoint = "https://api.example.com/data";
```

```
const params = { key: "API_KEY", query: "weather"
};

// Make the API call using axios
const response = await axios.get(apiEndpoint, {
params: params });

// Return the response data to n8n
return [
  {
    json: response.data,  // Pass the API response
to the next node
  },
];
```

This **JavaScript script** makes an HTTP request using the **axios** library, retrieves the data, and passes it on to the next node in the workflow.

11.5.3. Handling Errors in Custom Action Scripts

When writing custom scripts, it's important to handle potential errors (e.g., failed API requests, unexpected input data) to ensure smooth workflow execution.

How to Handle Errors in JavaScript:

1. **Use Try-Catch**: Wrap the JavaScript code in a **try-catch** block to catch any potential errors that may arise during execution.

javascript

```
try {
  const response = await axios.get(apiEndpoint, {
params: params });
  return [{ json: response.data }];
} catch (error) {
  throw new Error(`Error occurred:
${error.message}`);  // Throw a custom error
message
}
```

2. **Return Error Data**: In case of failure, you can return error details in a structured format (e.g., as JSON) to help with debugging and alerting.

javascript

```
catch (error) {
  return [
    {
      json: {
        error: true,
        message: `Failed to fetch data:
${error.message}`,
      },
    },
  ];
}
```

This ensures that the workflow logs the error and prevents it from silently failing.

11.5.4. Testing and Debugging Custom Action Scripts

Testing and debugging are crucial when writing custom scripts to ensure they work as expected.

Debugging Tips:

1. **Log Output Data**: Use **console.log()** to log data and inspect values during execution.

javascript

```
console.log("API Response:", response.data);  //
Log the API response
```

2. **Execution Logs**: Always check the **Execution Log** in **n8n** for error details and data flow between nodes. This log provides real-time feedback that helps pinpoint issues in custom scripts.

3. **Use the Function Node's "Test" Feature**: In the **n8n editor**, you can test the **Function node** with sample data to simulate the node's behavior before running the entire workflow.

11.6. Best Practices for Extending n8n's Native Capabilities

Extending **n8n** with custom nodes and scripts can significantly enhance its flexibility and power. However, to ensure that your extensions are maintainable, scalable, and compatible with other workflows, follow these best practices:

11.6.1. Design for Reusability and Maintainability

When writing custom code or creating new nodes, ensure that your scripts and extensions are **modular** and **reusable**. This will make it easier to maintain and extend the workflows over time.

Best Practices:

- **Modularize your code**: Break down complex tasks into smaller, reusable functions.
- **Write clear comments**: Add comments to explain the purpose of each function, making the code easier to understand for others (and yourself).
- **Use environment variables**: Store sensitive data like API keys in environment variables or **n8n credentials** to avoid hardcoding them in the script.

11.6.2. Optimize for Performance

When extending **n8n**, always consider the performance impact of your custom nodes and scripts. Inefficient code can slow down workflows and consume unnecessary resources.

Optimization Tips:

- **Use asynchronous functions**: For tasks like HTTP requests, always use `async/await` to ensure non-blocking behavior.
- **Batch processing**: Process data in smaller chunks instead of handling everything at once, especially for large datasets.
- **Optimize API calls**: Minimize the number of API calls made, and use **pagination** or **caching** where possible.

11.6.3. Ensure Compatibility and Avoid Breaking Changes

When creating custom nodes or scripts, ensure they are compatible with the rest of your **n8n workflows** and other **n8n nodes**.

Best Practices for Compatibility:

- **Versioning**: Use **semantic versioning** for custom nodes and actions. This will help you manage changes and ensure backwards compatibility.
- **Test with different workflows**: After creating custom nodes, test them in different workflows and with different data inputs to ensure they work across use cases.

11.6.4. Leverage n8n's Community

n8n has an active community that regularly contributes to the plugin ecosystem. If you're building custom integrations or nodes, consider:

- **Contributing to the community**: Share your nodes with the **n8n community** on **GitHub** or the **n8n marketplace**.
- **Seeking help and feedback**: Participate in the **n8n forums** or **Discord server** to ask for feedback or assistance from other developers.

In this chapter, we explored how to extend **n8n agents** by writing **custom action scripts** in **JavaScript** and following best practices for creating reusable, efficient, and maintainable extensions. We also covered key best practices for extending **n8n's** native capabilities, ensuring that your custom workflows are compatible, performant, and scalable.

11.7 Hands-on Example: Extending an Agent to Call Custom APIs

In this section, we'll walk through a hands-on example of extending an **n8n agent** to call a **custom API**. This will demonstrate how to use **JavaScript** in **n8n's Function node** to interact with an external API and process the data returned by the API. We'll create a simple **n8n agent** that fetches data from a custom API and processes it to fit into your workflow.

11.7.1. Scenario: Extending an Agent to Call a Weather API

Let's say you want to extend an **n8n agent** to get real-time weather data for a specified city using a **custom weather API** (for example, the **OpenWeatherMap API**). The goal is to create an agent that:

1. Takes a **city name** as input.
2. Calls the **OpenWeatherMap API** to fetch the weather data.
3. Processes the data and outputs the temperature, humidity, and weather condition.

Here's how we can achieve this using **n8n's Function node** to call a custom API and process the response.

11.7.2. Step-by-Step Implementation

Step 1: Create the n8n Workflow

1. **Create a New Workflow**:
   o Open the **n8n editor** and create a new workflow.
2. **Add a Trigger Node**:
   o Use a **Webhook Trigger node** as the starting point for the workflow. This node will listen for incoming requests with a city name that the agent will use to fetch weather data.

Example configuration for the Webhook node:

- o **HTTP Method**: POST
- o **Path**: /get-weather
- o **Parameters**: City name (e.g., city)

Step 2: Configure the Function Node to Call the Weather API

1. **Add the Function Node**:
   - o After the **Webhook Trigger node**, add a **Function node** to call the **OpenWeatherMap API**.
2. **Write the Custom API Call Logic in JavaScript**:
   - o In the **Function node**, write JavaScript code to make the API call to **OpenWeatherMap** and process the response.

Here's an example of what the JavaScript code in the **Function node** might look like:

```javascript

// Retrieve the city parameter from the incoming
webhook data
const city = $json["city"];  // The city name sent
in the request

// Define the API endpoint and your API key
const apiKey = 'YOUR_OPENWEATHERMAP_API_KEY'; //
Replace with your OpenWeatherMap API key
const apiUrl =
`https://api.openweathermap.org/data/2.5/weather?q=
${city}&appid=${apiKey}&units=metric`;  // URL to
fetch weather data

// Make the API call using n8n's request helper
const response = await this.helpers.request({
  url: apiUrl,
  method: 'GET',
  json: true,
});

// Process the response to extract relevant data
(temperature, humidity, weather)
```

```
const temperature = response.main.temp;
const humidity = response.main.humidity;
const weatherCondition =
response.weather[0].description;

// Return the processed data for use in the next
node
return [
  {
    json: {
      city: city,
      temperature: temperature,
      humidity: humidity,
      weatherCondition: weatherCondition,
    },
  },
];
```

Step 3: Handle Errors and Missing Data

If the **OpenWeatherMap API** returns an error (e.g., if the city is not found), we need to handle it gracefully. You can implement error handling in the **Function node** by adding a **try-catch** block around the API call to catch any errors.

Here's an updated version of the JavaScript code that includes error handling:

```javascript

try {
  // Retrieve the city parameter from the incoming
webhook data
  const city = $json["city"];

  // Define the API endpoint and your API key
  const apiKey = 'YOUR_OPENWEATHERMAP_API_KEY';   //
Replace with your OpenWeatherMap API key
  const apiUrl =
`https://api.openweathermap.org/data/2.5/weather?q=
${city}&appid=${apiKey}&units=metric`;   // URL to
fetch weather data
```

```
  // Make the API call using n8n's request helper
  const response = await this.helpers.request({
    url: apiUrl,
    method: 'GET',
    json: true,
  });

  // Process the response to extract relevant data
(temperature, humidity, weather)
  const temperature = response.main.temp;
  const humidity = response.main.humidity;
  const weatherCondition =
response.weather[0].description;

  // Return the processed data for use in the next
node
  return [
    {
      json: {
        city: city,
        temperature: temperature,
        humidity: humidity,
        weatherCondition: weatherCondition,
      },
    },
  ];
} catch (error) {
  // If there's an error (e.g., city not found, API
issue), return an error message
  return [
    {
      json: {
        error: true,
        message: `Failed to retrieve weather data
for ${$json["city"]}: ${error.message}`,
      },
    },
  ];
}
```

11.7.4. Step 4: Return the Data or Handle Errors

Once the **Function node** executes successfully, it will output the weather data (temperature, humidity, and weather condition). You can now either:

- **Log the data** for debugging or monitoring purposes.
- **Send the data** to another system, such as a **Google Sheets node** or **Slack node**, to display the results to the user.

11.7.5. Step 5: Test the Workflow

1. **Deploy the Workflow**: Once the workflow is configured, deploy it by clicking on the **Activate** button in the **n8n editor**.
2. **Test the Webhook**: Use an API testing tool like **Postman** or your browser's **developer tools** to send a **POST request** to your **n8n webhook** URL (e.g., `http://localhost:5678/webhook/get-weather`), passing the `city` parameter.

Example POST request (in **Postman**):

- **URL**: `http://localhost:5678/webhook/get-weather`
- **Body (raw JSON)**:

```json
{
  "city": "London"
}
```

Once the request is processed, the **n8n agent** will call the **OpenWeatherMap API**, extract the relevant data (e.g., temperature, humidity, weather condition), and output it in the response.

11.7.6. Optional: Send Results to Slack or Email

You can further enhance this workflow by sending the weather data to a **Slack channel** or an **Email** for notifications. Here's how to do this:

1. **Add a Slack Node**:
   - o Use the **Slack node** to send a message to a Slack channel with the weather data.

   Example configuration:

   - o **Channel**: `#weather-updates`
   - o **Text**: `Weather for {{city}}: {{temperature}}°C, {{humidity}}% humidity, Condition: {{weatherCondition}}`
2. **Add an Email Node**:
   - o Use the **Send Email node** to send the weather information to a recipient. Configure the email with the weather details as part of the message.

   Example email body:

```csharp

Subject: Weather Update for {{city}}
Body: The current temperature is
{{temperature}}°C with {{humidity}}% humidity.
The weather condition is {{weatherCondition}}.
```

In this hands-on example, we extended an **n8n agent** to call a **custom API** (the **OpenWeatherMap API**) to fetch weather data for a specified city. We used **JavaScript** in the **Function node** to make the API call, handle errors, and process the data. This type of extension allows you to create highly customized workflows that interact with any API or external service, providing dynamic and real-time data processing.

By following this process, you can build powerful **n8n agents** that interact with a wide range of external services, automate repetitive tasks, and integrate complex logic into your workflows.

Chapter 12: Advanced Topics in Automation with n8n Agents

In this chapter, we will explore advanced topics in automation using **n8n agents**. As businesses increasingly adopt **AI** and **machine learning** technologies, **n8n** provides powerful ways to integrate these capabilities into your workflows. We'll dive into how to use **n8n agents** for **predictive analytics** and integrate **AI** and **machine learning** models to enhance workflow automation.

12.1. AI and Machine Learning Integrations

Artificial Intelligence (AI) and **Machine Learning (ML)** are transforming the way businesses automate processes, analyze data, and make decisions. By integrating AI and ML with **n8n agents**, you can create powerful workflows that not only automate tasks but also leverage advanced algorithms to derive insights and make predictions.

In this section, we'll discuss how to integrate AI and machine learning capabilities into **n8n workflows** by using external AI services and custom models.

12.1.1. Why Integrate AI and Machine Learning with n8n?

Integrating AI and ML into your **n8n agents** allows you to:

- **Automate complex decision-making** based on data analysis.
- **Generate insights** from large datasets without manual intervention.
- **Personalize workflows** by leveraging **predictive models** (e.g., customer behavior, sales forecasting).
- **Enhance business processes** such as **recommendation systems**, **fraud detection**, or **image and text analysis**.

For example, a business could use **n8n agents** to:

- Analyze **customer reviews** using **sentiment analysis** (powered by AI).
- Build a **predictive model** to forecast sales based on historical data.
- Automate **recommendations** for users based on their browsing history using **machine learning** algorithms.

12.1.2. Popular AI and ML Integrations in n8n

There are several ways to integrate AI and ML models into **n8n**. You can either use **third-party AI services** or **deploy custom ML models** within your **n8n workflows**.

1. OpenAI GPT-3 Integration

OpenAI's GPT-3 is one of the most powerful AI models available for natural language processing. By integrating **GPT-3** with **n8n**, you can automate tasks like:

- **Text generation**: Automatically generate content (e.g., blog posts, emails, summaries).
- **Text summarization**: Summarize lengthy documents or articles.
- **Sentiment analysis**: Classify text as positive, negative, or neutral.

Example Workflow:

- **Trigger**: A new customer feedback form is submitted via **n8n's Webhook Trigger node**.
- **API Call**: The **n8n OpenAI node** sends the feedback text to GPT-3 for sentiment analysis.
- **Action**: Based on the sentiment, the system sends a personalized response (e.g., thanking customers for positive feedback or offering support for negative feedback).

2. Google Cloud AI Integrations

Google Cloud AI offers a wide range of services, such as **Vision AI, Natural Language Processing (NLP)**, and **AutoML**, that can be easily integrated into **n8n**.

- **Google Cloud NLP**: Analyze text for sentiment, entity extraction, or syntactic analysis.
- **Google Cloud Vision API**: Analyze and classify images (e.g., identifying objects or people in photos).
- **Google AutoML**: Train custom machine learning models on your data without needing deep ML expertise.

Example Workflow:

- **Trigger**: A new image is uploaded to **Google Cloud Storage**.
- **Action**: The **n8n Google Vision node** processes the image to detect objects and label them (e.g., identifying items in a product catalog).
- **Outcome**: The results are saved in a **Google Sheets node** or **CRM system**, allowing the business to automatically tag and categorize products.

3. IBM Watson AI Services

IBM Watson offers various AI services such as **Watson NLP, Watson Visual Recognition**, and **Watson Assistant** for building conversational agents. These can be integrated with **n8n** to automate tasks like:

- **Text analytics**: Sentiment analysis, entity extraction, and intent classification.
- **Image recognition**: Categorizing images or detecting faces.
- **Chatbots**: Automating conversations with customers using AI-powered chatbots.

12.1.3. Custom AI and ML Model Integrations

If you have custom AI or machine learning models, you can integrate them into **n8n** using **HTTP Request nodes** to call external endpoints, or by using **n8n's Function nodes** to handle the data processing.

Steps to Integrate a Custom ML Model:

1. **Prepare Your Model**:
   - Train your ML model using tools like **TensorFlow, PyTorch, or scikit-learn**.

- o Deploy the model to a cloud platform (e.g., **AWS SageMaker**, **Google AI Platform**, or **Heroku**) for easy access via an API.
2. **Integrate with n8n**:
   - o Use the **HTTP Request node** to send data (e.g., customer data, sales data) to the deployed API.
   - o Parse the model's predictions or output in **n8n's Function node**.
   - o Based on the results, take appropriate actions within the workflow (e.g., send recommendations, trigger email alerts).

12.1.4. Using AI for Data Transformation and Analysis in n8n

One of the powerful applications of AI in **n8n agents** is transforming and analyzing data before passing it to other systems or services. For example, you can use **n8n agents** to:

- **Perform data classification**: Automatically categorize data based on machine learning models (e.g., classifying customer feedback as positive or negative).
- **Create predictive models**: Use **historical data** to predict future outcomes, such as sales forecasts or customer churn.
- **Analyze and summarize** large datasets: Use **natural language processing** to summarize long documents, emails, or social media posts.

By combining **AI models** with **n8n workflows**, you can automate complex decision-making processes and gain valuable insights from your data.

12.2. Using n8n Agents for Predictive Analytics

Predictive analytics uses historical data and machine learning algorithms to make predictions about future events. Integrating **predictive analytics** into **n8n workflows** allows you to automate decision-making processes based on predictions. This section will explore how to use **n8n agents** for predictive analytics, focusing on key use cases and implementation strategies.

12.2.1. What is Predictive Analytics?

Predictive analytics involves using **historical data** and **machine learning algorithms** to forecast future outcomes. It is commonly used for:

- **Sales forecasting**: Predicting future sales based on historical data.
- **Customer churn prediction**: Identifying customers at risk of leaving based on their behavior.
- **Demand forecasting**: Predicting product demand to optimize inventory management.

In **n8n**, predictive analytics can be integrated to automate decisions, such as:

- **Identifying high-value customers**.
- **Predicting stock market trends**.
- **Forecasting sales performance**.

12.2.2. Use Case: Predicting Customer Churn

Predicting **customer churn** is one of the most common applications of **predictive analytics**. By using historical data (e.g., customer activity, purchase history, customer service interactions), businesses can predict which customers are likely to leave and take proactive steps to retain them.

Steps to Implement Predictive Analytics for Churn Prediction in n8n:

1. **Collect Data**:
    - Use **n8n's HTTP Request node** or **Database nodes** to gather historical customer data such as:
        - **Purchase history**.
        - **Customer support interactions**.
        - **Customer engagement metrics** (e.g., website visits, email opens).
2. **Train a Churn Prediction Model**:
    - Use **Python** or **R** to build a **machine learning model** that predicts churn based on the collected data. Popular algorithms for churn prediction include **Logistic Regression, Random Forests**, and **Support Vector Machines** (SVM).
3. **Deploy the Model**:

- Deploy your trained model to a cloud service or local server. Use **n8n** to make API calls to the model for predictions.
4. **Automate Predictions**:
    - Use the **HTTP Request node** in **n8n** to call the deployed model API and pass data to it (e.g., customer data).
    - Use the predictions from the model (e.g., "high churn risk") to trigger actions in your workflow (e.g., send a retention offer to the customer).

12.2.3. Example: Sales Forecasting

Another common use of **predictive analytics** is **sales forecasting**. By analyzing historical sales data, businesses can predict future sales trends and adjust their strategies accordingly.

Steps to Implement Sales Forecasting in n8n:

1. **Collect Sales Data**:
    - Use **n8n's Database node** or **Google Sheets node** to gather historical sales data (e.g., sales volume, revenue, customer data).
2. **Train a Sales Forecasting Model**:
    - Build a **predictive model** using **scikit-learn** or **TensorFlow** to predict future sales based on historical data. Common techniques for sales forecasting include **time series forecasting** and **regression analysis**.
3. **Integrate the Model**:
    - Deploy the trained model to an API endpoint (e.g., **AWS Lambda, Google AI Platform**).
    - Use the **HTTP Request node** to query the model with up-to-date sales data and get predictions for future sales.
4. **Automate Decisions**:
    - Based on the model's predictions, automate actions such as adjusting marketing spend, restocking products, or offering discounts to high-potential customers.

12.2.4. Best Practices for Implementing Predictive Analytics

- **Data Quality**: Ensure the data used for training the model is clean, complete, and accurate. Poor data quality leads to inaccurate predictions.
- **Feature Engineering**: Properly select and preprocess the features (variables) that will be used in your predictive model. The quality of the features can greatly impact the model's performance.
- **Model Selection**: Choose the appropriate machine learning model for the problem at hand. Different models perform better with different types of data.
- **Monitor Model Performance**: Continuously monitor the performance of your predictive models and retrain them as new data becomes available to ensure they remain accurate over time.

In this chapter, we explored how to integrate **AI** and **machine learning** into **n8n workflows** for advanced automation. We covered:

- **AI and ML integrations** using third-party services like **OpenAI**, **Google Cloud AI**, and custom machine learning models.
- **Predictive analytics** use cases like **customer churn prediction** and **sales forecasting**, demonstrating how to automate business decisions using predictive insights.

By integrating **AI** and **machine learning** with **n8n agents**, businesses can create intelligent workflows that automate decision-making, predict outcomes, and gain valuable insights from their data.

12.3. Implementing Real-Time Data Streaming with WebSockets

Real-time data streaming is crucial for applications that require instant data updates, such as live notifications, stock market tracking, social media updates, or IoT device monitoring. **n8n** can integrate **WebSockets** to enable real-time data streaming and enhance the responsiveness of workflows. In this section, we'll explore how to implement **WebSocket-based real-time data streaming** with **n8n agents**.

12.3.1. What is WebSocket and Why Use It?

WebSockets provide a full-duplex communication channel over a single, long-lived TCP connection. Unlike **HTTP**, which is request-response based, **WebSockets** allow for continuous communication between the client and server. This makes them ideal for scenarios where real-time data needs to be sent instantly without the overhead of constantly opening new HTTP requests.

Advantages of WebSockets:

- **Low latency**: Real-time data is sent immediately when available.
- **Efficient**: Unlike HTTP polling, WebSockets keep a single connection open, reducing resource usage.
- **Bidirectional communication**: Both the client and server can send data at any time.

12.3.2. Use Cases for WebSocket in n8n

n8n agents can be extended to support **real-time workflows** through WebSockets. Below are common use cases:

- **Live Data Feeds**: Monitor and process real-time data from APIs that use WebSockets (e.g., live stock prices, social media posts).
- **Event-Driven Automation**: Trigger workflows based on events that are pushed from external systems (e.g., changes in a database, new messages in a chat system).
- **IoT Device Integration**: Process data from IoT devices in real-time as they send data through WebSockets.

12.3.3. Steps to Implement Real-Time Data Streaming with WebSockets in n8n

To implement **WebSocket-based data streaming** in **n8n**, you'll need to follow these steps:

1. Set Up a WebSocket Client in n8n

You can use **n8n's WebSocket node** to connect to a WebSocket server, listen for incoming data, and trigger workflows based on that data.

1. **Add WebSocket Node**:
   - In your **n8n workflow**, add the **WebSocket node**.
   - Set the **WebSocket URL** (e.g., `wss://example.com/socket`).
   - Define the **action** (e.g., `Listen for Data`).

Example Configuration:

```plaintext

- WebSocket URL: wss://stocks.example.com/realtime
- Action: Listen for stock price updates
```

2. Process Incoming Data in n8n Workflow

Once the WebSocket node is connected and listening for real-time data, you can add nodes to process the data.

1. **Filter Data**: Use the **Set node** or **Function node** to extract and format incoming data as needed (e.g., stock price, market data).
2. **Trigger Actions**: Use the **If node** to create conditions based on real-time data. For example, trigger an alert when a stock price exceeds a certain threshold.
3. **Send Notifications**: Use **Slack** or **Email nodes** to notify users of significant changes in real-time.

Example Workflow:

1. **WebSocket Node**: Connect to a WebSocket server for stock price updates.
2. **Function Node**: Extract stock price from incoming data.
3. **If Node**: Trigger an action if the stock price rises above $100.
4. **Send Email Node**: Send an email notification to a user.

3. Handle WebSocket Disconnections and Reconnects

In production environments, WebSocket connections may occasionally drop. To handle this:

1. **Error Handling**: Implement error-handling logic using **Error Trigger nodes** or **Try/Catch blocks** in **Function nodes** to detect and handle connection failures.
2. **Reconnection**: Use **Delay nodes** and logic to automatically attempt reconnection when the WebSocket connection is lost.

12.3.4. Example Use Case: Real-Time Stock Price Monitoring

Let's say you want to create a real-time monitoring system for stock prices. You can set up a **WebSocket node** that listens to stock price updates and triggers an email when a stock price crosses a certain threshold.

Steps:

1. **WebSocket Node**: Listen to the WebSocket feed for stock price updates.
2. **Function Node**: Extract the stock price from the WebSocket message.
3. **If Node**: If the stock price is greater than $200, trigger the next action.
4. **Send Email Node**: Notify users via email about the stock price change.

12.3.5. Best Practices for Using WebSockets in n8n

- **Handle Disconnections Gracefully**: Always implement retry logic or reconnect features to handle temporary disconnections.
- **Optimize Data Handling**: Process incoming data efficiently to avoid overloading your **n8n** instance with large amounts of data.
- **Secure WebSocket Connections**: Always use **wss://** for secure WebSocket connections to ensure data privacy and security.

12.4. Hybrid Cloud and Edge Deployments with n8n

As businesses move toward more distributed architectures, the need for **hybrid cloud** and **edge deployments** is increasing. **n8n agents** can be deployed across **cloud environments** (e.g., AWS, Google Cloud) and **edge devices** (e.g., IoT devices, local servers) to provide high-performance automation and data processing closer to the data source.

In this section, we'll explore how to use **n8n agents** in **hybrid cloud** and **edge deployments** to create efficient, scalable automation solutions.

12.4.1. What is Hybrid Cloud and Edge Computing?

- **Hybrid Cloud**: A **hybrid cloud** deployment involves combining on-premises infrastructure (private cloud) with public cloud services. This allows businesses to have more control over critical applications while benefiting from the scalability and flexibility of the cloud.
- **Edge Computing**: **Edge computing** refers to processing data closer to the source (i.e., at the "edge" of the network) rather than sending it to a centralized data center. This reduces latency and bandwidth usage, making it ideal for applications that require real-time processing (e.g., IoT).

12.4.2. Deploying n8n Agents in a Hybrid Cloud Environment

n8n agents can be deployed across multiple environments (e.g., on-premises servers, cloud instances) to create a **hybrid cloud architecture**. This enables businesses to run workflows on their local infrastructure while leveraging cloud services for specific tasks (e.g., storage, compute, machine learning).

Steps for Hybrid Cloud Deployment:

1. **Install n8n on Cloud Instances**: Set up **n8n** on cloud services like **AWS EC2**, **Google Compute Engine**, or **Azure VMs**.
2. **Set Up On-Premises n8n Agents**: Deploy **n8n** on on-premises servers or private cloud instances that handle sensitive or localized tasks.
3. **Integrate Cloud and On-Premises Systems**: Use **API nodes** and **Webhook triggers** to integrate cloud-based workflows with on-premises workflows, enabling seamless data flow between the two environments.

Example Use Case:

A company could use **n8n** to automate **data processing** on cloud instances, but keep sensitive data processing (e.g., customer records) within a local private cloud or on-premises server. This hybrid approach enables efficient workflows while maintaining control over sensitive data.

12.4.3. Edge Computing with n8n

For applications that require **real-time data processing** (e.g., monitoring IoT devices), **edge computing** is an ideal approach. Deploying **n8n** on edge devices allows you to process data locally, reducing the need to send large amounts of data to the cloud and minimizing latency.

Steps for Edge Deployment:

1. **Install n8n on Edge Devices**: Deploy **n8n** on edge devices such as **Raspberry Pi**, **local servers**, or other IoT gateways. This allows workflows to run locally, processing sensor data, controlling devices, or triggering actions in real-time.
2. **Integrate with Cloud Services**: Use **n8n's Webhook nodes** and **API integrations** to send important data to the cloud when necessary (e.g., sending aggregated data or alerts).
3. **Automate Real-Time Decisions**: Use edge deployments to make real-time decisions (e.g., trigger alarms based on sensor data, process video feeds for immediate analysis).

Example Use Case:

An **IoT monitoring system** could use **n8n** deployed on edge devices to process data from sensors in real-time, triggering actions such as activating machines, sending alerts, or storing data in a local database. Periodically, critical data could be sent to the cloud for long-term storage or analysis.

12.4.4. Benefits of Hybrid Cloud and Edge Deployments with n8n

- **Reduced Latency**: By processing data closer to the source, edge computing reduces latency, providing faster response times for real-time applications.
- **Cost Efficiency**: **Hybrid cloud** and **edge deployments** allow you to optimize costs by using local resources for day-to-day processing and the cloud for scaling up during high-demand periods.
- **Scalability**: **Hybrid cloud** offers scalability when needed, while **edge computing** can handle local data processing without relying on cloud resources.
- **Data Privacy and Security**: Keep sensitive data within on-premises systems while taking advantage of cloud services for less sensitive operations.

12.4.5. Best Practices for Hybrid Cloud and Edge Deployments

1. **Data Segregation**: Ensure that sensitive data is processed on local devices or on-premises servers to meet compliance and security requirements.
2. **Seamless Integration**: Use **n8n's API** and **Webhook nodes** to integrate workflows between cloud and edge devices, ensuring smooth data transfer and communication.
3. **Automated Failover**: Set up automated failover mechanisms to ensure workflows continue running smoothly if an edge device goes offline or experiences issues.
4. **Edge Device Monitoring**: Monitor the health of edge devices using tools like **Prometheus** or **Grafana** to track resource usage, uptime, and workflow execution.

In this chapter, we explored **real-time data streaming with WebSockets** and how to leverage **hybrid cloud** and **edge computing** deployments with **n8n agents**. By integrating **WebSockets** for real-time data handling and using **n8n agents** in **hybrid cloud** and **edge environments**, you can create efficient, scalable workflows that process data in real time and improve overall performance.

12.5. Integrating n8n with IoT Devices for Automation

The Internet of Things (**IoT**) involves connecting everyday devices to the internet, enabling them to send data and perform actions automatically. **n8n** provides powerful capabilities to automate workflows involving IoT devices, enabling businesses to process real-time data and control devices without manual intervention. In this section, we will explore how to integrate **n8n** with IoT devices for automation, focusing on connecting IoT sensors, devices, and actuators to **n8n workflows**.

12.5.1. Why Integrate IoT Devices with n8n?

By integrating IoT devices with **n8n**, you can:

- **Automate real-time actions** based on sensor data (e.g., turning on lights when motion is detected).
- **Monitor IoT devices** remotely and receive alerts for specific events (e.g., temperature threshold exceeded).
- **Streamline workflows** by incorporating IoT data into business processes (e.g., triggering sales or inventory actions based on stock levels detected by sensors).
- **Control devices automatically** through workflows triggered by sensor input, remote signals, or external data.

12.5.2. Key IoT Integration Use Cases

Below are some common use cases where **n8n** can be used to automate workflows with IoT devices:

- **Smart Home Automation**: Automating home systems such as lights, thermostats, and locks based on sensor data or external triggers.
- **Industrial IoT (IIoT)**: Monitoring industrial equipment (e.g., temperature, pressure sensors) and automating maintenance workflows based on detected anomalies or threshold violations.
- **Environmental Monitoring**: Collecting data from environmental sensors (e.g., air quality, water temperature) and triggering actions such as sending alerts, generating reports, or controlling equipment.

12.5.3. Integrating IoT Devices with n8n Using Webhooks

One of the most common ways to integrate IoT devices with **n8n** is through **Webhooks**. **IoT devices** often support Webhooks to send real-time data to an endpoint when a certain event occurs. **n8n's Webhook node** allows you to listen to these Webhooks and trigger workflows in response to incoming data.

Step-by-Step Integration with IoT Devices Using Webhooks:

1. **Configure the IoT Device to Send Webhooks**:
   - Most modern IoT devices (e.g., smart cameras, motion sensors, temperature monitors) support **HTTP Webhooks** to send event data to a specified endpoint.
   - Set the device's **Webhook URL** to the **n8n Webhook URL**. For example, if you're using a **motion sensor**, configure the sensor to send data to the following **Webhook URL**:

   plaintext

   ```
   http://<n8n_instance_url>/webhook/motion-
   detected
   ```

2. **Set Up n8n Webhook Node**:
   - In **n8n**, create a **Webhook Trigger node** to listen for incoming data. This node will be triggered whenever the IoT device sends a webhook.
   - Configure the **Webhook node** with the same path as the device's Webhook URL (e.g., `/motion-detected`).

   Example configuration:

   - **Method**: POST
   - **Path**: `/motion-detected`
3. **Process Data from the IoT Device**:
   - Once the **Webhook node** is triggered, you can use other **n8n nodes** to process the incoming data. For example:
     - **Set node**: Extract relevant information from the incoming data (e.g., temperature, sensor ID).

- **Send Email node**: Notify users if a certain threshold is met (e.g., when the temperature exceeds a predefined limit).
- **HTTP Request node**: Send data to another system for further processing (e.g., updating an inventory system when a stock sensor triggers an event).

4. **Trigger Actions Based on IoT Events**:
   - After processing the data, you can trigger further actions, such as:
     - **Activating devices**: Turn on lights or air conditioning.
     - **Sending alerts**: Email or SMS notifications when a sensor detects a problem (e.g., water leak or motion detection).
     - **Logging data**: Storing sensor data for later analysis or reporting.

Example Workflow: IoT Motion Detection and Light Control

1. **Trigger**: A **motion sensor** sends a Webhook notification to **n8n** via the **Webhook node**.
2. **Action**: If motion is detected, use the **Set node** to process the data (e.g., storing sensor ID and timestamp).
3. **Condition**: Use an **If node** to check if the detected motion occurs during a specific time frame (e.g., evening hours).
4. **Action**: If the condition is true, use the **HTTP Request node** to send a command to a **smart light** API to turn on the lights.
5. **Notification**: Use the **Send Email node** to alert the user about the detected motion.

12.5.4. Integration with MQTT for IoT Device Communication

Another popular method for integrating IoT devices with **n8n** is using **MQTT (Message Queuing Telemetry Transport)**, a lightweight messaging protocol designed for **IoT devices**. **n8n** supports **MQTT nodes**, allowing you to integrate **n8n** with IoT devices that communicate via the MQTT protocol.

Steps to Integrate IoT Devices Using MQTT:

1. **Set Up MQTT Broker**:

- o Install an MQTT broker (e.g., **Mosquitto, HiveMQ, AWS IoT Core**) to handle communication between **n8n** and IoT devices.
2. **Configure IoT Devices to Publish Data**:
   - o Configure your IoT devices (e.g., temperature sensors, motion detectors) to publish messages to specific MQTT topics when certain events occur.
3. **Configure MQTT in n8n**:
   - o Add an **MQTT node** to **n8n**. Configure it to subscribe to the topics that your IoT devices are publishing (e.g., `home/living-room/temperature`).
4. **Process Data**:
   - o When a device publishes data to the MQTT broker, the **MQTT node** in **n8n** will trigger and allow you to process the incoming message.

12.6. Using n8n for Multi-Agent Systems in Complex Workflows

A **multi-agent system** (MAS) is a system that consists of multiple autonomous agents interacting with each other to achieve complex goals. In a **multi-agent system**, each agent has its own role, can perform tasks independently, and can communicate with other agents to achieve a common objective.

In this section, we will explore how to use **n8n agents** to create and manage **multi-agent systems** in **complex workflows**.

12.6.1. Why Use Multi-Agent Systems?

Multi-agent systems can be used to:

- **Parallelize tasks**: Multiple agents can work on different tasks simultaneously, increasing efficiency and speed.
- **Decentralized decision-making**: Agents can make decisions independently based on their own set of rules, allowing for more complex and dynamic workflows.

- **Distributed processing**: Tasks that require significant computing resources can be split across multiple agents, enabling better resource management and scalability.

12.6.2. Use Cases for Multi-Agent Systems in n8n

n8n is well-suited for building **multi-agent systems** due to its flexibility and ability to connect different nodes in workflows. Some common use cases for multi-agent systems include:

- **Collaborative Problem Solving**: Multiple agents can interact to solve complex problems, such as optimizing business processes, automating customer support, or performing complex data analyses.
- **Distributed Automation**: Different agents can handle different aspects of a business process, such as order fulfillment, customer communication, or inventory management.
- **Event-Driven Systems**: Agents can respond to specific events and interact in real-time, such as monitoring sensors, reacting to customer feedback, or handling alerts from IoT devices.

12.6.3. Setting Up Multi-Agent Workflows in n8n

To implement a **multi-agent system** in **n8n**, we can use the **Execute Workflow node**, which allows workflows to trigger other workflows. This approach enables the creation of **interdependent agents** that can work together to complete a task.

Steps to Create Multi-Agent Systems:

1. **Define Each Agent's Role**:
   o Break down the overall task into smaller, independent roles that can be assigned to different agents. For example, one agent may handle customer requests, while another agent handles data collection or reporting.
2. **Create Independent Workflows for Each Agent**:
   o Create separate workflows for each agent. Each workflow can be responsible for a specific task, such as sending an email, processing data, or interacting with an external API.

3. **Use the Execute Workflow Node**:
    o   Use the **Execute Workflow node** to allow agents to trigger one another. This enables agents to communicate and work together within a larger workflow.
4. **Coordinate Tasks Between Agents**:
    o   Use **n8n's data flow capabilities** to coordinate tasks between agents. For example, Agent 1 can send data to Agent 2 using the **Set node** or **Function node**, and Agent 2 can respond with a result that will be processed by Agent 1 or another agent.

Example: E-commerce Multi-Agent System

In an **e-commerce workflow**, you could have several agents:

1. **Agent 1**: Processes customer orders (e.g., validates order details).
2. **Agent 2**: Manages inventory (e.g., checks stock levels and updates product availability).
3. **Agent 3**: Sends notifications to customers (e.g., sends order confirmation emails).

The agents interact by passing data back and forth, each handling specific tasks independently but collaboratively to fulfill the overall workflow.

12.6.4. Best Practices for Multi-Agent Systems

1. **Decentralized Decision-Making**: Allow each agent to operate autonomously but ensure they have access to necessary data when needed to make decisions.
2. **Task Segmentation**: Divide workflows into manageable tasks that can be assigned to different agents.
3. **Communication Between Agents**: Use the **Execute Workflow node** and **Set node** to allow agents to communicate and share data in a clear, structured manner.
4. **Error Handling**: Implement robust error handling to ensure that when one agent fails, the workflow can continue or retry, without affecting other agents.

In this chapter, we covered the integration of **IoT devices** with **n8n agents** to automate tasks based on real-time data from sensors and devices. We also explored **multi-agent systems** and how to leverage **n8n** to build collaborative workflows that involve multiple independent agents working together toward a common goal. By integrating **IoT devices** and using **multi-agent systems**, you can create highly flexible and scalable automation solutions that improve efficiency and decision-making.

12.7 Hands-On Example: Building a Predictive Analytics Agent Workflow

In this section, we will walk through a hands-on example of creating a **predictive analytics** agent workflow in **n8n**. We will use a simple example to demonstrate how to leverage **historical data** to make predictions, automate business decisions, and integrate these predictions into real-world workflows.

For this example, we will create a predictive model to **forecast sales** using **historical sales data**, and use this prediction to trigger actions, such as sending an alert if the forecasted sales are above or below a specific threshold.

12.7.1. Scenario: Sales Forecasting with Predictive Analytics

We will use **historical sales data** (e.g., daily sales numbers from the past 6 months) to predict future sales. Based on the forecast, we will send an email notification if the predicted sales for the next month are higher than expected, triggering an alert for the sales team to prepare for a surge in demand.

Step-by-Step Implementation:

1. **Collect Historical Data**:
    - Start by using **n8n** to collect historical sales data from a source like a **database** (e.g., MySQL or PostgreSQL) or an **API** that provides this data.
2. **Train the Predictive Model**:
    - For simplicity, we'll assume that we have already trained a **predictive model** using **Python** and **scikit-learn** (or another

machine learning framework). This model predicts future sales based on historical data.

  o The model is deployed as a **REST API** (e.g., using **Flask** or **FastAPI**) to expose the prediction logic.
3. **Set Up the Workflow in n8n**:
  o Use the **HTTP Request node** in **n8n** to send historical data (e.g., the past month's sales data) to the **predictive model API** and receive the forecasted sales for the next month.

12.7.2. Workflow Steps

Step 1: Trigger Workflow

- Use a **Cron node** to schedule the workflow to run on a regular basis (e.g., at the end of each month) to predict sales for the next month.

Step 2: Retrieve Historical Sales Data

- Use the **Database node** (e.g., **PostgreSQL node**) to query and fetch the historical sales data. You might select the past 6 months of data for training purposes.

Example query:

```sql
SELECT date, sales_amount FROM sales WHERE date >=
NOW() - INTERVAL '6 months';
```

Step 3: Send Data to Predictive Model API

- Use the **HTTP Request node** to send the historical data to the predictive model API.

Configuration:

- **URL**: `http://your-api-url/predict-sales`
- **Method**: `POST`
- **Body**:

```json
{
  "historical_data": [
    {"date": "2025-01-01", "sales_amount":
500},
    {"date": "2025-01-02", "sales_amount":
450},
    // Include more historical data here
  ]
}
```

Step 4: Process the Forecasted Sales Data

- Once the API returns the forecasted sales for the next month, use the **Set node** or **Function node** to extract the forecasted value.

Example JavaScript code:

```javascript
const forecastedSales = $json["forecasted_sales"];
// Get the forecasted sales from the API response
return [{ json: { forecastedSales } }];
```

Step 5: Conditional Logic

- Use the **If node** to compare the forecasted sales against a predefined threshold (e.g., $10,000).
  - If the forecasted sales exceed the threshold, trigger a notification or alert.

Example condition:

- If forecastedSales > 10000, send an email alert.

Step 6: Send Notification

- If the condition is met, use the **Send Email node** to notify the sales team about the predicted surge in sales.

Example email:

```sql
Subject: Sales Surge Prediction for Next Month

Hello Team,

Our predictive model has forecasted that next
month's sales will exceed $10,000. Please prepare
accordingly for increased demand.

Best regards,
Sales Automation System
```

Step 7: Store Results

- Optionally, store the predicted sales in a **database** for tracking and reporting purposes.

12.7.3. Final Workflow Summary

1. **Trigger**: The workflow runs at the end of the month using a **Cron node**.
2. **Retrieve Data**: Historical sales data is pulled from a database using the **Database node**.
3. **Prediction**: The **HTTP Request node** sends the historical data to a **custom predictive model API** and receives the forecasted sales for the next month.
4. **Condition**: The **If node** checks if the forecasted sales exceed $10,000.
5. **Notification**: If the threshold is exceeded, a **Send Email node** sends a notification to the sales team.
6. **Store Results**: The predicted sales are stored in a **database** for future reference.

This is a simple predictive analytics workflow, but it can be scaled or adjusted based on more complex data or multiple predictive models.

12.8. Case Study: Building a Multi-Agent AI System with n8n

In this section, we will explore how to build a **multi-agent AI system** using **n8n** to solve complex problems by dividing tasks among different agents. Each agent will perform specific roles and collaborate with other agents to achieve a common goal. We will demonstrate how to integrate **AI models**, **n8n agents**, and **workflow automation** to create a powerful multi-agent system.

12.8.1. What is a Multi-Agent AI System?

A **multi-agent system** (MAS) consists of multiple **autonomous agents** that interact with each other to complete tasks. Each agent has its own specific role and can operate independently but will coordinate with other agents when necessary to achieve a common goal.

In the context of **n8n**, each **agent** can be represented as an independent **n8n workflow** that performs a specific task. These workflows can communicate with each other and share data via **API calls** or by passing data between workflows.

12.8.2. Use Case: AI-Powered Customer Support System

Imagine a **multi-agent AI system** designed to handle **customer support**. The system would include multiple agents, each responsible for a different part of the customer support workflow. The system might consist of the following agents:

1. **Agent 1**: Collects customer inquiries from email or a web form.
2. **Agent 2**: Classifies the inquiry based on predefined categories (e.g., technical issue, billing question).
3. **Agent 3**: Uses an **AI model** to automatically generate an initial response to the inquiry.
4. **Agent 4**: Sends the response back to the customer via email or other communication channels.
5. **Agent 5**: Logs the inquiry and resolution in a CRM system for tracking purposes.

12.8.3. Workflow Breakdown

1. **Agent 1: Collect Customer Inquiries**:
    o   A **Webhook Trigger node** is used to collect customer inquiries from an online form or email.
    o   The data (e.g., customer's question) is passed on to the next agent.
2. **Agent 2: Classify Inquiry**:
    o   A **Function node** is used to classify the inquiry based on keywords or predefined rules (e.g., technical vs. billing).
    o   Alternatively, an **AI model** (such as a pre-trained **BERT** model) can be integrated for more advanced classification.
3. **Agent 3: Generate AI Response**:
    o   The classified inquiry is passed to an **AI model** (e.g., using **GPT-3** or **IBM Watson**).
    o   The model generates a response based on the customer's question, which is returned as the output.
4. **Agent 4: Send Response**:
    o   Use the **Send Email node** to automatically send the AI-generated response to the customer's email.
5. **Agent 5: Log Inquiry**:
    o   The inquiry and its resolution are logged in a **CRM system** or **Google Sheets** for future reference and reporting.

12.8.4. Key Components of the Multi-Agent System

1. **Independent Workflows**: Each agent operates independently as a separate workflow. These workflows can be triggered by events (e.g., incoming inquiries) or scheduled to run at specific intervals.
2. **Data Flow Between Agents**: Data flows seamlessly between agents using **Set nodes** or **Webhook triggers**. Each agent receives relevant data from the previous agent and passes its results to the next agent.
3. **AI Model Integration**: **AI models** are integrated via **HTTP Request nodes** or custom API calls, allowing agents to make intelligent decisions or generate responses based on data.
4. **Error Handling and Retries**: Each agent has built-in **error handling** (e.g., using **Error Trigger nodes**) to ensure that failed tasks are retried or logged for manual intervention.

12.8.5. Benefits of a Multi-Agent AI System with n8n

- **Scalability**: New agents can be added to the system as needed (e.g., adding an agent for sentiment analysis or translation).
- **Parallel Processing**: Tasks can be processed in parallel, improving overall system efficiency.
- **Decentralized Decision-Making**: Each agent makes independent decisions based on its specific role, making the system more flexible and responsive.
- **Automation**: Automating the entire customer support process reduces manual effort and response time, enhancing customer experience.

12.8.6. Best Practices for Building Multi-Agent Systems

1. **Modular Design**: Keep each agent's workflow simple and modular. This allows for easier maintenance and scalability.
2. **Clear Communication Between Agents**: Ensure agents can share data effectively, either via direct API calls or through intermediary storage (e.g., databases, CRM systems).
3. **Error Handling**: Implement robust error handling to manage failures and ensure that the overall system remains operational even if one agent fails.
4. **Performance Optimization**: Monitor and optimize agent performance to prevent bottlenecks or slowdowns in large-scale systems.

In this chapter, we explored how to implement **predictive analytics** and **multi-agent systems** with **n8n**. We discussed how to build workflows that incorporate **AI-powered predictions** and create **multi-agent systems** that automate complex processes by distributing tasks across multiple agents. By using **n8n agents** for predictive analytics and multi-agent workflows, businesses can create scalable, intelligent automation systems that make real-time decisions and improve efficiency.

Chapter 13: Future of n8n and Automation with Agents

In this chapter, we will look ahead at the **future of n8n** and **automation with agents**, exploring the exciting developments on the horizon and the increasing role of automation in transforming the way businesses operate. We will discuss **n8n's roadmap**, upcoming features, and how **automation** will shape the **future of work**, particularly in the context of **agent-based automation**.

13.1. n8n's Roadmap and Upcoming Features

As **n8n** continues to evolve, the platform is expanding its capabilities to make automation workflows even more powerful, flexible, and easy to use. This section will provide a glimpse into **n8n's roadmap**, highlighting key features that are being planned or are already in development. These updates will significantly enhance the platform's ability to automate complex workflows, integrate new tools, and improve user experience.

13.1.1. Enhanced Agent Workflow Capabilities

n8n is continually improving its agent-based automation workflows, with features designed to:

- **Improve scalability**: Supporting larger workflows with more complex dependencies and integrations.
- **Enhance agent interaction**: Allowing agents to seamlessly communicate with each other, pass data, and work collaboratively within a workflow.
- **More dynamic workflows**: Incorporating advanced triggers, conditions, and looping mechanisms to create more flexible and dynamic workflows.

Upcoming Features:

- **Agent Coordination**: New features for better coordination between multiple agents, allowing agents to share context or collaborate on

shared tasks with more fine-tuned control over data flow and execution order.
- **Nested Workflows**: The ability to create **nested workflows** within agent workflows, making it easier to manage complex, multi-step tasks.

13.1.2. Advanced AI and Machine Learning Integrations

As AI and machine learning continue to gain traction, **n8n** will be increasingly incorporating more advanced integrations with AI services and machine learning models.

Key Features:

- **Pre-built AI nodes**: n8n plans to provide more pre-built nodes for integrating with popular AI platforms like **TensorFlow**, **Google AI**, and **OpenAI**, allowing users to easily incorporate machine learning models into their workflows.
- **Custom AI model support**: n8n will provide better support for integrating and using custom-trained machine learning models. This will allow businesses to build more sophisticated workflows that leverage the power of AI to automate decision-making.

13.1.3. WebSocket and Real-Time Data Processing

Real-time data processing through **WebSockets** is a crucial area of growth for **n8n**. In future releases, n8n plans to enhance its real-time capabilities, allowing for faster and more efficient handling of real-time events, such as:

- **Real-time event processing**: Allowing workflows to react instantly to incoming data, such as messages from IoT devices, webhooks, or live data feeds.
- **WebSocket improvements**: Better support for integrating with WebSocket APIs and handling long-lived connections efficiently.

13.1.4. Cloud-Native Capabilities and Hybrid Deployments

With the growing demand for cloud-native solutions, n8n will continue to evolve its capabilities to make deployment and management easier in cloud environments and hybrid architectures. This includes:

- **Cloud integrations**: More built-in integrations with cloud services such as **AWS**, **Azure**, **Google Cloud**, and **IBM Cloud**.
- **Containerized deployment**: Improvements to **n8n's containerization** using Docker and Kubernetes, making it easier for users to scale their workflows and agents across distributed environments.
- **Multi-cloud support**: New features will allow n8n to seamlessly operate across different cloud platforms, allowing for hybrid cloud architectures and edge computing.

13.1.5. Workflow Management and Collaboration Enhancements

As workflows grow in complexity and scale, managing and collaborating on them becomes increasingly important. n8n plans to enhance **workflow management** tools to improve collaboration among teams and ensure better control and monitoring over workflow execution.

Key Features:

- **Version control**: Enhanced version control support, allowing teams to track changes to workflows, roll back to previous versions, and manage updates across multiple users.
- **Collaborative workflows**: Tools for real-time collaboration on workflows, where multiple users can edit, comment, and track changes.
- **Role-based access control (RBAC)**: More granular user permissions to control access to different parts of workflows and agents, improving security and collaboration.

13.1.6. Integrations with More Tools and Services

As the demand for automation increases, n8n continues to add more **third-party integrations** to expand its capabilities. This includes integrations with more **CRM systems**, **project management tools**, **social media platforms**, and **business software**.

Upcoming Integrations:

- **CRM systems**: Deeper integrations with platforms like **Salesforce**, **HubSpot**, and **Zoho** for better automation in sales and customer relationship management workflows.
- **IoT platforms**: Enhanced support for IoT platforms like **AWS IoT**, **Google IoT Core**, and **Azure IoT Hub**, making it easier to automate workflows based on real-time data from IoT devices.
- **ERP systems**: Integrations with **ERP systems** such as **SAP** and **Oracle ERP** to automate business processes like inventory management, order fulfillment, and financial reporting.

13.2. The Role of Automation in the Future of Work

The **future of work** is increasingly intertwined with **automation**, and **n8n agents** are a key part of this transformation. By automating repetitive tasks, processing large volumes of data, and integrating AI-driven decision-making, automation is empowering workers to focus on more strategic, creative, and high-value activities.

In this section, we will explore the broader **role of automation** in the **future of work** and how **n8n agents** will contribute to this shift.

13.2.1. Increased Productivity and Efficiency

One of the main benefits of automation is the **significant increase in productivity and efficiency**. By offloading repetitive tasks to **n8n agents**, businesses can:

- **Reduce manual errors**: Automating manual tasks ensures greater accuracy and reduces the likelihood of human errors.

- **Increase speed**: Automation allows businesses to complete tasks faster, improving response times and overall throughput.
- **Free up employees for higher-value work**: Automation removes the burden of tedious tasks, allowing employees to focus on more strategic and impactful work.

Example:

In a **sales** environment, **n8n agents** can automate lead qualification, email follow-ups, and reporting. This allows sales representatives to focus on direct client engagement, strategy, and closing deals.

13.2.2. Empowering Data-Driven Decision Making

Automation allows businesses to integrate **real-time data** into their workflows, enabling **data-driven decision-making**. **n8n agents** can process and analyze large volumes of data from multiple sources, providing decision-makers with timely insights that improve their ability to make informed choices.

Example:

n8n agents can analyze customer behavior data in real-time and trigger personalized marketing actions, such as sending discounts or promotional emails to customers who are most likely to convert.

13.2.3. Transformation of Work Roles and Job Creation

While automation will reduce the need for some repetitive manual tasks, it will also create **new jobs** and **transform existing roles**. The rise of automation technology like **n8n agents** will lead to:

- **New roles in automation**: Positions such as **automation engineers**, **workflow designers**, and **AI specialists** will become more prevalent.
- **Job evolution**: Traditional roles will evolve to require new skills, such as working with automation tools, managing agents, and interpreting data-driven insights.

Example:

In customer service, automation will handle routine inquiries, but agents will focus on more complex issues, requiring them to acquire skills in both automation tools and customer engagement strategies.

13.2.4. Collaboration Between Humans and Machines

The future of work will involve **human-machine collaboration**, where **n8n agents** handle tasks that require speed, consistency, and scalability, while humans focus on areas that require creativity, emotional intelligence, and strategic thinking. This collaboration will create more efficient, innovative, and effective teams.

Example:

In a **creative agency**, **n8n agents** can automate the collection of customer data, analyze sentiment from social media, and generate reports, freeing up creative teams to focus on content creation, branding, and innovation.

13.2.5. Ethical Considerations and Automation

As automation grows, so do the ethical challenges surrounding it. Businesses must ensure that automation is implemented in ways that are fair, transparent, and aligned with their values. This includes:

- Ensuring **job fairness** by balancing automation and human labor.
- Addressing **bias in AI models** to ensure that automation does not inadvertently reinforce inequality.
- Maintaining **transparency** in automated decisions, particularly in customer-facing applications like credit scoring or recruitment.

In this chapter, we've looked at the exciting **future of n8n** and **automation** with agents. We explored **n8n's roadmap** for enhancing agent workflows, integrating AI and machine learning, and improving scalability in cloud-native environments. Additionally, we discussed the **role of automation** in the **future of work**, highlighting its potential to improve productivity, enable data-driven decision-making, and foster collaboration between humans and machines.

As automation continues to evolve, **n8n agents** will play a key role in shaping the future of business operations, enabling more intelligent, efficient, and scalable workflows.

13.3. How n8n Fits into the Broader Automation Landscape

As businesses look to streamline operations, reduce manual effort, and improve efficiency, automation technologies are rapidly becoming a cornerstone of modern business practices. In the **broader automation landscape**, **n8n** plays a key role by offering an open-source, highly flexible automation platform that enables developers and organizations to integrate, automate, and orchestrate processes across various systems and tools.

In this section, we will explore how **n8n** fits into the broader **automation ecosystem**, its role in the **low-code/no-code** automation movement, and how it compares with other automation solutions.

13.3.1. n8n: A Key Player in the Low-Code/No-Code Movement

The **low-code/no-code** automation movement is about empowering users with limited coding experience to create complex workflows without writing significant amounts of code. **n8n** is an open-source alternative in this space that balances ease of use with powerful customization capabilities.

n8n allows users to automate workflows using a visual interface with drag-and-drop nodes while still enabling developers to create custom nodes, connect to APIs, and implement advanced logic through scripting. This flexibility makes **n8n** an attractive option for both technical and non-technical users:

- **Non-technical users**: Can design workflows using **n8n's visual editor**, dragging and connecting nodes to automate tasks like data entry, reporting, and notifications.
- **Developers**: Have the ability to extend **n8n** by writing custom code, building new nodes, and integrating complex external systems.

Comparison with Other Low-Code/No-Code Platforms:

While **n8n** is primarily an automation platform, it competes with **low-code/no-code tools** like:

- **Zapier**: A popular automation tool that supports pre-built integrations with many apps. While Zapier is simple and easy to use, it can be limiting in terms of customization and scalability.
- **Integromat (Make)**: Similar to **n8n**, **Make** allows users to create powerful workflows through visual automation, but with a more restrictive pricing model and fewer customization options than **n8n**'s open-source framework.
- **Tray.io**: A more enterprise-focused platform that provides advanced automation tools with a rich API-first approach. It's more expensive and better suited for large organizations with more complex needs.

The key differentiator of **n8n** is that it is:

- **Open-source**: Unlike other platforms, **n8n** is free to use and can be self-hosted, which gives users complete control over their data and workflows.
- **Highly customizable**: **n8n** provides the flexibility for developers to extend the platform with custom code, create unique integrations, and scale workflows according to business needs.

13.3.2. n8n's Role in Enterprise Automation

In addition to being popular among individual users and small businesses, **n8n** is increasingly being adopted by enterprises for more advanced automation needs. It fits well into enterprise environments due to its **scalability**, **open-source nature**, and ability to integrate with a vast number of third-party tools.

Benefits for Enterprises:

- **Custom Integrations**: Enterprises often require **custom integrations** with internal systems or proprietary software. **n8n's extensibility** allows enterprises to create tailored workflows without having to rely on off-the-shelf solutions.

- **Flexibility and Control**: Enterprises can **self-host n8n**, ensuring full control over the platform, security, and data management.
- **Cross-Platform Automation**: **n8n** can integrate with cloud services, on-premise systems, and hybrid environments, making it ideal for enterprises that operate in complex, distributed environments.

Use Case: Automating IT Operations:

An enterprise IT team might use **n8n** to automate routine IT tasks, such as server monitoring, log management, software deployment, and alerting. The ability to integrate with internal systems, cloud platforms, and monitoring tools enables seamless automation across diverse infrastructure.

13.3.3. n8n in the Context of Robotic Process Automation (RPA)

Robotic Process Automation (RPA) refers to automating repetitive tasks that involve interacting with software applications. While RPA tools like **UiPath**, **Automation Anywhere**, and **Blue Prism** excel at automating UI-based tasks, **n8n** goes a step further by integrating with APIs and enabling the orchestration of processes that span multiple systems, services, and environments.

n8n provides a more **API-centric approach** to automation compared to traditional RPA tools, making it more suitable for modern software ecosystems where integrations with cloud platforms, databases, and APIs are essential.

n8n vs RPA:

- **RPA Tools**: Best suited for automating repetitive, UI-based tasks that require interaction with legacy applications or software interfaces (e.g., scraping data from websites, filling out forms, etc.).
- **n8n**: More focused on **workflow automation** involving API-based integration, database interactions, and service orchestration across different platforms.

13.3.4. n8n's Ecosystem and Community

One of **n8n's** greatest strengths is its **active and growing community**. The **n8n community** contributes to its ecosystem by building and sharing custom integrations, nodes, and extensions. This open-source collaboration makes it a powerful tool for businesses looking to integrate a wide variety of services and automate their workflows.

Key Ecosystem Features:

- **Custom Nodes**: Users can create custom nodes and share them with the community, allowing **n8n** to support a vast array of integrations.
- **Marketplace**: The **n8n marketplace** allows users to browse available workflows, templates, and nodes shared by the community.
- **Support for New Features**: Through contributions and community feedback, **n8n** continually evolves to support the latest automation trends, AI technologies, and enterprise needs.

13.4. Exploring AI-powered Agents in Automation

As automation continues to evolve, the integration of **AI-powered agents** into workflows is revolutionizing business operations. **n8n**'s ability to integrate **AI models** and **machine learning algorithms** into automation workflows is a game-changer. In this section, we will explore how **AI-powered agents** can be used to enhance the capabilities of **n8n agents**, enabling more intelligent, autonomous, and data-driven decision-making.

13.4.1. What Are AI-powered Agents?

An **AI-powered agent** is an intelligent software entity that can perform tasks autonomously, learn from data, and make decisions without human intervention. In the context of **n8n**, AI-powered agents can:

- **Analyze data**: AI can help automate data analysis, identifying patterns or trends in large datasets (e.g., sentiment analysis, anomaly detection).

- **Make decisions**: AI models can be used to make real-time decisions in workflows, such as recommending actions or predicting future outcomes.
- **Enhance customer interactions**: AI agents can automate customer service tasks, such as responding to emails, chatbot interactions, or issue resolution.

13.4.2. How AI-powered Agents Work in n8n

AI-powered agents in **n8n** are typically built using external AI services or custom machine learning models. These agents interact with **n8n workflows** by analyzing input data and making decisions based on their learnings.

Example AI-powered Agent Workflow:

1. **Collect Data**: Use the **HTTP Request node** to gather data from various sources (e.g., social media, customer reviews).
2. **Analyze Data**: Use **AI-powered nodes** (e.g., **Google Cloud NLP, IBM Watson** or **OpenAI** API) to analyze the data for sentiment, keywords, or intent.
3. **Make Predictions**: An **AI model** can predict the likelihood of a customer churning based on their behavior and interaction history.
4. **Take Action**: Based on the analysis, the agent can trigger a sequence of actions, such as sending a personalized offer to retain the customer or escalating the issue to a human agent.

Key AI Integrations:

- **Natural Language Processing (NLP)**: Sentiment analysis, language translation, and keyword extraction can help automate customer service and feedback analysis.
- **Predictive Analytics**: Using machine learning models to forecast future outcomes, such as sales, customer churn, or demand.
- **Image Recognition**: Integrating **image recognition models** to automate tasks such as categorizing images, detecting objects, or processing visual data.

13.4.3. Benefits of AI-powered Agents in n8n

AI-powered agents enhance the capabilities of **n8n** by:

- **Automating complex tasks**: AI can handle tasks that require significant cognitive capabilities, such as image recognition, language understanding, and decision-making.
- **Making data-driven decisions**: AI models can process large amounts of data and make predictions or recommendations in real-time, improving business efficiency.
- **Learning and adapting**: AI models can continuously learn from new data, improving their accuracy over time and adapting to changing business environments.

13.4.4. Use Cases for AI-powered Agents in n8n

1. **Customer Support**: Use AI agents to automatically categorize customer inquiries, provide answers via chatbots, or generate automated responses to emails.
2. **Sales and Marketing Automation**: Use predictive models to identify potential leads, personalize marketing campaigns, or forecast sales based on historical data.
3. **Business Intelligence**: Automate the analysis of large datasets, generate reports, and extract actionable insights for decision-making.

In this chapter, we explored the **future of n8n** and its integration with **AI-powered agents** in the automation landscape. We discussed how **n8n** fits into the broader **automation ecosystem**, providing businesses with a flexible, scalable solution that supports low-code automation, custom integrations, and complex workflows. Additionally, we examined the exciting potential of **AI-powered agents**, which enable intelligent, data-driven decision-making and automation.

As the demand for **automation** and **AI integration** continues to grow, **n8n** is positioned as a key player in the **low-code/no-code** and **enterprise automation** space.

13.5 The Impact of Automation on Businesses and Industries

Automation is transforming the way businesses and industries operate, reshaping workflows, improving efficiency, and driving innovation. With platforms like **n8n**, automation is becoming more accessible, enabling businesses to automate complex tasks and streamline operations across various departments. This section will explore the **impact of automation** on businesses and industries, highlighting the key benefits and challenges that come with adopting automation technologies.

13.5.1. Increased Operational Efficiency

One of the primary benefits of automation is the ability to **increase operational efficiency**. By automating repetitive tasks, businesses can:

- **Save time**: Automation reduces the amount of manual work required, freeing up employees to focus on higher-value tasks.
- **Reduce errors**: Automated systems are less prone to human error, ensuring greater accuracy in tasks such as data entry, calculations, and decision-making.
- **Enhance consistency**: Automation ensures that tasks are completed consistently every time, leading to more reliable results and fewer mistakes.

For example, **n8n agents** can automate a range of tasks, from data processing and customer service interactions to reporting and order processing. This leads to significant time savings and a reduction in operational costs.

Use Case: Customer Support Automation

Automating customer service workflows with **n8n agents** can improve response times and handle more inquiries simultaneously. For example, using **chatbots** or **AI-powered agents** to respond to common customer queries reduces the need for human intervention, enabling customer support teams to focus on more complex issues.

13.5.2. Cost Reduction and Resource Optimization

Automation enables businesses to **optimize resource allocation** and **reduce costs**. By automating repetitive tasks, businesses can:

- **Reduce labor costs**: Automation takes over low-value, manual tasks, allowing businesses to use their human resources more effectively.
- **Optimize resource use**: Automated systems can run 24/7 without the need for breaks or shifts, allowing businesses to utilize their resources more effectively and scale operations without additional overhead.

For example, in **n8n**, a company could automate tasks like inventory management, order processing, and data collection, reducing the need for manual oversight while ensuring that the processes are performed efficiently.

Use Case: Inventory Management Automation

Automating inventory management with **n8n** can help businesses maintain optimal stock levels, automatically reorder products when stock runs low, and track shipments without human intervention. This reduces labor costs and helps avoid stockouts or overstock situations.

13.5.3. Improved Decision-Making and Data Insights

Automation empowers businesses to make **better decisions** by providing real-time data insights and analytics. Automated systems can gather and process large volumes of data, helping businesses:

- **Analyze trends**: Automation enables businesses to collect, process, and analyze data in real-time, allowing them to identify trends, forecast future outcomes, and make informed decisions.
- **Make data-driven decisions**: Automated systems can provide actionable insights by processing data from multiple sources (e.g., customer feedback, sales, inventory), allowing businesses to make decisions based on current, relevant information.

With **n8n**, businesses can integrate **AI models** and **machine learning** to automate predictive analytics, customer segmentation, and sales forecasting, improving decision-making across departments.

Use Case: Sales Forecasting

By automating sales forecasting, businesses can predict demand, plan inventory, and allocate resources more effectively. **n8n agents** can integrate with machine learning models to forecast sales based on historical data and external factors, helping businesses optimize their strategies.

13.5.4. Enhanced Customer Experience

Automation has a significant impact on the **customer experience** by enabling businesses to respond faster, provide personalized services, and engage customers more effectively. With **n8n agents**:

- **Personalized communication**: Automation can help businesses tailor communication based on customer preferences, behavior, and history, providing a more personalized experience.
- **Faster response times**: By automating customer support and communication workflows, businesses can reduce response times, providing quicker resolutions for customer inquiries and issues.
- **Consistent service**: Automated systems can deliver consistent service across different channels, ensuring customers receive the same level of quality regardless of the interaction medium (e.g., email, chat, phone).

Use Case: Customer Retention Automation

Businesses can use **n8n agents** to identify at-risk customers and automatically send them personalized retention offers, such as discounts or special promotions, based on their behavior and interaction history.

13.5.5. Challenges of Automation Adoption

While automation offers numerous benefits, businesses face several challenges when adopting automation technologies:

- **Initial setup cost**: Implementing automation systems often requires an upfront investment in tools, technology, and training.

- **Change management**: Employees may be resistant to change or fear job displacement, requiring careful management and communication.
- **Integration complexity**: Integrating new automation systems with existing tools and processes can be complex and time-consuming.

Despite these challenges, the long-term benefits of automation far outweigh the initial hurdles, making it an essential strategy for businesses looking to stay competitive in the digital age.

13.6. Preparing for Future Innovations in Automation

As **automation** continues to evolve, new innovations are emerging that will further enhance business capabilities and revolutionize industries. In this section, we will explore some of the key trends in **automation**, how **n8n** fits into these trends, and how businesses can prepare for future innovations.

13.6.1. The Rise of AI and Machine Learning in Automation

One of the most significant trends in automation is the increasing integration of **AI** and **machine learning** into business processes. **n8n** is already supporting AI-powered agents in workflows, and in the future, we can expect even more advanced capabilities, including:

- **Predictive analytics**: Using machine learning models to forecast future events, such as sales, customer behavior, or inventory needs.
- **Intelligent decision-making**: AI agents that can autonomously make decisions based on data, without requiring human intervention.
- **Natural language processing (NLP)**: Integrating AI-powered NLP models to analyze text and make decisions based on unstructured data, such as customer feedback or social media posts.

Preparing for AI Integration:

To prepare for the rise of AI in automation, businesses should:

- Invest in **AI model training** and ensure they have the necessary data to power these models.

- **Adopt AI tools** like **n8n** to automate data collection, processing, and decision-making tasks that rely on AI.
- Train staff in **AI integration** and **machine learning** to take full advantage of these technologies.

13.6.2. The Growth of Edge Computing and IoT Automation

Edge computing and **IoT** are increasingly being integrated into automation systems to process data closer to the source, reducing latency and bandwidth usage. As **IoT devices** continue to proliferate, businesses will need automation solutions that can handle real-time data processing at the **edge**.

n8n is well-positioned to support **IoT and edge computing** integration, allowing businesses to automate workflows based on real-time data from **IoT sensors** and **edge devices**.

Preparing for Edge and IoT Automation:

- Invest in **IoT sensors** and **edge devices** that provide real-time data for automation workflows.
- Use **n8n's Webhook** and **MQTT nodes** to integrate real-time data from edge devices and create responsive workflows.
- Consider **edge computing infrastructure** to ensure that data can be processed locally before being sent to centralized systems for further analysis.

13.6.3. The Future of Low-Code and No-Code Automation

The **low-code/no-code** movement is empowering businesses to build automation workflows without the need for extensive programming knowledge. This trend is expected to continue, with more businesses adopting **low-code/no-code platforms** like **n8n** to automate processes across various departments.

As these platforms evolve, they will offer even more powerful features, such as:

- **Advanced AI integrations**: Allowing users to easily integrate AI models into workflows without coding.
- **Cross-platform workflows**: Enabling users to automate tasks across a broader range of platforms, including cloud, on-premises systems, and edge devices.

Preparing for Low-Code Automation:

- Encourage employees to adopt **low-code/no-code tools** like **n8n** to automate workflows across departments.
- Develop internal **automation centers of excellence** to promote the use of automation tools throughout the organization.
- Train staff on **workflow design** and **process optimization** to maximize the effectiveness of automation.

13.6.4. Automation in the Era of Digital Transformation

As part of **digital transformation**, automation will play a central role in helping businesses become more agile, responsive, and efficient. The future of automation will be deeply intertwined with **cloud technologies**, **AI**, and **big data**, enabling businesses to automate everything from customer service to supply chain management.

Preparing for Digital Transformation with Automation:

- Embrace a **digital-first mindset**, where automation is seen as a key enabler of business growth.
- Leverage **n8n's integrations** with cloud platforms and enterprise systems to automate workflows across the entire organization.
- Use **data-driven decision-making** to ensure that automation initiatives are aligned with business goals and deliver tangible results.

In this chapter, we explored the **impact of automation** on businesses and industries, highlighting its benefits, challenges, and transformative power. We also discussed the future of **n8n** in the context of emerging trends like **AI**, **machine learning**, **IoT**, and **low-code/no-code automation**. As automation continues to evolve, businesses that embrace these innovations will be well-positioned to thrive in the increasingly automated world of tomorrow.

Conclusion

In this final chapter, we reflect on the key concepts and takeaways from the book and provide guidance on how to continue your journey with **n8n** and **agent-based automation**. The rapidly evolving automation landscape holds enormous potential for businesses to streamline processes, improve efficiency, and innovate. **n8n** provides the flexibility, power, and ease of use to leverage these advancements.

14.1. Recap of Key Learnings

Throughout this book, we have covered a broad spectrum of concepts related to **n8n agents**, automation, and integration. Here's a recap of the key lessons and takeaways:

1. **Introduction to n8n and Automation**:
   - We began by exploring **n8n**—a powerful, open-source automation platform that enables users to automate workflows without needing extensive coding experience.
   - The concept of **n8n agents** was introduced, explaining how agents can execute specific tasks within workflows, coordinate with other agents, and work autonomously.
2. **Setting Up and Using n8n**:
   - We covered how to **install, set up**, and **configure n8n**, including its interface, dashboard, and initial workflow creation.
   - We discussed essential **n8n concepts**, such as nodes, triggers, actions, and variables, and how they interact within workflows.
3. **Building and Extending Agent Workflows**:
   - We delved into creating **simple agent workflows** and advanced workflows using **n8n's functionality**. You learned how to implement features like looping, branching, error handling, and interacting with external systems through APIs.
   - We explored the **power of WebSockets** for real-time data processing, as well as how to integrate **AI** and **machine learning** models to build smarter workflows.
4. **Integrating with External Systems**:

- o Detailed walkthroughs covered **integrating n8n with IoT devices, databases, APIs,** and **cloud services,** allowing you to automate a wide range of business processes, from inventory management to customer support.
  - o We also explored the use of **predictive analytics** and **multi-agent systems** to handle more complex tasks like forecasting and collaborative decision-making.
5. **Advanced Topics**:
   - o The book explored future trends in **n8n** and automation, including **AI-powered agents, hybrid cloud and edge deployments,** and how **IoT** is revolutionizing automation workflows.
   - o We discussed the **challenges and opportunities** of implementing automation in businesses, including how to manage change, overcome integration hurdles, and ensure a smooth transition into automated environments.
6. **The Future of Automation**:
   - o We explored the growing role of **automation** in business and the **future of work**, emphasizing how **AI-powered agents** and **n8n's flexibility** will continue to shape workflows in a rapidly changing world.

14.2. Next Steps: Building Your Own Custom Agent Workflows

Now that you have a solid foundation in **n8n agents** and automation, you are ready to take the next step and start building your own custom workflows. Here are some actionable steps to continue your journey with **n8n**:

1. **Start with Simple Workflows**:
   - o Begin by automating small, repetitive tasks that you currently perform manually. For example, create a workflow that automatically collects data from a form and stores it in a Google Sheet, or set up email alerts for specific conditions.
2. **Explore n8n's Ecosystem**:
   - o Leverage the **n8n community** and **plugin marketplace** to find pre-built nodes, templates, and workflows. By examining these, you can gain insights into best practices and learn new ways to extend **n8n's capabilities**.
3. **Build Advanced Custom Agents**:

- As you become more comfortable with **n8n**, start building **more complex agent workflows**. Experiment with **custom nodes** that integrate with external systems or use **AI models** to automate decision-making. You can create workflows for business processes such as customer support, data analysis, and sales forecasting.

4. **Experiment with AI and Machine Learning**:
   - Try integrating **AI-powered agents** into your workflows. For example, you can create an agent that analyzes customer feedback using **sentiment analysis**, or build a predictive model to forecast sales.
   - Explore **machine learning** APIs and services (e.g., **OpenAI**, **Google Cloud AI**) to improve the intelligence of your workflows and automate decision-making.

5. **Integrate with IoT and Real-Time Data**:
   - Set up **real-time data streaming** in **n8n** by using **WebSocket** or **MQTT nodes** to connect to IoT devices. Automate processes based on real-time sensor data or system alerts.

6. **Optimize for Scalability and Performance**:
   - As you build more complex workflows, keep an eye on **scalability** and **performance**. Use **n8n's built-in error handling**, **logging**, and **debugging tools** to troubleshoot issues and ensure your workflows run efficiently.

7. **Explore Cloud and Hybrid Deployments**:
   - If you need to scale, consider deploying **n8n** on **cloud platforms** like **AWS**, **Google Cloud**, or **Azure**. Alternatively, experiment with **hybrid cloud and edge deployments** to optimize real-time data processing and ensure the efficiency of your workflows.

8. **Collaborate and Share Your Workflows**:
   - Share your workflows and templates with the **n8n community** to contribute to the ecosystem. You can also collaborate with other users or developers to solve complex problems and enhance your workflows.

9. **Stay Updated with New Features**:
   - **n8n** is continually evolving. Keep an eye on new **features**, **integrations**, and **improvements** announced in the **n8n community** and **release notes**. This will ensure you stay at the forefront of automation technology and continue to leverage the latest advancements.

10. **Focus on Continuous Improvement**:

- o   As your workflows mature, continuously refine and optimize them. Experiment with new **n8n nodes**, integrate **new tools**, and test different automation strategies to improve workflow efficiency and business outcomes.

Final Thoughts

By now, you should have a clear understanding of how **n8n agents** and automation workflows can be used to improve business processes, save time, and enhance decision-making. With **n8n**, you have the tools and flexibility to design custom workflows tailored to your business needs, from simple automations to advanced AI-powered agent systems.

The journey towards building intelligent, automated workflows is ongoing, and **n8n** provides a robust platform to explore and implement automation at every level. We hope this book has equipped you with the knowledge to take the next steps in creating powerful, efficient workflows that can drive business success.

Good luck as you start building your own **n8n agent workflows** and continue to innovate in the world of automation!

14.3. Resources for Continued Learning and Community Engagement

As you continue your journey with **n8n** and automation, it's important to stay updated and engaged with the **n8n community** and **learning resources**. Here are some valuable resources to help you deepen your knowledge, share your work, and stay connected with the **n8n ecosystem**.

14.3.1. Official n8n Resources

- **n8n Documentation**: The official **n8n documentation** provides in-depth guides, tutorials, and reference materials to help you get started and master advanced features.
  - o   n8n Documentation

- **n8n Academy**: A platform offering structured learning resources, from beginner tutorials to advanced courses, helping you get hands-on with **n8n**.
  - o n8n Academy
- **n8n GitHub Repository**: The **n8n GitHub repo** contains all the code, examples, and resources for developers who want to contribute or explore **n8n's open-source** project. It's a great resource for developers looking to understand **n8n's internal architecture** or contribute to new features.
  - o n8n GitHub
- **n8n Blog**: Stay informed about the latest features, use cases, and integration tips with **n8n's blog**.
  - o n8n Blog

14.3.2. Community Engagement

Being part of the **n8n community** can provide valuable insights, allow you to contribute to the project, and help you connect with other **n8n users** and **developers**. Here are some platforms for engagement:

- **n8n Community Forum**: The official **n8n forum** is where you can ask questions, share your workflows, and interact with other **n8n users**. It's a great place to get help, share ideas, and stay updated on new developments.
  - o n8n Community Forum
- **n8n Discord Server**: Join the **n8n Discord server** to engage with the community in real-time, get support, and chat about automation workflows, ideas, and challenges.
  - o n8n Discord Server
- **n8n on Stack Overflow**: For more technical questions, **n8n** has a **Stack Overflow** tag where you can find answers or post your own queries related to the platform.
  - o n8n Stack Overflow
- **Social Media**: Follow **n8n** on platforms like **Twitter**, **LinkedIn**, and **YouTube** to stay updated with the latest announcements, video tutorials, and community discussions.
  - o n8n Twitter
  - o n8n LinkedIn
  - o n8n YouTube

14.3.3. Learning Platforms and Courses

For those looking for a more structured approach to learning **n8n**, several online platforms offer courses that can help you master the platform and automate business processes:

- **Udemy**: Look for comprehensive **n8n automation courses** on platforms like **Udemy** that walk you through building workflows and integrating third-party services.
  - Udemy
- **LinkedIn Learning**: LinkedIn Learning offers courses on **workflow automation** and related topics that can help deepen your understanding of automation tools, including **n8n**.
  - LinkedIn Learning

14.3.4. Books and Guides

As you advance your knowledge of **n8n** and automation, consider looking for additional books or eBooks that dive deeper into specific areas of automation, such as:

- **Automation with AI**: Explore **AI-powered automation**, predictive analytics, and machine learning integrations.
- **API Integrations**: Books that cover API integrations and building custom nodes in platforms like **n8n**.

14.3.5. Contribution and Open Source Involvement

- **Contributing to n8n**: One of the best ways to engage with **n8n** and learn more about the platform is by **contributing** to its development. Whether it's submitting bug fixes, creating new nodes, or improving documentation, there are plenty of ways to get involved. The **n8n GitHub repository** has a wealth of information on how to contribute.
  - Contribute to n8n
- **Creating Custom Nodes**: If you have experience with programming and want to extend **n8n**'s capabilities, consider creating and sharing

custom nodes for others to use. This allows you to address specific needs that aren't currently met by existing nodes and contribute to the broader **n8n ecosystem**.

14.4. Final Thoughts on Automating Smart Workflows with n8n Agents

As we conclude this book, it's important to recognize the incredible potential that **n8n** offers in the world of **automation**. The platform's flexibility, open-source nature, and ease of use make it a powerful tool for automating a wide range of workflows, from simple tasks to complex, multi-agent systems.

Through this journey, you've learned how to:

- Set up **n8n** and create automation workflows using its visual editor.
- Integrate **n8n agents** into workflows that interact with external systems, APIs, and services.
- Use **AI and machine learning** to power intelligent workflows that can make real-time decisions.
- Handle real-time data processing, integrate IoT devices, and scale automation systems for enterprise use.

Key Takeaways:

- **n8n** empowers you to automate your workflows in a way that suits both **technical and non-technical users**, offering a perfect blend of flexibility and accessibility.
- **n8n agents** allow you to break down tasks into smaller, manageable steps, automating complex processes and improving operational efficiency.
- The platform is continuously evolving, with new integrations, AI capabilities, and performance improvements ensuring that **n8n** remains at the forefront of automation technology.

The Future of Automation:

The future of work is increasingly driven by **automation**, and **n8n** is perfectly positioned to play a pivotal role in this transformation. Whether you're automating business processes, integrating AI into your workflows, or managing a **multi-agent system**, **n8n** offers the tools to help you unlock the full potential of your operations.

Now that you have a solid foundation, you can continue building, experimenting, and expanding your automation capabilities with **n8n**. Whether you're automating your personal projects or transforming entire business operations, the power of **n8n** agents is at your fingertips.

We hope this book has inspired you to explore new ways to automate workflows and use **n8n** to solve real-world challenges. Let us know how you're applying **n8n** in your projects, and continue to stay engaged with the community to learn and grow as automation technology evolves.

Happy automating!

Appendices

A. n8n Node Reference

The **n8n Node Reference** is a comprehensive guide to the various nodes available in **n8n**, detailing their functionality, configurations, and use cases. Nodes are the building blocks of **n8n workflows**, and each one performs a specific task, such as triggering an event, performing an action, or interacting with an external service. This reference will help you understand how to use **n8n nodes** effectively in your workflows.

A.1. Overview of n8n Nodes

n8n nodes can be broadly classified into several categories based on their functionality:

- **Trigger Nodes**: Initiate workflows based on specific events or incoming data (e.g., webhook triggers, cron schedules).
- **Action Nodes**: Perform tasks such as sending data, making API calls, or processing information (e.g., email, HTTP requests).
- **Condition Nodes**: Help implement logic within workflows, such as if-else conditions or data filtering (e.g., If node, Switch node).
- **Utility Nodes**: Handle general operations, such as data manipulation, file handling, and error logging (e.g., Set node, Function node).
- **External Service Nodes**: Enable integration with third-party services, APIs, and platforms (e.g., Google Sheets, Slack, AWS S3).

Each node has a distinct purpose and can be connected with other nodes to form a complete automation workflow.

A.2. Trigger Nodes

1. **Webhook Trigger Node**
   Purpose: Listens for incoming HTTP requests and triggers workflows based on data received.
   Use Cases:

- Webhooks for receiving data from external systems (e.g., incoming form submissions, third-party API responses).
- Real-time event-driven workflows.
  Key Parameters:
- **HTTP Method**: Defines the HTTP method (GET, POST, etc.) used for the request.
- **Path**: Specifies the URL path for the webhook endpoint.
- **Response Format**: Defines the structure of the response to the sender.

Example: Set up a webhook to receive customer feedback via an API and trigger an automated response based on sentiment.

2. **Cron Node**
   Purpose: Triggers workflows based on a scheduled time or interval (e.g., daily, weekly, specific times).
   Use Cases:
   - Automating routine tasks like sending daily reports or syncing data.
   - Running maintenance tasks at regular intervals.
     Key Parameters:
   - **Cron Expression**: Defines the schedule for running the workflow (e.g., every day at 8 AM).

Example: Use the **Cron node** to trigger a workflow that sends weekly reports to the team.

A.3. Action Nodes

1. **HTTP Request Node**
   Purpose: Sends HTTP requests to external services (e.g., making API calls).
   Use Cases:
   - Interacting with third-party APIs to retrieve or send data.
   - Performing integrations with external platforms like CRM, payment gateways, or social media.
     Key Parameters:
   - **URL**: The endpoint URL of the API.
   - **Method**: Defines the HTTP method (GET, POST, PUT, DELETE).

o **Body Parameters**: Allows sending data in the request body, such as JSON or form data.

Example: Use the **HTTP Request node** to send user data to a CRM platform (e.g., Salesforce, HubSpot).

2. **Email Node**
   Purpose: Sends emails based on the workflow's triggers and actions.
   Use Cases:
   o Sending confirmation emails after form submission.
   o Automating customer notifications or internal alerts.
     Key Parameters:
   o **Sender Email**: Defines the email address from which the email will be sent.
   o **Recipient Email**: The email address to which the email will be sent.
   o **Subject/Body**: Defines the content of the email.

Example: Automatically send an email when a new order is placed on your e-commerce website.

A.4. Condition Nodes

1. **If Node**
   Purpose: Implements basic conditional logic to control the flow of the workflow.
   Use Cases:
   o Make decisions based on data (e.g., if the stock level is low, send an alert).
   o Implement if-else logic for branching workflows. **Key Parameters**:
   o **Condition**: Defines the condition (e.g., if a value is greater than a threshold).
   o **True/False Actions**: Specifies what actions to take if the condition is met or not met.

Example: Use the **If node** to check if a customer's subscription is about to expire, and send a renewal reminder if true.

2. **Switch Node**
   Purpose: Provides more complex conditional logic by allowing multiple branches based on different conditions.
   Use Cases:
   - Routing data to different actions depending on a variety of conditions.
   - Handling multiple outcomes from a single source of data.
     Key Parameters:
   - **Cases**: Defines different conditions and corresponding branches in the workflow.

   Example: Use the **Switch node** to handle different types of customer feedback (e.g., positive, neutral, negative) and respond accordingly.

A.5. Utility Nodes

1. **Function Node**
   Purpose: Executes custom JavaScript code to manipulate or process data within the workflow.
   Use Cases:
   - Perform calculations or data transformations.
   - Apply custom logic that is not available through other nodes.
     Key Parameters:
   - **JavaScript Code**: The custom code to run, which can manipulate input data or return specific values.

   Example: Use the **Function node** to calculate the total order value from individual item prices in an e-commerce workflow.

2. **Set Node**
   Purpose: Modifies or sets data values within the workflow.
   Use Cases:
   - Create new data fields or modify existing ones.
   - Store values for use in later nodes.
     Key Parameters:
   - **Values to Set**: Define the data or variables to be set.

   Example: Use the **Set node** to store user input from a form into a variable for further processing.

A.6. External Service Nodes

1. **Google Sheets Node**
   Purpose: Integrates **Google Sheets** with **n8n**, allowing data to be read from or written to Google Sheets.
   Use Cases:
   - Syncing customer data with Google Sheets.
   - Collecting form submissions into a spreadsheet.
     Key Parameters:
   - **Spreadsheet**: The Google Sheet you want to access.
   - **Action**: Specify whether you want to read or write data.

   Example: Automatically log form submissions into a Google Sheets document for later analysis.

2. **Slack Node**
   Purpose: Sends messages to **Slack** channels or users.
   Use Cases:
   - Sending alerts or notifications to a Slack channel.
   - Automating messages for specific events (e.g., new orders, customer inquiries).
     Key Parameters:
   - **Channel**: The Slack channel where the message will be sent.
   - **Message**: The content of the message.

   Example: Notify a team in Slack when a critical error occurs in a business process.

A.7. Best Practices for Using n8n Nodes

1. **Break Workflows into Modular Pieces**: Use multiple nodes to break your workflow into smaller, manageable steps. This makes it easier to maintain and debug workflows.
2. **Use Variables and Dynamic Data**: Leverage **variables** and **dynamic data** wherever possible to ensure your workflows are flexible and can adapt to different inputs.

3. **Test Workflows Regularly**: Test workflows at different stages to ensure everything is functioning as expected. Use the **Test node** feature in the **n8n editor** to simulate real-world execution.

The **n8n Node Reference** provides an overview of the essential nodes that make up **n8n workflows**. By understanding and utilizing these nodes, you can create highly customized, dynamic automation workflows that integrate with a wide variety of tools and services. The flexibility and power of **n8n nodes** allow you to automate complex tasks, handle real-time data, and create intelligent workflows that optimize business processes.

As you continue building your workflows in **n8n**, refer to this node reference to learn more about each node's capabilities and how it can be used in your automation projects. Happy automating!

B. Troubleshooting Guide

Automation workflows, especially those involving complex systems like **n8n agents**, can sometimes encounter issues that require troubleshooting. This guide provides you with steps to identify, diagnose, and resolve common issues that may arise while building or executing **n8n workflows**. By following these troubleshooting steps, you can quickly address problems and get your workflows back on track.

B.1. General Troubleshooting Steps

Before diving into specific issues, here are some general troubleshooting steps you should follow when something goes wrong in your workflow:

1. **Check Workflow Logs**:
   - **n8n** provides detailed **execution logs** that can help identify where the issue occurred. Always start by examining the **execution logs** for any error messages, warnings, or unexpected behavior. This can give you a clear idea of what went wrong.
   - To view logs, click on the **Execution Log** tab for a workflow and review the data returned from each node.

2. **Review Node Configurations**:
   - o Ensure that each node in your workflow is configured correctly. Double-check the settings, API keys, URLs, and parameters.
   - o Many issues arise from misconfigured nodes, such as incorrect API URLs, missing credentials, or improperly set conditions in nodes like **If**, **Switch**, or **Set**.
3. **Validate Credentials**:
   - o If your workflow interacts with external services (e.g., databases, cloud storage, APIs), make sure the credentials are correct and up-to-date.
   - o Go to **n8n's Credentials** section and ensure that the credentials for each integrated service are properly configured and authenticated.
4. **Test Nodes Individually**:
   - o Use **n8n's "Test" feature** to execute individual nodes in isolation. This helps isolate where the problem may be occurring. Run each node with sample input to verify that it's performing the intended action.
5. **Review Data Flow Between Nodes**:
   - o Check how data flows from one node to the next. Sometimes, the issue can arise from data not being passed correctly between nodes or unexpected null/empty values.
   - o Use **Set nodes** to inspect and modify data as it flows between stages of the workflow.
6. **Check for API Rate Limits**:
   - o If your workflow makes repeated calls to third-party APIs, ensure that the API doesn't have rate limits or usage restrictions that might be causing the issue.
   - o Check API documentation for information about rate limits and adjust the frequency of requests accordingly.

B.2. Common Issues and Fixes

B.2.1. Workflow Is Not Triggering

Problem: The workflow does not trigger as expected (e.g., Webhook, Cron, or Event-based triggers are not activating).

Possible Causes:

- The trigger node is not properly configured.
- Incorrect Webhook URL or missing parameters in the trigger URL.
- Cron expressions for scheduled triggers are not set correctly.

Fixes:

1. **Webhook**: Ensure the Webhook URL is correctly configured in both the **n8n** editor and the external service sending data to the webhook.
   - Verify the URL: `http://<n8n_instance>/webhook/<webhook_path>`.
   - Use tools like **Postman** or **curl** to send test requests to the Webhook URL and see if it triggers the workflow.
2. **Cron**: Double-check the **Cron expression**. Use online tools to validate your cron expression syntax to ensure it matches your desired schedule.
3. **Event-based Triggers**: Ensure that the external system is correctly sending events and that they match the expected format or parameters.

B.2.2. Invalid API Response or Data Fetching Issues

Problem: Nodes that interact with external APIs (e.g., HTTP Request, Google Sheets, Salesforce) return an **error** or **unexpected response**.

Possible Causes:

- Invalid API endpoint, method, or parameters.
- Missing or incorrect authentication (API key, OAuth tokens).
- API rate limiting or timeouts.
- Incorrectly structured data from the API.

Fixes:

1. **Verify the API Endpoint**: Double-check the **URL, HTTP method,** and **parameters** used in the API request. Refer to the API documentation to confirm that the request is properly formed.
2. **Check Authentication**: Ensure that the API credentials (API key, OAuth token, etc.) are correctly configured. Check **n8n's credentials settings** for each service.

3. **Test API Response**: Use **Postman** or **cURL** to send a test request to the API and confirm the expected response. Look for any **error messages** or changes in the API.
4. **Handle API Errors Gracefully**: In cases where the API is unreliable or prone to errors, use error-handling techniques in **n8n**, such as adding **Retry** logic, using the **Error Trigger** node, or implementing fallback actions.

B.2.3. Workflow Execution Takes Too Long or Timeouts

Problem: Workflows are taking too long to execute or timing out.

Possible Causes:

- Inefficient workflows or excessive API calls.
- Large data processing or slow third-party services.
- Workflow loops or recursive calls causing delays.

Fixes:

1. **Optimize Workflow Design**:
   - Break large workflows into smaller, more manageable pieces.
   - Avoid unnecessary loops and recursive calls that may cause excessive delays.
   - Reduce the number of redundant actions (e.g., avoid multiple API calls for the same data).
2. **Batch Processing**: Use **Batch nodes** to handle large datasets in smaller chunks rather than processing everything at once.
3. **Reduce External Calls**: Minimize the number of external API calls or services that the workflow interacts with. Use **caching** for data retrieval or fetch only the necessary data.
4. **Increase Timeout Settings**: If using an **HTTP Request node**, increase the **timeout** value for external requests if the response time is generally long.

B.2.4. Data Is Not Passed Between Nodes Correctly

Problem: The data passed between nodes is missing or incorrectly formatted.

Possible Causes:

- Misconfigured **Set nodes** or **Function nodes** that alter the data.
- Incorrectly mapped variables or outputs from earlier nodes.
- Data fields not being set or missing from inputs.

Fixes:

1. **Inspect Data**: Use **Set nodes** and **Function nodes** to inspect the data as it flows between each node. Use `console.log()` or `JSON.stringify()` to check the data at each step.
2. **Ensure Proper Variable Mapping**: Double-check that the data being passed between nodes is correctly referenced. Ensure you are using the correct data paths (e.g., `$json["field_name"]`).
3. **Test with Sample Data**: If possible, test your workflow using sample data that can be manually inserted into nodes to ensure it is passing through the workflow correctly.
4. **Use the Set Node to Fix Data**: If a node requires specific data to be set, use the **Set node** to ensure that the correct value is available for the subsequent nodes.

B.2.5. Workflow Errors or Failures

Problem: The workflow encounters an error during execution and fails unexpectedly.

Possible Causes:

- Invalid data or missing parameters in nodes.
- Errors in custom scripts or code within **Function nodes**.
- Workflow dependencies are not met (e.g., required data not available, API services down).

Fixes:

1. **Check Node Configuration**: Ensure each node is configured with the correct input data, parameters, and credentials.
2. **Use Error Handling**: Add an **Error Trigger node** to detect errors in specific parts of your workflow and automatically take corrective actions (e.g., retries or notifications).
3. **Use Try-Catch Blocks**: For custom scripts in **Function nodes**, implement **try-catch** blocks to catch and log errors:

```javascript
try {
  // Your code here
} catch (error) {
  throw new Error(`Error occurred:
${error.message}`);
}
```

B.3. Advanced Debugging Tips

When troubleshooting more complex workflows, you may need to dive deeper into debugging:

1. **Enable Debug Mode**: If the workflow has complex logic, enable **debug mode** in **n8n** to view detailed logs during execution.
2. **Examine Node Outputs**: Always check the output of each node. This will help you understand how the data is transformed as it flows through the workflow.
3. **Simplify Workflows for Testing**: If the issue is hard to pinpoint, simplify the workflow by breaking it down into smaller parts and testing each part individually.

Conclusion

This **Troubleshooting Guide** provides you with the tools and techniques to diagnose and resolve common issues in **n8n workflows**. By following the general troubleshooting steps, addressing specific issues like **API errors**, **data flow issues**, and **workflow delays**, and leveraging debugging features, you can ensure that your automation workflows run smoothly and efficiently.

If you encounter issues that aren't addressed here, don't hesitate to explore the **n8n community forums** or **Discord server**, where you can get help from other users and the **n8n team**.

Happy troubleshooting and automating!

C. GitHub Repository & Example Workflows

This section provides a detailed overview of the **n8n GitHub repository** and how to leverage example workflows for building more complex automation systems. Whether you're looking to explore the **n8n codebase**, share your custom workflows, or find inspiration from existing workflows, this section will guide you on how to make the most of **n8n's GitHub repository** and **example workflows**.

C.1. Overview of the n8n GitHub Repository

The **n8n GitHub repository** serves as the central hub for all things related to **n8n**'s open-source development. It contains the **core code**, **documentation**, and **community contributions**, as well as the **official releases** and **extension packages**. Here's what you can find in the **GitHub repository**:

- **n8n Core Code**: The primary source code for **n8n**, which includes the underlying infrastructure and automation logic that powers the platform.
- **Nodes**: All the built-in **n8n nodes** and custom integrations with third-party services. You can find and modify node templates here.
- **Community Contributions**: Community members often share their **custom nodes, workflows**, and **plugins** in pull requests.
- **Extensions**: **n8n** supports custom node creation, and the repository contains examples of how to build and contribute your own nodes or workflows to the **n8n ecosystem**.
- **Documentation**: **n8n's GitHub repository** provides documentation for developers, including how to extend **n8n**, create custom nodes, set up the platform, and more.

You can explore the **n8n GitHub repository** at:

- n8n GitHub Repository

C.2. Cloning the Repository and Setting Up n8n Locally

To get started with the **n8n GitHub repository**:

1. **Clone the Repository**:
   - Clone the **n8n repository** to your local machine to inspect or contribute to the code.

   bash

   ```
   git clone https://github.com/n8n-io/n8n.git
   cd n8n
   ```

2. **Set Up Your Local Environment**:
   - Follow the setup instructions in the repository to get **n8n** up and running locally.
   - Install the necessary dependencies:

   bash

   ```
   npm install
   ```

3. **Start n8n Locally**:
   - After installation, run **n8n** locally with:

   bash

   ```
   npm run start
   ```

C.3. Example Workflows in the n8n Repository

The **n8n GitHub repository** includes a folder dedicated to **example workflows** that demonstrate how **n8n agents** and nodes can be used to automate a variety of tasks. These workflows provide great starting points for understanding how to structure workflows, integrate services, and use different **n8n nodes** effectively.

C.3.1. How to Find Example Workflows

To find example workflows in the **n8n GitHub repository**:

1. Navigate to the **Examples** folder in the repository.
2. Browse through the example workflow files, which may include:
   - **Basic automations** (e.g., sending emails, integrating with Google Sheets).
   - **Complex workflows** (e.g., multi-step automation involving APIs, databases, and third-party services).

Each example comes with detailed comments on what each part of the workflow does, making it easy for you to adapt these examples to your own needs.

C.3.2. Examples of Common Workflow Use Cases

Here are a few common examples you can find or build upon using **n8n**:

1. **Automated Data Sync between Google Sheets and a Database**:
   - Automate the process of syncing data between **Google Sheets** and a **SQL database**. This is useful for maintaining an up-to-date copy of data across platforms, especially in collaborative environments.
2. **Social Media Monitoring and Reporting**:
   - Monitor mentions on social media platforms (e.g., **Twitter**) using **n8n's social media nodes** and generate a report every week summarizing engagement, sentiment, or specific hashtags.
3. **Customer Feedback Analysis with Sentiment Analysis**:
   - Collect customer feedback from forms or surveys and run it through a **sentiment analysis** API (e.g., **Google Cloud NLP** or **IBM Watson**). Trigger actions based on sentiment (e.g., escalate negative feedback, send automated responses).
4. **E-commerce Order Processing Automation**:
   - Automatically process orders from an e-commerce platform by integrating with payment gateways, inventory management systems, and shipping providers.

C.3.3. Sharing Custom Workflows with the Community

As you build your own workflows, consider sharing them with the **n8n community**:

- **Contributing Workflows**: Share workflows that you create or adapt from examples by opening a **pull request** in the **n8n GitHub repository**.
- **Workflow Templates**: Publish templates to the **n8n Community Forum** or in the **n8n Workflow Marketplace**. This allows others to explore, use, and improve upon your work.

C.4. Creating Custom Nodes and Contributions

If you have a specific need that isn't met by **n8n's existing nodes**, you can create **custom nodes** to extend the platform's capabilities.

C.4.1. Creating Custom Nodes

To create a custom node for **n8n**, follow these steps:

1. **Set up the Development Environment**:
   - Install **n8n** on your local system and set up the necessary tools for node development.
2. **Create Your Custom Node**:
   - Follow the guidelines in the **n8n GitHub repository** to create a custom node.
   - Define your custom node's behavior (e.g., handling API requests, processing data).
3. **Test Your Node**:
   - Use **n8n's local development environment** to test your custom node before integrating it into your workflows.
4. **Submit a Pull Request**:
   - Once your custom node is ready, **submit a pull request** to the **n8n GitHub repository** for review and integration into the main codebase.

C.4.2. Example: Custom API Integration Node

For instance, if you are working with a specific service that isn't natively supported by **n8n**, you can create a custom node to interact with the service's API. The node might:

- Make **API requests** to the service.
- Handle responses and errors.
- Pass data into subsequent nodes for further processing or storage.

C.5. Best Practices for Contributing to n8n

When contributing to the **n8n repository**, follow these best practices to ensure your work aligns with the project's standards:

1. **Write Clear Documentation**: Always document your nodes, workflows, and contributions so other users can understand and use them effectively.
2. **Follow Coding Standards**: Adhere to the coding conventions and standards outlined in the **n8n GitHub repository** to ensure consistency and readability in the code.
3. **Test Extensively**: Before submitting your contributions, test them thoroughly to ensure that they work as expected and do not introduce any bugs.
4. **Be Transparent in Communication**: Use clear and concise messages in your pull requests and discussions with the community to promote collaboration and feedback.

The **n8n GitHub repository** is an essential resource for extending **n8n's capabilities**, sharing workflows, and contributing to the open-source project. By exploring the **example workflows**, creating custom nodes, and actively engaging with the community, you can continuously enhance your **n8n automation** workflows and contribute to the growth of the platform.

Whether you're a beginner or an advanced user, the **n8n GitHub repository** is a valuable tool for learning, experimenting, and growing as you build more powerful automation solutions.

D. Glossary of Terms

In this glossary, we define key terms and concepts used throughout the book to help clarify the language of **n8n**, automation, and related technologies. Understanding these terms will assist you in navigating the **n8n platform** and applying its features effectively in your workflows.

A

- **API (Application Programming Interface)**: A set of protocols and tools that allow one software application to interact with another. APIs are used to connect **n8n** with external services and data sources.
- **Agent**: In the context of **n8n**, an **agent** is an autonomous workflow or process that can be set up to perform a task based on specific conditions, inputs, or events.
- **Automation**: The use of technology to perform tasks without human intervention. **n8n** automates workflows, integrating various systems and services to streamline operations.

B

- **Batch Processing**: The execution of a series of tasks or operations in a group or "batch," typically without interaction. In **n8n**, batch processing can be used for large sets of data to optimize execution.
- **Bug**: An error or flaw in the software that causes it to behave unexpectedly. Debugging involves identifying and resolving bugs in workflows or nodes.

C

- **Cloud Automation**: The use of cloud computing technologies to automate IT and business processes, such as the use of **n8n** for automating cloud-based workflows and integrations.

- **Cron Expression**: A string of characters that defines the schedule for recurring tasks. **n8n** uses **Cron expressions** for scheduling workflows, such as running tasks at specific times or intervals.
- **Custom Node**: A node that extends **n8n**'s functionality, created by developers to integrate a specific service or action that isn't supported by default.

D

- **Database Node**: A type of node in **n8n** that enables integration with databases such as **MySQL**, **PostgreSQL**, or **MongoDB** to perform actions like reading, writing, or updating data.
- **Debug Mode**: A mode in **n8n** that allows for detailed inspection of workflow execution, helping users identify where issues or errors may occur.

E

- **Event-Driven Automation**: Automation triggered by an event (e.g., receiving a message or an API request). **n8n** enables event-driven workflows using **webhooks** or other triggers.
- **Error Handling**: The process of managing and responding to errors that occur during workflow execution. **n8n** offers built-in error handling and retry logic to ensure workflows run smoothly even when problems arise.

F

- **Function Node**: A node in **n8n** that allows users to run custom JavaScript code, enabling data manipulation, calculation, and advanced logic within a workflow.
- **Flow**: A series of connected nodes in **n8n** that define a process or set of tasks to be executed in sequence.

G

- **GitHub Repository**: The central source of code and resources for **n8n**, where the open-source project is maintained. It includes documentation, bug reports, feature requests, and contributions.
- **Google Sheets Node**: A node in **n8n** that allows for integration with **Google Sheets**, enabling users to automate data entry, retrieval, and updates.

H

- **HTTP Request Node**: A node in **n8n** that allows users to send HTTP requests to external services or APIs, enabling integration with third-party tools and data sources.
- **Hybrid Cloud**: A computing environment that uses both **private** and **public** cloud resources. **n8n** workflows can be deployed in hybrid cloud environments for greater flexibility and scalability.

I

- **If Node**: A conditional node in **n8n** that allows users to define logic and make decisions within workflows based on data or variables.
- **Integration**: The process of connecting different services, applications, or systems to work together. **n8n** is used to integrate multiple platforms, APIs, and databases into a unified workflow.

J

- **JavaScript**: A programming language commonly used for web development. **n8n** utilizes **JavaScript** for custom coding in nodes, particularly the **Function node**, to process and manipulate data.

K

- **Kubernetes**: An open-source platform used to manage containerized applications. **n8n** can be deployed on **Kubernetes** for automated scaling and management of workflows in cloud-native environments.

L

- **Low-Code/No-Code**: A type of software development that allows users to build applications and workflows with minimal or no coding. **n8n** provides a **low-code** interface for building workflows, making automation accessible to both technical and non-technical users.
- **Looping**: A workflow pattern that repeats actions until a certain condition is met. **n8n** supports loops in workflows to automate tasks that require repetitive actions or data processing.

M

- **Machine Learning**: A subset of **artificial intelligence (AI)** that allows systems to learn and improve from data without being explicitly programmed. **n8n** can integrate with machine learning models to automate decision-making based on predictive analytics.
- **Multi-Agent System**: A system that consists of multiple agents (autonomous workflows) that work together to accomplish tasks. **n8n** enables the creation of **multi-agent systems** by allowing workflows to interact and share data.

N

- **Node**: A basic unit of work in **n8n**, representing an action, task, or integration within a workflow. Nodes can trigger actions, make API calls, handle logic, and manage data.
- **n8n**: An open-source automation platform that allows users to create workflows to automate processes across various services, APIs, and databases. It supports a wide range of integrations, triggers, actions, and custom logic.

O

- **Open Source**: A type of software whose source code is freely available for modification and distribution. **n8n** is an open-source project, allowing anyone to contribute to its development or customize it for their specific needs.
- **OAuth**: An open standard for access delegation commonly used in APIs. **n8n** supports **OAuth** authentication for securely connecting third-party services like **Google**, **Facebook**, and **Slack**.

P

- **PostgreSQL Node**: A node that allows **n8n** to interact with **PostgreSQL** databases, enabling users to perform actions like data retrieval, updates, and deletes within workflows.
- **Predictive Analytics**: The use of statistical models and machine learning to analyze historical data and predict future outcomes. **n8n** can integrate with predictive models to automate decision-making based on these forecasts.
- **Pull Request (PR)**: A method of contributing changes to the **n8n** codebase through GitHub, where developers propose changes that are reviewed and merged into the repository.

Q

- **Queue**: A data structure used to manage tasks that need to be processed. In **n8n**, workflows can be queued to ensure tasks are executed in sequence or based on priority.

R

- **REST API**: A popular API architecture that allows for communication between systems over HTTP. Many of **n8n's nodes** integrate with **REST APIs**, allowing workflows to interact with external services such as CRM, marketing platforms, and databases.

- **Retry Logic**: The process of automatically retrying a failed task or action after a certain amount of time or conditions are met. **n8n** supports retry logic for tasks like API calls or long-running processes.

S

- **Set Node**: A node in **n8n** that allows users to create or modify data within a workflow. It's useful for setting variables or structuring data before passing it to other nodes.
- **SQL Node**: A node that allows **n8n** to execute SQL queries against relational databases like **MySQL** or **PostgreSQL**, enabling data manipulation and retrieval as part of automation workflows.

T

- **Trigger Node**: A node in **n8n** that starts a workflow when a specific event occurs (e.g., receiving a Webhook, running on a schedule via Cron).
- **Token**: A string of characters used for authentication in APIs, often used in OAuth-based systems to access resources securely.

U

- **User Interface (UI)**: The visual interface in **n8n** that allows users to build and manage workflows. It provides drag-and-drop functionality, node configuration options, and visualization of workflow execution.
- **Utility Nodes**: Nodes that provide basic functionality for workflow manipulation, such as modifying data, performing calculations, or handling errors.

V

- **Version Control**: A system that tracks changes to software or workflows over time. **n8n** supports version control for workflows, allowing teams to manage updates and track changes.

W

- **Webhook Node**: A trigger node in **n8n** that listens for HTTP requests from external services. It's commonly used to start workflows based on real-time data from APIs or systems.
- **Workflow**: A series of connected nodes that define a process in **n8n**. Workflows can automate tasks, integrate with APIs, and trigger actions based on various conditions.

X

- **X-Axis/Timeline**: In automation workflows, the **X-axis** often refers to the time or sequence in which nodes or actions are executed. Understanding the sequence of tasks is essential for debugging workflows.

Y

- **YAML**: A human-readable data serialization format commonly used for configuration files. **n8n** uses **YAML** for defining parameters and settings in certain use cases (e.g., node configurations).

Z

- **Zero-Downtime Deployment**: The process of deploying updates to a system without taking it offline. **n8n** supports zero-downtime deployment strategies, especially when integrated with tools like **Docker** or **Kubernetes** for scalable, cloud-native setups.

This **Glossary of Terms** provides definitions for key concepts and terms that are frequently used in **n8n** and automation. Understanding these terms will help you navigate the platform more effectively and build powerful workflows that leverage the full potential of **n8n**.

Feel free to refer back to this glossary as you continue developing your workflows and automation projects with **n8n**!

E. Further Reading and Resources

As you continue your journey with **n8n** and automation, it's important to keep learning, exploring new tools, and expanding your knowledge of related technologies. Below, we've compiled a list of **further reading** and resources that will help you deepen your understanding of **n8n**, **workflow automation**, **AI**, and **integration platforms**.

E.1. Official n8n Resources

1. **n8n Documentation**
   The official **n8n documentation** is the primary resource for understanding the platform's capabilities, configuration options, and workflows. It's ideal for getting a deep dive into **n8n's features** and learning how to integrate various services.
   - n8n Documentation

2. **n8n Academy**
   n8n Academy offers structured courses to help you learn how to automate workflows effectively. Whether you're a beginner or an advanced user, the academy provides lessons for mastering **n8n**.
   - n8n Academy

3. **n8n GitHub Repository**
   For developers, the **n8n GitHub** repository is where you can access the **source code**, **community contributions**, and **custom nodes**. You can contribute to **n8n**, review the codebase, and find examples for extending **n8n's functionality**.
   - n8n GitHub

4. **n8n Blog**
   The **n8n blog** features articles, tutorials, and product updates. It's a

great resource for keeping up with new features, integrations, and community use cases.
- o n8n Blog

E.2. Workflow Automation and Integration

1. **Zapier Documentation**
   Zapier is one of the most popular no-code tools for workflow automation. While **n8n** is an open-source alternative, **Zapier's documentation** can help you understand how simple integrations and triggers can be set up.
   - o Zapier Documentation
2. **Integromat (Make) Documentation**
   Integromat (now called **Make**) is another powerful tool for automating workflows and integrating apps. Their tutorials and resources can help you understand advanced integrations and automation.
   - o Integromat (Make) Documentation
3. **Microsoft Power Automate**
   Microsoft Power Automate is a popular automation tool for businesses using Microsoft products. If you work with Microsoft services like Office 365, SharePoint, or Teams, their **Power Automate documentation** is invaluable.
   - o Microsoft Power Automate Documentation
4. **Apache Airflow**
   If you're looking to scale your workflows or work in a more enterprise environment, **Apache Airflow** is a powerful tool for orchestrating complex workflows. It's widely used in data engineering and machine learning pipelines.
   - o Apache Airflow Documentation

E.3. Automation and AI-Driven Workflows

1. **The AI-Powered Enterprise: Designing the AI-powered organization of the future** by **Gary D. S. Miller**
   This book explores how **AI-driven workflows** are transforming businesses and how organizations can use AI for process automation,

decision-making, and more. It's a great read for understanding the role of **AI in automation**.
- o The AI-Powered Enterprise
2. **Machine Learning Yearning** by **Andrew Ng**
Written by **Andrew Ng**, this book is a must-read for anyone interested in the intersection of **machine learning** and automation. It provides a strategic guide for building AI systems and integrating them into workflows.
- o Machine Learning Yearning
3. **Automate This: How Algorithms Came to Rule Our World** by **Christopher Steiner**
This book offers a look at how **automation** and **algorithms** have already changed industries, with a focus on real-world examples. It's a great resource to understand the broader context of automation and its societal impact.
- o Automate This: How Algorithms Came to Rule Our World
4. **AI for Everyone** by **Andrew Ng** (Coursera)
This is a great online course by **Andrew Ng** that introduces the fundamentals of **AI** and its application in business and automation. The course is beginner-friendly and highly relevant for those integrating AI into **n8n workflows**.
- o AI for Everyone

E.4. Books on Automation, APIs, and Integrations

1. **The Automation Advantage: Embrace the Future of Work** by **Ravi Kumar**
This book focuses on the strategic implementation of automation across industries. It's especially useful for business leaders and decision-makers who want to integrate automation into their operations.
- o The Automation Advantage
2. **RESTful Web APIs: Services for a Changing World** by **Leonard Richardson**
This book covers the best practices for creating **RESTful APIs**, which are essential for integrating various tools and systems in **n8n** workflows. It's a valuable resource for understanding how **n8n** interacts with external services via APIs.
- o RESTful Web APIs

3. **Building Microservices: Designing Fine-Grained Systems** by **Sam Newman**
   Microservices are a crucial component in automation and distributed systems. This book provides an in-depth understanding of **microservices architecture**, which can be applied when building complex workflows with **n8n**.
   o   Building Microservices
4. **Learning Python for Automation** by **Al Sweigart**
   For those interested in adding custom **Python scripts** into **n8n workflows**, this book is an excellent resource. It teaches how to automate tasks using **Python**, which can then be incorporated into **n8n** workflows for added flexibility.
   o   Learning Python for Automation

E.5. Online Communities and Forums

- **n8n Community Forum**
  A great place to ask questions, share workflows, and get advice from other **n8n users**.
  o   n8n Community Forum
- **n8n Discord**
  Join the **n8n Discord server** to chat with developers, share ideas, and get real-time help with workflows.
  o   n8n Discord
- **Stack Overflow**
  For more technical questions, the **n8n tag on Stack Overflow** can be a valuable resource for troubleshooting and solving programming-related challenges.
  o   n8n Stack Overflow

The resources listed here provide a variety of learning opportunities, from official documentation and books to community platforms and online courses. Whether you are looking to deepen your understanding of **n8n**, expand your knowledge of **AI** and **automation**, or learn more about **API integrations**, these resources will help you stay ahead in the rapidly evolving world of automation.

Keep exploring, keep experimenting, and continue building your workflows with **n8n** as you embark on a journey of automation and innovation!

F. Index

A

- **AI and Machine Learning Integration**
  165, 180, 192
- **Agent**
  25, 45, 57
- **API (Application Programming Interface)**
  11, 52, 138
- **Automation**
  4, 13, 22
- **Authentication**
  87, 96
- **Azure**
  184, 185

B

- **Batch Processing**
  95, 104
- **Bug**
  118, 120
- **Browser**
  154

C

- **Cloud Automation**
  71, 130
- **Cron Expression**
  75, 82
- **Custom Nodes**
  134, 153, 157
- **Condition Nodes**
  64, 66

The **Index** is a helpful tool to quickly navigate through key topics and concepts discussed in this book. Whether you're looking for specific details about **n8n agents**, **workflow automation**, or technical troubleshooting, this index allows you to easily locate the relevant sections of the book.

If you need further clarification on any topic or want to explore more advanced use cases, the **resources** section and the **community forums** can provide additional insights and examples. Happy automating!

www.ingramcontent.com/pod-product-compliance
Lightning Source LLC
LaVergne TN
LVHW081515050326
832903LV00025B/1501